News Media in India

The Impact of Globalization

News Media in India

The Impact of Globalization

By

Madhuri Madhok

Assistant Professor,
Journalism and Mass Communication,
Indian Institute of Mass Communication, New Delhi

New Century Publications
New Delhi, India

NEW CENTURY PUBLICATIONS
4800/24, Bharat Ram Road,
Ansari Road, Daryaganj,
New Delhi - 110 002 (India)

Tel.: 011-2324 7798, 4358 7398, 6539 6605
Fax: 011-4101 7798
E-mail: indiatax@vsnl.com • info@newcenturypublications.com
www.newcenturypublications.com

Editorial office:
LG–7, Aakarshan Bhawan,
4754-57/23, Ansari Road, Daryaganj,
New Delhi - 110 002

Tel.: 011-4356 0919

First Published: **July 2013**

ISBN: **978-81-7708-353-8**

Published by New Century Publications and printed at Salasar Imaging Systems, New Delhi.

Designs: Patch Creative Unit, New Delhi.

PRINTED IN INDIA

About the Book

Globalization has set in a new trend in Indian news media wherein the once leading news agencies are steadily losing their traditional hold on daily newspapers and slowly getting marginalized in the process. The shrinking presence of news stories from leading news agencies in news dailies is a sure indicator of the ill-effects of globalization on Indian news media. The role of news agencies, as the main supplier of news, has steadily declined over the past two decades.

The present study considers the quantum of news stories from the Indian news agencies to critically examine their position in the overall news coverage, both from temporal and cross-sectional perspective.

The study utilizes content analysis, a specific research approach used frequently in all areas of the media, to examine the contents of the newspapers to test the validity of the argument that the role of Indian news agencies is shrinking in the wake of globalization. The study aims at identifying and analyzing distinct trends in the world of news agency journalism with the help of data generated after content analysis of five leading dailies—four in English and one in Hindi.

Four English dailies representing four regions of the country are *The Times of India* from the West, *The Tribune* from the North, *The Statesman* from the East, and *The Hindu* from the South. The Hindi daily is *Punjab Kesari.*

National news agencies covered under the study are PTI, UNI (English) and Hindusthan Samachar (Hindi).

Specifically, the study examines the quantum and percentage of news items taken from Indian news agencies both before and after globalization.

The temporal axis analysis covers a period of 20 years beginning with 1985 at a five year gap, i.e. 1985, 1990, 1995, 2000 and 2005 for a period of one week each for content analysis.

Author's Profile

Dr. Madhuri Madhok has been associated as Assistant Professor, Journalism and Mass Communication, Indian Institute of Mass Communication, New Delhi. She is an author, freelance journalist and media academic. She joined the Press Trust of India (PTI), India's premier news agency in 1986, shortly after completing her post-graduation from University of Delhi. Her incisive news features on India's bilateral trade relations with various countries earned her Media Fellowship to Israel. She has aired talks on current affairs on All India Radio and scripted documentary features for television.

She has been a visiting faculty at the University of Delhi and counsellor to the Indira Gandhi National Open University (IGNOU). She has participated in various national and international seminars/conferences organized by UNESCO, UNDP, FICCI and CII. She is currently engaged in media research, training and consultancy.

Contents

About the Book..*v*
Author's Profile..*vi*
Preface...*viii-x*

1. Linkages between Globalization and Media **1-27**

2. Globalization and Indian Mass Media **28-41**

3. Literature on News Media **42-47**

4. The Times of India **48-82**

5. The Tribune **83-117**

6. The Statesman **118-151**

7. The Hindu **152-187**

8. Punjab Kesari **188-214**

9. Data Analysis and Interpretation **215-239**

10. Conclusions **240-254**

Bibliography **255-264**

Index **265-270**

Preface

Globalization has ushered a new trend in Indian news media where the once leading news agencies are steadily losing their traditional hold on daily newspapers and slowly getting marginalized in the process.

The shrinking presence of news stories from leading news agencies in news dailies is a sure indicator of the ill-effects of globalization on Indian news media. According to an estimate, the role of news agencies as the main supplier of news has steadily declined in newspapers over the past two decades or so. However, it has also been seen that with little imagination and shrewd thinking, some news agencies have managed to bounce back to regain their hold.

The present study considers the quantum of news stories from the Indian news agencies to critically examine their position in the overall news coverage, both from temporal and cross-sectional perspective.

The study utilizes content analysis, a specific research approach used frequently in all areas of the media, to examine the contents of the newspapers to test the validity of the research hypothesis. The study aims at identifying and analyzing distinct trends in the world of news agency journalism with the help of data generated after content analysis of five leading dailies—four in English and one in Hindi.

Four English dailies representing four regions of the country are *The Times of India* from the West, *The Tribune* from the North, *The Statesman* from the East, and *The Hindu* from the South. The Hindi daily is *Punjab Kesari.*

National news agencies covered under the study are PTI, UNI (English) and Hindusthan Samachar (Hindi).

Specifically, the study examines the quantum and percentage of news items taken from Indian news agencies both before and after globalisation.

The temporal axis analysis covers a period of 20 years beginning with 1985 at a five year gap, i.e. 1985, 1990, 1995,

2000 and 2005 for a period of one week each for content analysis to test the hypothesis with regard to aforementioned national news agencies.

The method employed for the study is *content analysis of the* leading Indian newspapers to see how many stories from Indian news agencies are getting published in the given time period. As is well-known, content analysis is a method of studying and analyzing communication in a systematic, objective and quantitative manner for the purpose of measuring variables. This definition has three concepts.

First, content analysis is systematic, i.e. the content to be analyzed is selected according to explicit and consistently applied rules. It simply means that only one set of guidelines is used for evaluation throughout the study.

Second, content analysis is objective in the sense that personal views, idiosyncrasies and biases of the researcher do not enter into the findings. However, the researcher is free to exercise subjective choice in the selection of unit of analysis and the precise make-up and definition of relevant categories.

Third, content analysis is quantitative, i.e. the goal of content analysis is the accurate representation of a body of messages. Quantification is important in fulfilling that objective as it helps find precision in the study. Quantification allows the researcher to summarize the results and to report them succinctly. Besides, it helps in interpretation and analysis of results.

The selection of 20 year period from 1985 to 2005 is significant. In the 1980s dawned the realization that if a country with roughly 15 percent of world population had to grow and prosper, then it must shed the mixed economy baggage and integrate with the world economy in a more direct way. The need for opening the economy was felt more keenly during Prime Minister Rajiv Gandhi's government and some reductions in tariff rates were activated in early 1980s. However, the real support for globalization, liberalization and reduction in protectionism came in the late 1980s. Hence, 1985 comes towards the end of the first phase of Indian economy from 1950 to 1985–a period which saw the stagnation of trade and economy.

The week selected for the study is the first week of each quinqunnial beginning with the year 1985 on to 1990, 1995, 2000 and 2005. All newspapers are studied in a sequence to understand the broad trends available regarding the use of news agency stories by them.

In this study, the units of analysis are the various news items–stories and features–released by and credited to these news agencies. This analysis revealed the actual allocation of space to national news agency stories by the newspapers in the given time period.

Further, all the five newspapers were subjected to cross-sectional analysis to find out which one of them gave the maximum and minimum coverage to news agency news stories and why.

I place on record my deep sense of gratitude to the following scholars and media experts who helped and encouraged me at various stages of the completion of this work: Dr. Kuldeep Chand Agnihotri, Professor Ashok Tandon, Shri H.K. Dua, Shri Harish Khare, and Shri Keith Flory.

I am indebted to my sister Shakti for being a source of continuous support and encouragement. My greatest debt undoubtedly is to my father for strengthening my resolve to pursue this research work. Finally, I humbly dedicate this book to my late mother, Saubhagyawati Shrimati Kamla Madhok, whose love and divine inspiration made it happen.

New Delhi **Madhuri Madhok**

1

Linkages between Globalization and Media

Globalization, which means interconnection and interdependence of all global areas as a result of free movement of capital, goods, services and people, is the key idea behind the transition of human society into the third millennium. It is central to the arrival of 'the information age' also called the 'third wave' after the agricultural and industrial eras—of human civilization. [1]

Globalization: Conceptual Framework

Globalization, as a concept as is known today, gained currency in the 1990s which saw the collapse of communism, the disintegration of the Soviet Union and the Eastern Bloc. End of the Cold War paved way for the rise of pan-capitalism through global economic integration accompanied by growing international trend towards liberalization, deregulation and privatization.

According to the UNESCO's World Communication Report, "The world of communication is gradually changing from an economy of scarcity and government-structured controls to a free economy oriented towards abundant supply and diversity. This change quickens the pace of the elimination of monopolies in the delivery and distribution of information, in both telecommunications and the audiovisual fields." (UNESCO, 1997: 11)

Thus, opening up of the global communication system paved way for the corporatization and concentration of global information and communication networks resulting in trans-nationalization of media and communication industries. This trend widely influenced the location of production, transmission and reception of media contents making it global in nature, scope, audience, ownership, capabilities and also, in political loyalties. Today, the mass media is characterized by unprecedented power, speed, reach and influence of transnational media organizations and conglomerates in penetrating every nook and corner of the 'global village'. [2]

However, for many like George Soros, Peter Singer and Amartya Sen, this village is, in fact, just a global landscape of gross inequalities. "The central issue of contention is not globalization itself, nor is it the use of the market as an institution, but the inequality in the overall balance of institutional arrangements—which produces very unequal sharing of the benefits of globalization. The question is not just whether the poor, too, gain something from globalization, but whether they get a fair share and a fair opportunity." [3]

"Global capitalism is much more concerned with expanding the domain of market relations than with, say, establishing democracy, expanding elementary education, or enhancing the social opportunities of society's underdogs...As George Soros has pointed out, international business concerns often have a strong preference for working in orderly and highly organized autocracies rather than in activist and less-regimented democracies, and this can be a regressive influence on equitable development.

Further, multinational firms can exert their influence on the priorities of public expenditure in less secure third-world countries by giving preference to the safety and convenience of the managerial classes and of privileged workers over the removal of widespread illiteracy, medical deprivation, and other adversities of the poor. These possibilities do not, of course, impose any insurmountable barrier to development, but it is important to make sure that the surmountable barriers are actually surmounted." [4]

Given the strong linkages between globalization and media and development, this brings us to the central question of our research work i.e. is globalization benefiting only the transnational media at the cost of national news agencies whose access and reach can be gainfully utilized in meeting the development objectives of the developing world.

As such, the coverage of rural India in television news bulletins as well as daily newspapers is abysmal - barely two percent as compared to over 60 percent of news emanating from four metros like Delhi, Mumbai, Kolkata and Chennai and other big cities. Even the role of news agencies—national, regional and smaller ones—is consistently declining.

Globalization, as is understood today, is a process of increasing interconnectedness and the resultant 'time-space compression' [5]; as the growing recognition of the worldwide human commonality; as the ultimate expression of capitalism, where "the market" alone determines the restructuring of economic, political and cultural life; and also as the reorganization of networks and institutions across global space. In other words, it refers to the universal interdependence of nations due to physical compression or 'shrinking' of the world into single entity and the intensification of a new 'global consciousness' of the world as a whole. [6]

According to the Oxford Dictionary of New Words, the term 'global consciousness...draws on the fashion of consciousness-raising in the sixties' (1991) among the young in numerous parts of the world on themes like love and liberation at both individual and collective level. This consciousness in turn sharpened the sense of what was supposedly common to all at the global level. The noun globalization has therefore come to symbolize global consciousness as an aspect of everything cantered upon global meaning thereby, worldwide or the whole. Enthusiasts see globalization as a vehicle for the spread of modernity that involves 'the development of something like a global culture'. [7]

In this spread of global consciousness, societies relate to a single system of societies, while individuals relate to a single sense of humanity becoming more and more aware of their new global existence. In this world society, cultures become relativized to each paving way for a global culture or global homogenization. [8] This homogenization, popularly called westernization, is seen as 'the direct consequence of the expansion of European culture across the planet via settlement, colonization and cultural mimesis'. [9] And, as a vehicle for the spread of modernity and a tool for global homogenization, globalization also involves extension of the nation-state system, the world capitalist economy, the world military order and the international division of labour. [10] However, critics of globalization prefer to call it 'triadization' rather than the globalization of world economy as many of the indices of globalization are concentrated within the OECD countries, especially between the USA-EU-Japan triad. [11]

Historically, the genesis of the ideation of a global society *without a world state and without world government* [12] can be traced back to the ancient Vedic dictum of '*Vasudhaiva Kutumbakam'* that holds the planet earth and mankind as one family. This has been the spirit behind the wonder that is India–its wisdom, philosophy, art and culture–since antiquity.

Globalization, thus, is not a novel concept. It assumed different forms in the past owing to the influence of world religions, imperialistic conquests and trade networks. In fact, it only changed shape, direction and intensity from one epoch or phase of social development to another.

The emergent concept of globality or global humanity in a single world system symbolizes continuity and change within the complex matrix of cultural dynamics which embraces the formation of nation state, industrialization, urbanization, techno-rationality and democratization. [13] It sees the world society as an irrevocable fact and one which is characterized as being multidimensional, polycentric, contingent and political. [14] The *globality* of this world society is opposed to a view which can understand the world in terms of nation-states (i.e. an international view). The resultant non-state society means that there are political players other than states, institutions and even corporations.

The economic conception of globalization denotes a paradigm shift away from a national to a globalized economy wherein although national economies continue to predominate within nations, they are often subordinate to transnational processes and transactions. [15] The phenomenon, often described as pan-capitalism, is characterized by international trend towards liberalization, deregulation and privatization in what is known as capitalist market as a global system. It is also argued that in the globalized economy, the nation-state has become irrelevant and market capitalism is producing a 'cross-border civilization'. [16]

The resultant 'deterritorialization' along with the expansion of information and communication technologies coupled with market-led liberal democracies is paving way for the emergence of a global civil society or a global village. However, this process is fraught with tensions between forces of globalization and fragmentation. [17] This tension is resolved through the concept of 'glocalization', a term whose origins are in the discipline of marketing, to express the global production of the local and the localization of the global. [18]

International Media and Globalization

In this process, international media and communication networks act as forces of globalizing culture and contribute to the process of homogenization due to diffusion of western media and cultural products. It is even considered global Westernization that followed the Industrial Revolution, the Enlightenment and the Renaissance. A liberal interpretation of globalization views it as fostering global integration by promoting global liberal capitalism through global markets. It is seen as promoting liberal democracy through its increasing emphasis on global governance, [19] 'cosmopolitan democracy' [20] and even 'cosmopolitics'. [21]

In this dominant view of globalization, the expansion of information and communication technologies coupled with market-led liberal democracies are contributing to the creation of what has been called a global civil society in a globalized economy. The globalized economy denotes a paradigm shift away from largely national to internationalized system of manufacture and production, to growing world trade, international capital flows and the role of transnational corporations. Thus, liberal interpretations of globalization see markets playing the key role at the expense of the states.

Also, there are other related issues like history of conquests, colonialism and alien rule that connect globalization to Western imperialism. Here, the historical continuity is quite evident. From the nineteenth century imperialism to the 'electronic empires' of the 21st century, the big powers have dominated the global information and communication networks.

Information is power and as the key strategic resource, information plays a central role in the international economy, the distribution, regulation, marketing and management of which are becoming increasingly important. "Information is the new coin of the international realm...and the United States is better positioned than any other country to multiply the potency of its hard and soft power resources through information". [22]

Globalization is thus viewed as an instrument of American hegemony or Western dominance or continuation of Western imperialism as "(the) global traffic in information and ideas. American music, American movies, American television, and American software are so dominant, so sought after, and so visible that they are now available literally everywhere on the Earth. They influence the tastes, lives, and aspirations of virtually every nation. [23]

Historical Kaleidoscope

Moving away from the polemics of an intellectual debate and discussing globalization as an historical fact, Amartya Sen holds that the active agents of globalization were located far from the West. [24]

"To illustrate, consider the world at the beginning of the last millennium rather than at its end. Around 1000 A.D., global reach of science, technology, and mathematics was changing the nature of the old world, but the dissemination then was, to a great extent, in the opposite direction of what we see today. The high technology in the world of 1000 A. D., included paper, the printing press, the crossbow, gunpowder, the iron-chain suspension bridge, the kite, the magnetic compass, the wheelbarrow, and the rotary fan. A millennium ago, these items were used extensively in China–and were practically unknown elsewhere. Globalization spread them across the world, including Europe.

"A similar movement occurred in the Eastern influence on Western mathematics. The decimal system emerged and became well developed in India between the second and sixth centuries: it was used by Arab mathematicians soon thereafter. These mathematical innovations reached Europe mainly in the last quarter of the tenth century and began having an impact in the early years of the last millennium, playing an important part in the scientific revolution that helped to transform Europe.

"The agents of globalization are neither European nor exclusively Western, nor are they necessarily linked to Western dominance. Indeed, Europe would have been a lot poorer–economically, culturally, and scientifically–had it resisted the globalization of mathematics, science, and technology at that time. And today, the same principle applies, though in the reverse direction (from West to East).

"Over thousands of years, globalization has contributed to the growth and development of the world and mankind through trade, travel, migration, spread of cultural influence and dissemination of knowledge and understanding (including science and technology)...For instance, the origin of modern word *sine* in mathematics can be traced back to India in 499 A.D. when the fifth-century Indian mathematician Aryabhatta had discussed the concept of sine in his classic work on astronomy and mathematics called it by its Sanskrit name, *jya-ardha* (literally, "half-chord"). This word, first shortened to *jya* in Sanskrit, eventually became the Arabic *jiba* and later, *jaib,* which means "a cove or a bay". Gherardo of Cremona, in his translations from the Arabic, rendered *jaib* as the Latin *sinus,* the corresponding word for a cove or a bay. And this is the source of modern word *sine.* [25]

The historicity of globalization process is further reinforced by the spread of knowledge about the use of paper, the printing press, the crossbow, gun-powder, the iron-chain suspension bridge, the kite, the magnetic compass, the wheel-barrow, and the rotary fan from China to the West. Similarly, the West imported the well-developed decimal system from India between the second and sixth centuries. It was used by Arab mathematicians soon thereafter. These mathematical innovations reached Europe towards the end of the tenth century and played a key role in the scientific revolution of the last millennium that helped transform Europe. [26]

Likewise, scholars like Robertson view globalization as a five-phase temporal-historical path marked by a very high degree of global density and complexity. [27]

Phase I: The Germinal Phase: Lasting in Europe from the fifteenth until the mid-eighteenth century; Incipient growth of national communities and downplaying of the medieval 'transnational' system; Expanding scope of the Catholic church; Accentuation of concepts of the individual and of ideas about humanity; Heliocentric theory of the world and beginning of modern geography; spread of Gregorian calendar.

Phase II: The Incipient Phase: Lasting, mainly in Europe, from the mid-eighteenth century until the 1870s; Sharp shift towards the idea of the homogenous, unitary state; crystallization of conceptions of formalized international relations, of standardized citizenry individuals and a more concrete conception of humankind; Sharp increase in legal conventions and agencies concerned with international and transnational regulation and communication; International exhibitions; Beginning of problem of 'admission' of non-European societies to 'international society'; Thematization of nationalism-internationalism issue.

Phase III: The Take-off Phase: Lasting from the 1870s until the mid-1920s. 'Take-off' here refers to a period during which the increasingly manifest globalizing tendencies of previous periods and places gave way to a single, inexorable form cantered upon the four reference points, and thus constraints, of national societies, generic individuals, a single 'international society', and an increasingly singular, but not unified conception of humankind...Very sharp increase in number and speed of global forms of communication. Development of global competition, for example, the Olympics and Nobel prizes; Implementation of world time and near-global adoption of Gregorian calendar; First World War.

Phase IV: The Struggle-for-Hegemony Phase: Lasting from the mid-1920s until the late-1960s; Disputes and wars about the fragile terms of the dominant globalization process established by the end of the take-off period; Establishment of the League of Nations and then the United Nations; Principle of national independence established; The Cold War; Nature of and prospects humanity sharply focused by the Holocaust and use of the atomic bomb; The crystallization of the Third World.

Phase V: The Uncertainty Phase: Beginning in the late 1960s and displaying crisis tendencies in the early 1990s; Heightening of global consciousness in late 1960s; Moon landing Accentuation of 'post-materialist' values; End of the Cold War and manifest rise of the problem of 'rights' and widespread access to nuclear and thermonuclear weaponry; Number of global institutions and movements greatly increases; Sharp acceleration in the means of global communication; Societies increasingly facing problems of multi-culturality and poly-ethnicity; Conceptions of individuals rendered more complex by gender, sexual, ethnic and racial considerations; Civil rights become a global issue. International system more fluid–end of bipolarity; Concern with humankind as a species-community greatly enhanced, particularly via environmental movements; Arising of interest in world civil society and world citizenship, in spite of the 'ethnic revolution'; Consolidation of global media system, including rivalries about such; Islam as a deglobalizing/reglobalizing movement; Earth Summit in Rio De Janeiro."

In each of these phases, the process of globalization was driven by communication and communication technology, which in turn, was influenced by global interconnectedness. This was quite obvious as global fluidity would not have been possible without communication as a relating tool.

Thus, the influence of technology on global interconnectedness and as a *change agent* can be clearly traced back to the invention of paper and printing type sets by the Chinese in mediaeval times. From eighth century onwards, Chinese paper replaced the Roman parchment. In late fifteenth century, the technique of movable printing typesets reached Europe from China. Johann Gutenberg of Germany developed the first European movable type printing press which transformed the European society and culture. Scriptures were now printed in various European languages other than Latin.

It led to the Renaissance and Reformation led by Luther, Calvin, Zwingley and many others. This in turn led to the Enlightenment and the emergence of the idea of the modern nation state based on cultural identity through language and literary tradition. Calvinist ethics contributed to the accumulation of capital which promoted both the mercantile activity and technological inventions that led to the Industrial Revolution.

Printing Press as an Agent of Change

Industrial Revolution led to colonization of resource-rich areas of Asia, South America and Africa. It led to transplantation of communication systems from the colonial powers to the colonies. The invention of the printing press in the fifteenth century by Johann Gutenberg and the subsequent reproduction of written material from the copyist's desk to the printer's workshop revolutionized all forms of learning. The colonial powers used printed books and papers to undermine local languages and culture.

The first to do this were the Portuguese who opened printing presses in Goa in 1557 and Macau in 1588. By the early 19th century, power press printing brought the newspaper which posed the greatest challenge to the printed book. The journey from the invention of the printing press to the birth of a newspaper and the consequent rise of the reading public constitutes the *first wave* of communication revolution that went hand in hand with the rising tide of globalization in Europe.

Till now, information travelled only as fast as the messenger who carried it. However, with the expansion of colonial empires the imperial powers needed to exercise political control and regulate the economies of their colonies with effectiveness and confidentiality. This required a speedy yet secret communication system. Such a system was provided through the invention of the Telegraph cable by Sir Charles Wheatstone and Samuel Morse in 1837. The first public telegraphic message was transmitted in 1844. Telegraphy was first used by the mercantile sections of European society to seek profit and international expansion. Telegraphy played an important role in the unification of the British Empire. The public telegraph system, established in England in 1851, also provided a money order service. It made instant communication and transfer of money between India and England possible.

In the middle of the nineteenth century, Telegraphy had significant military implications. The French used the Telegraph cable laid in Algeria in 1842 to occupy and subsequently colonise it. During the Crimean War, the French and the British exchanged the military intelligence against the Russians through the Telegraph cable laid under water in the Black Sea. It was through these cable information that the reporter of 'The Times' London, William Howard Russell made a mark in journalism.

The Telegraphy played an important role in the American Civil War. It was used to connect America with Europe particularly Britain where the everyday account of the Civil War was publicized by the newspapers. The later half of the nineteenth century saw laying Telegraph cable across the North Atlantic, the Mediterranean, the Indian Ocean and the Persian Gulf, China and Japan seas. The transpacific cable completed in 1902 provided information for the Russo-Japanese War of 1904-05. Thus, by the turn of the century, the Telegraph cable had become the essential part of the new imperialism. [28] But it also had a logistic repercussion. It could be cut thereby causing a total failure of communication.

This weakness was overcome by the invention of wireless telegraphy or radio telegraphy. This was invented in 1901 by Marconi. Initially, the telegraphy company set up by Marconi enjoyed the monopoly of manufacturing the transmitters and providing the transmission services but in 1906 an International Radio Telegraph Union was born. Initially, radio was used only as a medium of entertainment as it had created a new audience for music and drama. But national leaders, especially in times of crisis, soon discovered the advantage of speaking directly to the population instead of waiting for their utterances to be reported in the newspapers.

Thus, propaganda became the integral part of radio broadcasts and radio emerged as the key element in psychological warfare. During the First World War, the power of radio was quickly recognized as vital both to the management of public opinion at home and propaganda abroad. "During the war period it came to be recognized that the mobilization of men and means as not sufficient; there must be mobilization of opinion. Power over opinion, as over life and property, passed into official hands". [29]

By the time, the Nazis came to power in Germany in 1933, radio broadcasting had become an extension of international diplomacy. The head of Hitler's Propaganda Ministry, Josef Goebbels, believed in the power of radio broadcasting as a tool of propaganda. "Real broadcasting is true propaganda. Propaganda means fighting on all battlefields of the spirit, generating, multiplying, destroying, exterminating, building and undoing." [30] The Second World War saw an explosion in international broadcasting as a propaganda tool on both sides. Prominent broadcasters of the time like the British BBC, the American Voice of America (VOA), Radio Moscow, Radio Free Europe and Radio Liberty carried on the propaganda battle during the Cold War era.

One invention followed another with increasing speed. The phonograph was invented by Thomas Edison early in the second part of the nineteenth century. With his invention of a phonograph, movie camera and a projector, Edison made it possible to store sound and moving picture. This changed the character of dissemination of news during the Manchurian Crisis of 1931. The Japanese newspaper Asahi Shimbum hired movie cameramen who captured the visual footage of war in Manchuria and canned the reel in boxes and sent it in the evening through Japanese air-force planes back to Japan where these were shown in public parks of Osaka and Tokyo. This is how the 'news reel' came into being.

De Forest's invention of the triode vacuum tube in 1907 opened up the new worlds of radio and television. This path-breaking invention launched the audio-visual revolution in the field of communication. Television broadcasting began in 1930s, ten years after the radio broadcasting. In McLuhan's words, "if the movie was the mechanization of movement and gesture, TV was the electronification of the same". [31] The world was transformed into a global village with satellite communication via television. Thus the journey from the invention of the telegraph to television comprised the *second wave* of communication that influenced the tide of globalization in an unprecedented manner.

Then followed computers and the concept of information retrieval in what is now called the *Third Wave* [32] of human civilization after the agricultural and industrial eras. The communication technologies of the computer, including its various applications (in telecommunications, radio, television, cable, satellite, the Internet etc.) have led to the creation of global media that has actually turned the whole world into a global village with its instant connectivity and interactivity. The emergent global society is also known as the Information Society. [33] Here the convergence of telecommunications and computing technologies will digitally link all homes via the Internet–the network of networks.

The information grid of networked computers, like the electricity grid, will link every home, office and business, to create a networked society, based on what has been termed as 'knowledge economy'. [34] These networks have become the information superhighways, providing the infrastructure for a global information society. Here the computer plays the same role that steam engine played in the Industrial Society. Significantly, the third wave of modern communication or global media was set in motion almost at the same as the first, but climaxed only in the 20th century.

Thus, globalization emerged as the natural corollary of Industrial Revolution that came after the Renaissance and the Enlightenment in Europe. The communication technologies came handy in fostering strong links between communication and empire-building through the mechanics of distributed government, military campaigns and trade linkages.

Transnational News Agencies

The first true global media were the transnational news agencies set up in the nineteenth century. Much of the world's international news, especially the financial news, was collected through them as they enjoyed the twin advantages of economy of scale and patronage by the imperial forces. Hailed as agents of globalization and empire-building, news agencies altered the process of news dissemination, nationally and internationally. Their establishment, therefore, was the most important development in the field of newspaper industry of that time.

The increasing demand for commercial information–on business, stocks, currencies, commodities, harvests–resulted in steady growth of news agencies. Their power and reach grew proportionately to their influence on business clients and colonial masters. 'The major European agencies were based in imperial capitals. Their expansion outside Europe was intimately associated with the territorial colonialism of the late nineteenth century'. [35]

The first news agency to be founded was the French Havas News Agency (1835). It was followed by the German agency Wolff in 1849 and the British Reuters in 1851. The U.S. agency, Associated Press (AP) was established in 1848. To begin with, only the first three European agencies began as international news agencies. AP joined their league only towards the turn of the century around 1860. Reuters confined its operations to commercial and financial information while Havas was to combine information and advertising.

Together all three of them controlled information markets in Europe and were aiming at expanding their operations beyond the continent. In 1870, they signed a treaty to divide the world market between the three of them. The resultant association of agencies became known as the League of Allied Agencies, the World League of Press Associations or just the 'Ring Combination'. [36] This was more or less a kind of news cartel whose influence on world opinion was used by colonial powers to suit their own interests. Reuters dominated the Ring Combination of these global news agencies due to larger territory and bigger pool of staff and stringers.

Its importance was further enhanced by Britain's wide-ranging commercial, financial and imperial activities. [37] The cartel continued to dominate the international news distribution till AP began to expand internationally. The decline in cartel's influence coincided with the weakening of the European empires after the First World War.

Reuters: The most famous international news agency owes its name to its founder Paul Julius Reuter. The fortunes of Reuters ran parallel with the growth of the British Empire. The expansion of trade and investment during the nineteenth century and the resultant demand for news helped Reuters to expand. It exploited the growing demand for news with the help of electric telegraph. Reuters' telegrams became an essential reading for the latest news from the various corners of the British Empire. By 1861, Reuters was dispatching news from all the major British colonies including India, Australia, New Zealand and South Africa.

In 1871, Shanghai became the headquarters of the growing Reuters presence in East Asia, and after the beginning of the commercial gold mining in southern Africa in the late nineteenth century, Cape Town became another nodal point in Reuter's global network. By 1914, Reuters news service had three main channels covering the empire: London to Bombay; London to Hong Kong via the Mediterranean to Cairo, Aden, Ceylon and Singapore, and another to Cape Town, Durban, Mombasa, Zanzibar, the Seychelles, and Mauritius. [38]

Reuters keenly watched the interests of the British Empire. In 1910, it started an imperial news service and a year later, the agency made a secret arrangement with the British Government under which it offered to circulate on its wires official speeches to every corner of the Empire. During the First World War, Reuters launched a wartime news service by arrangement with the Foreign Office, which by 1917 was circulating about one million words per month throughout the Empire. In 1942, it signed a wartime news-sharing agreement with its rival AP to create a new cartel of news. In the post-war period, Reuters continued to focus on commercial information around the clock and around the world.

At the turn of the millennium, Reuters was one of the world's biggest multimedia corporations dealing in the business of information, supplying global financial markets and the news media. With over 400 client network around the world, it was supplying satellite feeds of about 25 minutes. These were then sent out scheduled for local news production. It has thus emerged as the one of the world's largest media and information corporations, with regional headquarters in London, New York, Geneva and Hong Kong and offices in 217 cities.

Associated Press (AP): Reuters' hegemony over global news is shared by the Associated Press which came into existence in 1860. Although the decision to launch a news agency by the name Associated Press was taken as early as 1948 at the meeting of leading of newspaper publishers of New York, it actually came into being only 12 years later. It was founded mainly to share the cost of telegraphing the news brought by ship to different ports in the U.S. Initially, AP had to face stiff competition and rivalry from its European counterparts.

Under the 1893 news exchange contract, Reuters, Havas and the Wolff had restricted its entry into the British Empire area. Although AP was able to establish foreign bureaus before the First World War, it could not sell news abroad. The long and arduous struggle which ended in 1934, resulted in the creation of the AP World Service in 1946. Since then, it has expanded its services to include economic and financial international news service called AP-DJ (Dow Jones). This service is run in conjunction with Dow Jones Inc., publisher of the Wall Street Journal and with Telerate, a major US-based financial data service.

Agence France Presse (AFP): AFP is a post-war successor to the Agence Havas, founded in 1835. The French newspapers controlled the agency by having the maximum representation on its board of directors. Through a wide network of bureaus within the country and abroad, AFP is regarded as one of the major global news agencies.

The AFP grew out of a translation agency, which sold the translations to various newspapers. Two of its employees, Paul Julius Reuter and Bernard Wolff started news agencies in the UK and Germany. All these three countries–the UK, France and Germany were the leading European empires of that time. Accordingly, the news agencies, Havas, Reuters and Wolff took control of the large segments of the world for news coverage. This laid the foundation for a close relationship between communication and empire-building.

United Press International (UPI): The phenomenal rise of AP led Edward Wyllis Scripps, the founder of the famous Scripps chain of newspapers in the US, to form the United Press Association in 1907.

Initially, he started two regional news services to cater to his own newspapers. At the same time, there was another association, the Publishers' Press Association formed in1898 by the non-AP newspapers. In 1907 itself, Scripps merged his United Press Association with the Publishers' Press Association to form the United Press Association. This association could enter areas which AP could not due to contractual limitations. Also, unlike AP's straight reporting, UPA was doing an excellent job with human interest stories. The backgrounds and personal accounts enabled it to score over AP and its influence grew.

In 1918, another press association, the International News Service (INS), appeared on the scene. It faced severe competition from AP. To offset this pressure, INS focused on good writers who could do extensive and well-researched pieces. The newspapers never considered it a major source of news but subscribed to it for its well-written stories and major news beats. Although, by 1956, INS emerged as a major news service, it decided to merge with the UPA to form United Press International or UPI. Unlike the AP and Reuters, the UPI has not diversified much into specialized economic services. However, its broadcast related services are its forte.

Telegrafnoi Agentsvo Sovetskavo Soyusa (TASS): In terms of influence, impact, coverage during the Cold War, TASS is one of the five 'globals' as the transnational news agencies are referred to. The news agency which began as the St. Petersburg Telegraph Agency (SPTA) in 1904, underwent a number of name changes before becoming Telegraph Agency of the Soviet Union (TASS) in 1925. Earlier, in 1914, it was renamed as the Petrograd Telegraph Agency (PTA). In 1917, it was made central news agency; a year later the PTA and the Cominform (Communist Information Bureau) were united to form the Russian Telegraph Agency (ROSTA).

TASS was one of the major publicity organs in the erstwhile USSR. It supplied news through a network of correspondents in all regional and territorial centres. Officially, its role was to supply balanced information, objectively reflecting the economic life of all republics, territories and regions by taking into account their economic potential and peculiarities. It had around 20,000 subscribers both domestic and foreign. Actually, its communist propaganda, a central component of the post-war Soviet diplomacy, was primarily aimed at the Eastern Bloc.

The work of TASS was complemented by another information agency, *Novosti Press Agency (APN*). This was established in 1961 by the Union of Soviet Journalists, the Union of Soviet Writers and a few other organizations. The objective was to promote information for peace and friendship among nations. In comparison to TASS which claimed to be the single state system of information, APN became the organ of public organization in the Soviet Union.

During the Cold War years, TASS remained a major source of news among the media in eastern bloc countries. Its Marxist propaganda, couched in the language of the class struggle between the capitalist bourgeoisie and the global proletariat, was the ideological clash between communism and imperialism aimed at countries colonized by European powers.

Following the collapse of the USSR, TASS and APN

merged to form a new Russian information agency called ITAR (the Information Telegraph Agency of Russia). The TASS trademark has now changed to ITAR-TASS. It was decided that the TASS logo would remain in its news reports, as in 'ITAR-TASS'.

In a separate agreement, the heads of 14 national news agencies of former Soviet republics–also former branches of TASS–decided to cooperate in preserving ITAR-TASS' extensive information and communication structures in the post-Soviet era as well as to maintain its central databank.

Together, these five globals comprised the five-headed monster of transnational agencies that barring the last continue to dominate the information flow in the globalized world.

Unlike the Soviet news agency, the western news agencies were established not so much to create an informed international citizenry but to make money. Their histories are witness to their struggles to secure and expand markets for their news. These markets are often delineated by the territorial limits of their home countries' empires or spheres of influence.

Issues in International News Flow

In the backdrop of what has been discussed so far, it would not be wrong to say that global news agencies acted as colonial agents of globalization. They not only propelled the process of globalization across continents in a tightly wired world but also helped in empire-building by relaying important financial and economic news and information about the colonies back to their political masters. They thus helped the imperial colonizers to milch the resource-rich colonies with impunity. The resultant impoverishment of colonies and growing prosperity of their colonizers resulted in an acutely imbalanced world between resource and information rich North and resource-hit and information-poor, South.

The uneven news flows between regions–from the richer countries of the North to the South–greatly exceeds the quantity going in other direction. The quality and quantity of news flows from South to North is very low. In contrast, the consumption of news between countries of the North is very high. The international news agencies, the elite newspapers and magazines of North America and Europe along with the global TV networks such as CNN have news bureaus in all major capitals of the world. The poor and low quantity and quality South-South flow is in sharp contrast to the extremely high quantitative and qualitative North-North flow.

The structure of global news flows from the international wire services to global satellite TV networks and to interactive multimedia systems have only increased the quantity and quality of information flows in what is now called information blizzard but it has not changed the basic hierarchical structure of the news flows.

Western domination of news media made the Third World media thoroughly dependent on the former. It was this imbalance that led Wilbur Schramm, the author of seminal work, *Mass Media and National Development* published in 1964 in conjunction with UNESCO, to consider mass media as a 'bridge to wider world', as the vehicle for transferring new ideas and models from the North to the South and, within the South, from urban to rural areas. Accordingly the task of the mass media of information and 'new media' of education is to speed and ease the long and slow social transformation required for economic development, and, in particular, to speed and smooth the task of modernizing human resources behind the national effort. [39]

'The mass media in the South', he wrote, 'face the need to rouse their people from fatalism and a fear of change. They need to encourage both personal and national aspirations. Individuals must come to desire a better life than they have and to be willing to work for it'. [40]

However, this imbalance was not just confined to information flow between the North and the South. Nearly thirty years later, the MacBride Commission appointed to study the International Communication Problems, noted that the imbalance in news circulation turned out to be a far more complex and varied phenomenon.

It was found to occur at different levels and in different forms: (a) between developed and developing countries, insofar as the information flow is governed by the existence or non-existence of appropriate infrastructures; (b) between countries having different political and socio-economic systems; (c) between developed countries belonging to the same political system, particularly between the smaller and bigger ones; (d) between the Third World countries themselves; (e) between political news and news concerning the social, economic and cultural life of countries battling with the ills of underdevelopment; (f) between what is conventionally called 'good' news 'bad' news i.e. news of catastrophes, failures, conflicts, set-backs, follies and excesses; and finally (g) between topical news of current events and information dealing in greater depth with issues important in the daily lives of peoples and nations. [41]

The Non-Aligned Movement, through the Group of 77, established in 1964, played a major role in the evolution of ideas concerning the dependence of the media, the imbalance and inequality in news flows and global communication patterns and the negative effects of this imbalance. They have advanced the view that the vast majority of countries are reduced to the state of passive receivers of information put out by a few centres. This is how the call for a 'new order' as distinct from the 'old order' in the field of communication and information came into being.

In order to remove these imbalances in news circulation, the concept of 'free flow of information' was coined. Although, the 'free flow' doctrine was essentially a part of the liberal, free market discourse that championed the rights of media proprietors to sell wherever and whatever they wished, here it was meant to serve both economic and political purposes of the Third World. Although this concept ultimately helped the media proprietors in the Western countries, its essence was utilized by newly independent nations of Asia, Africa and Latin America to harness the vast potential of mass media for national development. The birth of national news agencies in these countries was the first step towards establishing a 'new order' to fulfil the promise of democracy, freedom of expression, the media's role as 'public watchdog' and their national and global relevance.

At this point in time, the idea of a new world information and communication order was an open-ended conceptual framework aimed at the following: (a) defining the problems affecting the building of a freer and better balanced international communication system; (b) facilitating coherent discussion at the international level; and (c) clarifying the political options involved. [42]

All this was aimed at countering the increasingly monopolistic trend in global news media as per the Universal Declaration of Human Rights that states that everyone has the right to freedom of opinion and expression; this right includes freedom to hold opinions without interference and to seek, receive and impart information and ideas through any media and regardless of frontiers. The concept of freedom of information with its three main components, namely: the right "to seek" and "to impart" as well as right "to receive" information and the much-trumpeted 'Right to Information" is in fact an extension of this basic tenet of human rights. Over-emphasis of any kind on the 'right to receive' information not only restricts the full rights of the individual to both 'seek' and 'impart' information but also creates unwanted obstacles to and restrictions on the free flow of information.

Role of National News Agencies

Information is power. An informed nation is a strong nation. Knowledgeable and informed citizenry is the power house of a nation-state. A responsible citizen must be adequately informed about the local, national and even international levels to make rational choices. Any lacunae or distortion in information hampers the process of correct assessment and correct judgment. It is, therefore, imperative that no such flaw is allowed to affect the process of an informed and rational decision-making.

Accurate, relevant and timely information is not just required for public alone. Even governments and many public and private bodies may also be in dire need of correct information. It is for this reason the role of national news agencies as channels of authentic and relevant news gains significance.

Also factors like distortion of news due to inaccuracies or biases; cultural alienation due to mindless media encroachment particularly television into traditional societies; and external influence in the wake of western media and cultural intrusion are also major issues that need to be countered in a systematic way. The best way to do is to utilize the network of domestic news agencies.

A news agency, according to the United Nations Educational, Scientific and Cultural Organisation (UNESCO), is "an undertaking of which the principal objective, whatever its legal form, is to gather news and news material of which the sole purpose is to express or present facts, and to distribute this to a group of news enterprises, and in exceptional circumstances to private individuals with a view to providing them with as complete and impartial a news service as possible against payment, and under conditions compatible with business laws and usage".

The primary functions of a news agency is to provide news reports of current events to newspapers and others who subscribe for its service; news agencies are, therefore, expected to work with integrity and disinterestedness, besides being as comprehensive in their coverage as possible. There has to be freedom of bias in the collection of news, particularly political news. News agencies are not expected to have any specific editorial policy apart from following an impartial, disinterested policy where collection and selection of facts are concerned. Social responsibility would, however, apply to news agencies also. There has been an element of comment in the name of interpretation intruding into the dissemination of news.

As wholesale suppliers of news and news related material, news agencies are supposed to play a crucial role in the modern information system. They exercise considerable influence on building opinion and orienting perceptions of peoples and governments on major issues of the day.

"The establishment of a news agency, like the acquisition of a parliament, a flag and a currency became one of the sine qua non of modern European nationhood. Thus, in the aftermath of the Versailles Treaty a cluster of new news agencies emerged, which all depended upon one form of subsidy or another and have done so ever since". [43]

Today, almost every country of the world has a news agency of its own. Be it Rashtriya Samachar Seva or RSS of Nepal or TNA i.e. Thai News Agency of Thailand or PTI–The Press Trust of India–all are playing a key role in information gathering and dissemination.

End Notes

1. Toffler, A. (1980), The Third Wave. London: Collins.
2. McLuhan, Marshall (1960), *Explorations in Communication* (ed.), E.S. Carpenter, Boston: Beacon Press.
3. Sen, Amartya (2002), How to Judge Globalism?, The American Prospect, 13, 1, January, 1-14.
4. Ibid.
5. Harasim, L. (ed.) (1994), Global Networks: Computers and International Communication, Cambridge, MA: MIT Press, p. 81.
6. Robertson, Roland (1992), Globalization: Social Theory and Global Culture. London: Sage Publications, p. 8.
7. Ibid.
8. Ibid.
9. Waters, M. (1995), Globalization. London: Routledge, pp. 23-24.
10. Giddens, A. (1990), The Consequence of Modernity,

Cambridge: Polity Press.

11. Ferguson, M. (1992), The Mythology About Globalization, European Journal of Communication, 7, 1, pp. 69-93.
12. Beck, U. (2000), What is Globalization? Oxford, Polity Press, p. 78.
13. Giddens, 1990, pp. 112-13.
14. Ibid.
15. Hirst. P. and Thompson, G. (1996), Globalization in Question: The International Economy and the Possibilities of Governance, Cambridge: Polity Press, pp. 45-46.
16. Ohmae, K. (1995), The End of the Nation State: The Rise and Fall of Regional Economies, London: HarperCollins, p. 89.
17. Clarke, I. (1997), Globalization and Fragmentation: International Relations in the 20th Century, Oxford: Oxford University Press, pp. 39-40.
18. Robertson, R. (1992), Globalization: Social Theory and Global Culture, London: Sage Publications, pp. 173-174.
19. UN (1995), Our Global Neighbourhood: The Report of the Commission on Global Governance, Oxford: Oxford University Press.
20. Archibugi, D. and Held, D. (eds.) (1995), Cosmopolitan Democracy, Cambridge: Polity Press.
21. Cheah, P. and Robbins, B. (eds.) (1998), Cosmopolitics: Thinking and Feeling beyond the Nation, Minneapolis: University of Minnesota Press.
22. Nye, J. and Owens, W. (1996), America's Information Edge, Foreign Affairs, March-April, pp. 20-36.
23. Rothkopf, D. (1997), In Praise of Cultural Imperialism? Foreign Policy, Summer, pp. 38-53.
24. Sen, Amartya (2002), How to Judge Globalism? The American Prospect, 13, 1, January, pp. 1-14..
25. Sen, Amartya (2002), How to Judge Globalism?, The American Prospect, 13, 1, January, pp. 1-14.
26. Ibid.
27. Robertson, Roland (1992) Globalization: Social Theory and Global Culture, London: Sage Publications, pp. 58-59.
28. Headrick, D. (1981), The Tools of Empire: Technology and European Imperialism in the Nineteenth Century, New York: Oxford University Press, pp. 48-49.
29. Lasswell, H. (1927), Propaganda Techniques in the World War,

New York: Alfred Knopf.

30. Hale, J. (1975), Radio Power: Propaganda and International Broadcasting, London: Paul Elek.
31. McLuhan, M. (1964), Understanding Media, London: Methuen, p. 69.
32. Toffler, A. (1980), The Third Wave, London: Collins.
33. Ibid.
34. Stehr, N. (1994), Knowledge Societies, London: Sage Publications.
35. Boyd-Barrett, O. (1980), The International News Agencies, London: Constable, p. 36.
36. Desmond, R. (1978), The Information Process: World News Reporting to the Twentieth Century, Iowa City: University of Iowa Press, p. 89.
37. Read, D. (1992), The Power of News: The History of Reuters, 1849-1989, Oxford: Oxford University Press, pp. 90-91.
38. Ibid.
39. Schramm, W. (1964), Mass Media and National Development: The Role of Information in the Developing Countries, Stanford, CA: Stanford University Press, pp. 28-34.
40. Ibid.
41. Many Voices, One World (1982), Paris: UNESCO, pp. 36-39.
42. Many Voices, One World (1982), Paris: UNESCO, pp. 36-39.
43. Smith, A. (1973), The Politics of Information, London: Macmillan, p. 18.

2

Globalization and Indian Mass Media

Advent and History of News Agencies in India

The credit for conceiving the idea and establishing an Indian news agency goes to K.C. Roy who, as a special correspondent at the headquarters of the Government of India at Bombay and Calcutta, took special interest in the ways and means of popularizing news. He was keen to assist Indian newspapers with an affordable news service. His efforts bore fruit with the birth of the *Associated Press of India (API)* in 1910. His coordinators in this venture were Everard Coates, the special correspondent of the Statesman, the Madras Mail, the Advocate of India and the London Daily Mail, and Edward Buck, Reuters Agent with the Government of India.

To facilitate its smooth functioning, Roy used his influence to amend the Indian Telegraph Act thereby making provisions for news agencies to be registered for the purpose of accepting "bearing" press telegrams, a privilege hitherto confined to the newspapers registered with the Director General of Posts and Telegraphs. [1] The establishment of API came as a big boon to Indian newspapers which were always in short supply of news about India within the country itself due to undeveloped communication lines and inefficient reporting.

Roy was assisted in his endeavour by a band of loyal workers who selflessly shared his vision. Notable among them were Dallas of the Indian Daily News and Usha Nath Sen. Sen was instrumental in opening the Madras office of the API with the cooperation of two leading newspapers, the Hindu and the Swadesmitram. The formation of API replaced the "distinctively personal touch of Indian Journalism by impersonal service of news". [2]

According to M. Chalapathi Rau, K.C. Roy was the dominant figure in the formation of the first news agency in India. "In scenting news, in getting it from the highest sources in the land, and in transmitting it, he was considered exceptionally agile and intelligent." [3]

However, Roy's days in API proved to be numbered as he fell out with his corraborators over the issue of internal management of the news agency. Roy left API to launch a competing organization called the *Indian News Bureau* along with Sen and other Indian friends and well-wishers. Roy's exit from API and subsequent launch of the News Bureau did not help either of the two. Rather competition hurt of both of them, particularly the News Bureau as Roy faced considerable financial strain to sustain it.

In 1919, at the suggestion of Coates, Baron de Reuters bought off the interests of Coates and Roy in API and News Bureau to launch a domestic news service in India for assimilation and dissemination of news. The resultant *Eastern News Agency* had the interests of Reuters, the API and News Bureau. Roy was made its Managing Director and Chief Editor. Sen succeeded Roy on the latter's death in 1931. Both of them were given free hand in building up service to cater to India's needs while Reuter took care of its financial aspect.

This combination of Reuters, API and News Bureau in early twenties proved ineffective in supplying hard news wanted by the freedom loving Indian people. It turned out to be self-defeating venture as it invited official control over its contents. It could only supply official news, and the activities of commercial magnates, big landlords and other vested interests. It failed to channelise and express the aspirations of countless nationalists.

To counter it, the *Free Press of India News Agency* was started to 'correct the balance' with a view to develop 'healthy public opinion which was moulded entirely by the news supplied from day to day'. Free Press of India emerged as an independent nationalist news agency to safeguard the nationalists' view and to contradict and counteract the API whenever it was found necessary. Its eminent sponsors included Dr. Annie Besant, M.R. Jayakar, Sir Purushottamdans Thakurdas, G.D. Birla, Sir Phiroze Sethna and Walchand Hirachand.

S. Sadanand, the moving spirit behind the venture, did not bow before government repression and financial troubles. Under the press ordinance of May 1930, newspapers publishing Free Press news faced penalties, and the agency's telegrams were subject to strict censorship; newspapers were reluctant to publish news supplied by the agency. In order to make the Free Press more popular and secure, the management of the news agency started an English daily, the *Free Press Journal* in June 1930. It featured the telegrams of the parent agency.

Unwilling to give up so easily, Sadanand fought back by starting the Free Press Journal as a morning daily in June 1930 from Bombay and other associated newspapers to publish Free Press news exclusively. Both Reuters and Associated Press objected to a news agency running a chain of newspapers and refused to sell their services to those dailies which subscribed to any other service. When his newspapers' securities were confiscated, Sadanand had to close down his agency in 1935. [4]

The vacuum created by the closure of the Free Press was filled by the *United Press of India* (UPI). It was started by B. Sen Gupta, the Calcutta editor of the Free Press. It was a small concern with only 16 newspapers of Calcutta and Lahore subscribing to it. The API continued to be its chief rival. Despite stiff competition, it went on undaunted. It organized a skeleton foreign service with an office in Fleet Street, London, supplying Indian news to the British Press and cabling foreign news to the Indian papers. Steadily, it gained a foothold both within and outside India. It established 20 branch offices in the country and appointed a large number of provincial and national correspondents.

It supplied news to over 90 newspapers all over India, including the British-owned newspapers. Its clientele, among others, included the All India Radio, the Government of India and many provincial governments. It also went ahead and forged trade links with the leading French news agency the Agence France Presse. The API was ahead of UPI due to its better communication facilities. To meet this challenge, the UPI also started its teleprinter service in 1948. Dr. Rajendra Prasad, the first President of India, inaugurated the teleprinter service for speedy transmission of news. Within three years by 1951, UPI was in a position to provide full and comprehensive world news to its subscribers. It continued to do so for the next five years till 1956. It was the first news agency to flash the news of the Mahatma Gandhi's assassination. [5]

While the nationalist view-point was given by nationalist news agencies like the Free Press and UPI, the separatist perspective was reflected in the dispatches of news agency like the *Orient Press of India*. Started in 1941 by Syed Mohammad as its managing Director, it was exclusively meant to safeguard the Muslim interests by serving the Muslim League and catering to the Urdu Press. It got financial help from the Government and a few wealthy states like Hyderabad as well as prominent Muslim businessmen. It had limited clientele and no foreign subscribers at all. It did not make much progress as a news agency and closed down in 1947 at the time of partition.

Another contemporary but lesser known news agency was the *Globe News Agency* established by a British journalist and a successful newspaper proprietor, Edward Hulton. It was an independent and non-subsidized news service with head office in Calcutta and other offices in Bombay, Madras, Delhi and Bangalore. With senior journalist like Satyendranath Majumdar as its editorial head, the Globe secured the services of experienced journalists and correspondents to spread its network all over India and the world.

The advent of freedom brought a new dawn for the Indian

Press. The need for a national news agency was strongly felt. The Indian newspapers formed the Press Trust of India, the successor to the Associated Press of India (API) on the basis of cooperative ownership. It was registered as a company in August 1947 and went into operation from February 1949. Sardar Vallabh Bhai Patel, the then Home Minister, had refused to renew Reuter Teleprinter lease in July 1947 unless the ownership was transferred to an Indian agency. PTI arrived at a three-year agreement with Reuters under which it took over the Associated Press and joined Reuters as a partner in the collection and dissemination of news.

It was assigned a zone from Cairo to Singapore for covering news for the Reuters world pool. It was made primarily responsible for the control and direction of correspondents in that zone. Consequently, it maintained correspondents at important news centres like Bangkok, Cairo, Colombo, Dacca, Georgetown, Johannesburg, Karachi, Kathmandu, Lahore, New York, Rangoon, Singapore and Tokyo.

The preamble of the agreement between the Reuters and the PTI was the article of faith that stated: "both parties declare that they are news agencies serving no other purpose than the dissemination of truthful unbiased news, that they are free from any Government or tendentious control and that the news, which they supply to each other, shall be compiled and selected solely on its objectivity of news value. They have entered into this agreement in full accord and understanding as to the basic principles of integrity of news". [6]

The PTI provides full and comprehensive world and Indian news service to the newspapers and several types of commercial services to trading and industrial houses. As a trust, it is a non-profit sharing company.

In 1953, PTI entered into a significant bilateral news sharing arrangement with the Reuters. As per the arrangement, PTI buys Reuters world-wide news service to sell to Indian newspapers. Similarly, it sells Indian news to the Reuters for its world service. The All India Radio, the Government of India and the State governments are the largest single source of revenue of the PTI.

For over ten years, PTI enjoyed complete monopoly as the only national news agency of free India. To promote healthy competition and improve quality of news service, the United News of India (UNI) was sponsored by a group of 40 leading newspapers of India including the Statesman, the Times of India and the Hindu. These newspapers shared the view of the first Press Commission that there should be "at least two news agencies each competing with the other and also acting as a corrective to the other". It was registered in 1959 but it started service on March 21, 1961. It also entered into a tie-up with the Associated Press of America for distribution of foreign news.

Hindusthan Samachar was started as a private limited company in 1948 by Shri S.S. Apte. It became a cooperative society of the workers in 1957. It is meant to cater to the needs of the Language Press. The agency has an objective view in the dissemination of news. Through its network of reporters in rural areas and by the establishment of the first Dev Nagari teleprinter service, it has carved a niche for itself in the country.

The Hindusthan Samachar provides news in eight Indian languages, besides service in English. As a multi-lingual news agency, it is of great help to regional newspapers. In 1975, it had 21 bureaus offering services in the Indian languages to 135 subscribers. In 1967, another news agency, the Samachar Bharati, began operations as a second Indian language agency. In 1975, it had 13 bureaus and revenue of about half a million rupees.

During the Emergency, all the four news agencies were compelled by the Indira Government to merge into Samachar on 24 January 1976. The resultant news agency received a government grant of half a million rupees during 1976-77 to facilitate increase in pay and allowances and towards discharge of old liabilities. The Janata Government which came to office in 1977 did away with press censorship and abolished Samachar. The four agencies resumed functioning separately as before from 14 April 1978.

Globalization in India

Now we come to the central point of our discussion i.e. the globalization in India. As we know, modern concept of globalization refers to a process of deepening economic integration, increasing economic openness and growing economic interdependence between countries in the world economy. "It is associated not only with a phenomenal spread and volume of cross border economic transactions, but also with an organization of economic activities which straddles national boundaries". [7]

Globalization in India is generally taken to mean integration of the Indian economy with the world economy. The main push towards globalization was provided by the new economic policy introduced by the Government of India in July 1991 at the behest of the International Monetary Fund (IMF) and the World Bank. Steps were taken to facilitate the flow of foreign direct investments or FDI in various sectors of the economy by allowing entry of multinational companies or MNCs in the country. Indian companies were also allowed to enter into foreign collaborations within the country and also encourage them to set up joint ventures abroad. A number of policy initiatives were also undertaken to make this happen. The economy was opened up through dilution and subsequent scrapping of restrictive laws like FERA (Foreign Exchange Regulation Act) and carrying out massive import liberalization programmes and opting for exchange rate adjustments for promoting exports.

In fact, India's leap towards globalization was the result of 'stabilisation and structural adjustment programme' which the Government of India was compelled to undertake by the IMF and the World Bank as a necessary pre-condition for credit availability to ward off default on debt in June 1991. With the downgrading of India's credit rating by some international agencies consequent upon the large deficit in India's balance of payments in 1990-91 and the political uncertainties at home, the investor's confidence in the Indian economy was shaken badly and there resulted a substantial capital out-flight.

Despite drawing US$ 1.8 billion from the Contingency Compensatory Financing Facility (CCFF) in January 1991, adopting import compression measures, and pledging gold abroad, the crisis could not be stemmed. Foreign exchange reserves dwindled to US$ 1.1 billion in June 1991–less than sufficient for two weeks of import requirements. Default on debt servicing appeared imminent and the Government of India was pushed towards the wall. Default could be avoided only if credit was made available from the IMF and the World Bank. Assistance was indeed made available by these institutions but on their own terms and conditions. And, these terms and conditions entailed adoption of a 'stabilisation and structural adjustment programme' by India.

This programme had three main components namely: (a) stabilization which basically implies cutting down fiscal deficit and the rate of growth of money supply, (b) domestic liberalization which consists of relaxing restrictions on production, investment, prices and increasing the role of market signals in guiding resource allocation, and (c) external sector liberalization or relaxing restrictions on international flows of goods, services, technology and capital. [8]

Thus, India embraced globalization under 'desperate conditions of 1990 and 1991' despite the fact that already a number of committees in the 1980s had strongly advocated substantial liberalization of the industrial, trade and other sectors of the economy. [9] A powerful public opinion in favour of liberalization had also emerged within the country. As a result, wide ranging changes in industrial and trade policies were introduced in the 1980s as many concessions were granted to the foreign capital, MNCs were allowed to enter a number of crucial sectors to which their entry was previously restricted or banned, provisions of FERA were not strictly enforced, import liberalization process was accelerated considerably and downward adjustment in the exchange rate of the rupee was resorted to.

However, the real opening up of the economy and attempts at integrating it with the world economy came up only in 1991 consequent upon the adoption of the structural adjustment programme. In the following years, the globalization process was carried still further by the government.

Among the many steps towards globalization initiated by the government, the three most important ones have been the following.

1. **Exchange Rate Adjustment and Rupee Convertibility:** The most import measure for integrating the country's economy is to make its currency fully convertible. As a first step towards this measure, the IMF insisted on the devaluation of the Indian rupee. According the Government of India made a two step downward adjustment of 18-19 percent in the exchange rate of the rupee on July 1 and 3, 1991. Thus, the most important condition of the IMF for the grant of assistance was met.

   In the following years, the government progressively moved towards full convertibility. For instance, in the 1992-93 Budget, dual exchange rate system implying partial convertibility of rupee was introduced. The 1993-94 Budget introduced full convertibility of the rupee on trade account and switched over to a unified exchange rate system. India achieved full convertibility on current account on August 19, 1994.
2. **Import Liberalisation:** India redesigned its import policy to ensure freer entry of capital goods, intermediate goods, raw materials and consumer goods into the Indian economy. The supplementary trade policy announced on August 13, 1991 decanalised the import of 20 items. In addition, the import duty has also been reduced

successively. Also, as a member of the World Trade Organisation (WTO), India is committed to the phasing out of quantitative restrictions over a six-year period beginning 1997. The standard argument for import liberalization is that competition from imports would improve efficiency, quality and technology besides making international quality capital goods and inputs available to Indian export industries thereby increasing their competitive strength in the international markets.

3. **Opening up to Foreign Capital:** In 1991, the government announced a specified list of high technology and high-investment priority industries wherein automatic permission was granted for direct foreign investment up to 51 percent foreign equity. The limit was raised from 51 percent to 74 percent and subsequently to 100 percent for many of these industries. Presently, Foreign Direct Investment (FDI) is permitted up to 100 percent on the automatic route in most sectors subject to sectoral rules/regulations applicable. FDI is prohibited only in the following sectors: (1) retail trading (except single brand product retailing), (2) atomic energy, (3) lottery business, and (4) gambling and betting.

Globalization and Indian Mass Media

Liberalization, privatization and globalization (LPG) policies of the Government of India have resulted in unprecedented changes in the Indian media scene. This includes 100 percent FDI in enterprises that sustain and support country's mass media. Together, they determine the direction taken by the Indian media.

The process of allowing FDI in media started in 2003 when 26 percent foreign equity was allowed into newspapers. Over and above, FDI of 20 or 26 percent foreign institutional and non-resident Indian investment was also allowed. Together, it amounted to nearly 46 percent in the case of news media, DTH, cable TV and FM radio. Non-news media, both in print and broadcasting, is allowed 100 percent FDI. The related areas like advertising, market research, films and other entertainment ventures are also included in this package.

The resultant exponential growth of mass media in terms of size, reach and access is evident both in print as well as electronic media. The number of television channels has crossed over 500 against hardly ten or so a decade ago. Of these, there are over 45 round the clock news channels. With neighbourhood or cable channels also in the fray, the total television coverage is over 50 percent of country's population as against 35 percent of newspapers of all periodicity. [10]

Table 2.1: Foreign Direct Investment (FDI) Allowed in Media (April 2013)

Media	Percent of FDI
Technical Journals	100
Films	100
Advertising	100
Market Research	100
Public Relations	100
Printing Plants	100
TV-Non News	100
Cable Networks	74
DTH	74
Newspapers	26
Radio-FM	26
TV News	26

Source: *Consolidated FDI Policy, April 2013*, Department of Industrial Policy and Promotion, Ministry of Commerce and Industry, Government of India.

Even in rural India, the print medium is covering about 15 percent of the population against about 45 percent reached by television. Not to be left behind, the good old radio and cinema both witnessed an equally interesting revival in the last couple of years.

The turnover of the fast-expanding media sector is more than ₹ 400 billion and growing at around 18 percent annually since 2003. As a result, media is recognized as among the top five priority sectors for investment in the country. This is very well reflected in the voluminous size of the Indian media. In particular, the electronic media has registered a tremendous growth during the 2000-2005 period.

This growth has affected the print media in a major way. With 24-hour news channels beaming news bulletins round-the-clock, the newspapers have lost their enviable position of 'primary' and 'most credible' source on political, business, financial and sports news. The 'breaking news' syndrome of TV news channels is at the forefront of this change.

This explains the Page 3 phenomenon in bigger and multi-edition news dailies to woo readers who are increasingly relying on television news channels for their daily doze of current news and affairs. Even the small and medium sized newspapers with limited means and localized readership are in the grip of Page 3 mania.

This trend has given way to a certain homogenization in media contents and changing values of media. The emerging media scenario is thus characterized by increasing consumerism and corporatization of Indian media. The keen interest of media mogul like Rupert Murdoch (Star Group) in various sectors of the Indian media industry proves this point. He already enjoys key strategic partnership with leading individuals and businesses with annual turnover of ₹ 12,000 crore next only to the Times of India group with ₹ 15,000 crore. According to Business World, by the end of 2004, the reach of Star Group (TV and radio) was at 55.9 million viewers as against the Times of India's reach of 6.1 million readers and Doordarshan's 233 million viewers. Almost 70 percent of Star's total earnings are from India alone.

Thus, the globalization process in India has brought about unprecedented changes in the role and function of mass media. With the entry of foreign players, mergers, acquisitions and cross-media holdings have become the order of the day. The situation is further compounded by the global consumerist culture ultimately setting the media priorities. Gone are the days of public service broadcasters who were once hailed as *change agents*. As a result, with just one-third share of the overall broadcast scene in the country, the once all-in-all Doordarshan, despite its wide reach and access, has virtually become a fence-sitter.

Not because it lacks technical finesse but because the agenda setting function of the mass media, particularly the news media, has taken a severe beating by the avalanche of market forces unleashed by global capital. According to an estimate, foreign channels together (Star, Sony, ESPN, Star Sports and Discovery, etc) earned about ₹ 2,500 crore in advertising revenue in 2002-2003 as against ₹ 400 crore in 1998-99.

Further, in roads made by Pay TV, DTH, set-top-box in addition to expanding domain of the Internet and 24-hour news channels have further eroded the ground held by traditional media. Winds of change are blowing hard. The fury of this blizzard is evident in the changes witnessed in the print media whose main sources of news and information have been national news agencies which too are losing ground in the emergent media scene. Their steady marginalization is a matter of concern and therefore a fit subject of this research study.

End Notes

1. Murthy, Nadig Krishna (1966), Indian Journalism, University of Mysore Press, Mysore, pp. 66-67.
2. Ibid.
3. Chalapathi Rau, M. (1974), The Press: National Book Trust, India, New Delhi.
4. Chalapathi Rau, M. (1974), The Press: National Book Trust, India, New Delhi.
5. Murthy, Nadig Krishna (1966), Indian Journalism: University of Mysore Press, Mysore, pp. 394-397.
6. Murthy, Nadig Krishna (1966), Indian Journalism: University of Mysore Press, Mysore, pp. 394-397.
7. Nayyar, Deepak (1988), Globalisation: What Does it Mean for Development? in Bibek Debroy (ed.) Challenges of

Globalisation: New Delhi, p. 15.
8. Ray, Alok (1993), External Sector Liberalisation in India, Economic and Political Weekly, October 2, 1993, p. 2161.
9. Swamy, Dalip S. (1994), The Political Economy of Industrialisation, New Delhi.
10. CMS Media Lab Compilation.

3

Literature on News Media

Globalization together with rapid innovation in communication technology and information explosion has revolutionized the media scene and led to unprecedented changes in the working mechanism of news agencies, both national and international. As is well-known, the national news agencies were generated within a global news system controlled by the 19th century news cartel comprising the 'big four' western news agencies namely the AFP, AP, Reuters, UPI. The two leading news agencies of the communist world, TASS of the erstwhile Soviet Union and Xinhua of expansionist China served their allies in the eastern bloc and communist Asia.

The main objective behind the establishment of national news agencies was to project the 'national image' of their respective countries on the global stage. Their agenda was to inform the world about their point of view as distinct from the perspective often projected by their highly resourceful global competitors. The United Nations, through UNESCO, was keen to help newly independent nations develop their national news agencies and encourage a credible news-exchange mechanism between them. Again the western-based international news agencies saw a great business potential in these upcoming national news agencies and readily established local business links with the former. The national news agencies thus became a conduit for providing international news to the local media and releasing domestic news to the wider world.

Media scholars like Daniel Lerner [1], Pye [2] and Wilbur Schramm [3] found great promise in news agencies for their integrated media approach to pursue the agenda of national development through mass media. In his book *Passing of*

Traditional Society, Lerner emphasized the correlation between economic productivity and the media provisions in different countries. In his view, mass media could be an ideal tool for promoting empathy in individuals in particular and society at large for development and better living conditions.

Diffusion of new ideas and practices being the crucial component of modernizing practices, both Lerner and later Rogers [4] considered mass communication an effective medium for creating awareness, development of favourable attitudes and adaptation by inter-personal channels, particularly the opinion leaders. This function could be performed effectively be news agencies in the Third World they opined. Later Wilbur Schramm in his magnum opus 'Mass Media and National Development' which was produced by the UNESCO conceptualized the development communication in a systematic manner. Here, he hailed the mass media as *magic multiplier* and stressed the importance of media content as the key for development. And, since the news agencies were the only reliable medium of mass communication available in resource starved under-developed countries of Asia, Africa and Latin America, both UNESCO and communication scholars alike stressed their role as development agents and magic multipliers.

As political instability, poverty, illiteracy, unemployment and corruption emerged as salient features of a developing society, the International Commission for the study of communication problems, '*Many Voices, One World*' [5] identified imbalance in the news flow from the developed to the non-developed countries as the key concern in international communication.

According to the report, a handful of transnational media giants like the AP, AFP, the Reuters, UPI, ITAR-TASS etc were monopolizing the entire news and information flow. Their monopoly was causing 'one-way flow' of news and information which was highly detrimental to the interests of Third World countries. It was, therefore, decided to offset the harm caused by the Western media empires by creating a new international information climate. The launch of Non-Aligned News Agencies Pool in 1975 followed by the establishment of many other news distribution systems at national, regional and international levels was an important step towards this direction.

The entire 1970s was consumed by this debate till the acceptance of the MacBride Commission report by UNESCO in 1981 which saw the NWICO as "a multistage, dynamic and evolutionary process". [6]

During this time, most of the media research pertaining to news agencies focused either on the NWICO debates and various policy initiatives at various national and international levels as suggested by the MacBride Commission report or to analyse and evaluate the imbalance in the so called free flow doctrine of news flow in international communication.

Scholars like Herbert Schiller have minced no words in saying that free flow of information was essentially meant to safeguard the economic growth of the West and any attempt to regulate the flow of information beyond borders was seen as a threat to Western economies. Calling it a blatant interference in the basic human right, he wrote: "A powerful communication system exists to secure, not grudging submission by an open-armed allegiance in the penetrated areas, but by identifying the American presence with freedom–freedom of trade, freedom of speech and freedom of enterprise". [7]

Describing the nature of news and information flow as "imbalanced, iniquitous, sometimes even biased and West-oriented, impervious to the needs of the developing world", noted journalist D.R. Mankekar [8] wrote that the monopoly of transnational media empires was detrimental to the interests of developing nations.

Dissecting the entire NWICO debates threadbare, Wolfgang Kleinwachter [9] said all forces in the South, in the East and the West are forming a consensus on the basic issue of freedom of speech and information which is universal and should be respected nationally and internationally.

Sophia Peterson of the West Virginia University attempted a useful study of the Third World news coverage by the Western news agencies and the Times (London). [10] She mainly explored three questions:

1. Do Western news agencies tend to under-report Third World countries?
2. Is news coverage of Third World countries by the Western news agencies more negative than news coverage of First World countries?
3. How does an elite Western newspaper compare with the news agencies, both in the amount and type of news coverage of Third World countries?

This study was undertaken in the light of the assumption that Western news agencies provide better coverage of the Third World than is appreciated but that Western newspapers do not select a representative sample of agency news for publication.

Chris Paterson's study of the news agency stranglehood on global political discourse [11] looks at the concentration of corporate control over public affairs in the context of emerging news distribution mechanisms in the light of dominance of AP and Reuters as reflected in the dominance of a Western agenda in international news.

A research study about the State of news agencies– Government's last media stronghold by Goran Verzic [12] of SEEMO (Southeast European Media Organisation) discusses how while the states are renouncing newspaper ownership and turning TV and Radio stations into public services, they are not giving up news agencies in order to retain their political control and influence. In this way, the state exerts three monopolies: information, market using citizen's money and political monopoly. Through news agencies, they continue to disseminate their political views freely. The money set aside for news agencies depend directly upon the state's wealth.

However, from purely Indian perspective, I could find only one research conducted on the subject of news agencies entitled "News Agency Journalism in India" by Malay Mitra from the Department of Journalism, University of Calcutta, in 1993. It was supervised by Sunil Kumar Mukhopadhyaya. [13]

Then in 2009, the Indian Institute of Mass Communication, New Delhi, undertook a study on Indian news agencies with the following broad objectives: to assess the process of news exchange between Indian News Agencies and their counterparts abroad; to study the procurement, processing and utilization of foreign news content by looking at:

1. Projection of India's image through news content provided by the News Agencies and its utilization by foreign newspapers and
2. Foreign news sourced by News Agencies in India and its utilization by the Indian press.

Thus, it is clear from the aforementioned review of the body of work already existing in the field of news agency journalism that there is no research done to study the impact of globalization on domestic news agencies of India. The research study undertaken by me focuses solely on the impact of globalization on Indian news media with particular reference to national news agencies.

End Notes

1. Lerner, D. (1958), The Passing of Traditional Society, New York, Free Press.
2. Pye, L. (1963), Communications and Political Development, Princeton, NJ: Princeton University Press.
3. Schramm, W. (1964), Mass Media and National Development, Stanford: Stanford University Press.
4. Rogers, Everett M. (1983), Diffusion of Innovations, The Free Press, New York.
5. 1989, Paris, UNESCO (MacBride Commission Report).
6. Ibid.
7. Schiller, H.I. (1971), Mass Communication and American Empire, Boston: Beacon Press, p. 68.
8. Mankekar, D.R. (1981), Whose Freedom? Whose Order? New

Delhi: Clarion Books.

9. Kleinwachter, W. (1993), Three Waves of the Debate in Global Media Debate: Its Rise, Fall and Renewal (eds.) Gerbner, G., Mowlana, H., Nordenstreng, K., Ablex Publishing Corporation, Norwood, NJ, p. 16.
10. Peterson, S. (1980), A Case Study of Third World News Coverage by the Western News Agencies and the Times (London), Studies in Comparative International Development (CSID), Springer, New York, pp. 62-98.
11. Paterson, Chris (2003), Media Research, Journal of the Centre for International Communication Research.
12. www.mediaonline.ba of Southeast European Media Journal (2005).
13. www.inflibnet.ac.in.

4

The Times of India

The Times of India (TOI) is one of India's leading daily newspapers and the highest circulation English language daily broadsheet in the world. It was founded in 1838 as *The Bombay Times and Journal of Commerce* and served the British residents of western India. It adopted its present name in 1861. It is published by India's largest media group, Bennett, Coleman & Co. Ltd. This company along with its other group companies are more popularly known as *The Times Group,* which also publishes *The Economic Times, the Navbharat Times,* and the *Maharashtra Times.* It is most widely read in Gujarat and Maharashtra particularly Mumbai and Ahmedabad.

The Times of India (1985) [1]

Times of India, Bombay, Tuesday, January 1, 1985: The front page of the first issue of Times of India dated January 1, 1985 displayed an eight-column banner headline saying *Rajiv and 39 ministers sworn in* credited to TOINS or the Times of India News Service. Next major headline was a six column PTI story saying *8th LS Formed* along with another boldly displayed story about the *List of Portfolios* spread over two columns. A news feature entitled *Rajiv's ascent from pilot to PM* spread over four columns was credited to UNI. These stories were part of the total 12 stories that appeared on the front page of Times of India that day.

Of these, PTI had two stories, UNI had three while the remaining stories were credited to TOINS. Pages 2 and 4 of the same issue were devoted to commercial advertisements. Page 3 had a total of 8 stories of which just one story jointly belonged to the agencies i.e. UNI and PTI. The remaining were all in-house stories. Page 5 had a total of 15 stories of which only two belonged to PTI. Of the remaining, five were district news from the staffers and just one story was credited to AFP. Likewise, Page 6 was again reserved for advertisements and Page 7 had a total of six stories of which three belonged to PTI and the remaining to TOINS.

Page 8 was the editorial page. Page 9 contained a total of 18 stories of which there were three PTI stories, two UNI and the remaining six foreign stories were equally shared by AP, UPI and Reuters. Page 10 has 20 commodity news stories of which three belonged to PTI and just one to UNI. The sports page (Page 11) had all the 12 stories credited to TOINS. The following Page 12 also was a sports page with just four stories of which two belonged to PTI. Page 13 had a total of three news features of which one belonged to PTI.

Page 15 had just two stories by the TOI's own foreign correspondents while page 15 had a total of seven stories of which PTI had three and one each by Oana-Kyodo, AP, Reuters and AFP. Pages 17 and 18 were again reserved for advertisements and Page 18 had just two stories by TOINS staffers. Page 19 had three stories of which the credit of one story was jointly shared by PTI and TOINS. Page 20 and 21 had pictures of winners and losers both. Page 22 had two news features of which one belonged to PTI while page 23 had just one feature by TOINS. Page 24 again was filled with advertisements. Hence, there were a total of 113 news stories in the issue of which 25 were credited to PTI and eight to UNI and 10 to other foreign news agencies namely Reuters, AP, UPI, Oana-Kyodo and AFP.

Times of India, Bombay, Wednesday, January 2, 1985: The front page headlines included TOINS' *Hegde wants early poll* and *Cuban revo defies US schemes* credited to Reuters. Of the total 12 stories, PTI and UNI shared two stories each while AP had one story to its credit. Pages 2, 4 and 6 were reserved for commercials, while Page 3 had a total of 13 stories of which PTI had four and UNI just one. Page 5 had a total of 18 stories of which five were credited to PTI and three to UNI. Page 7 had eight stories of which two were by PTI and three by UNI.

Page 8 was the editorial page. Page 9 had the maximum number of 21 news stories of PTI and UNI had five each while AP had three. Page 10 had 14 stories of which two stories were credited to PTI, two to UNI and two to AP. Likewise, Page 11 had seven stories of which two belonged to PTI and three to UNI while Page 12 was reserved for advertisements. Page 13 had 17 stories of which three were PTI's and one each of UNI's and AP. Page 14 had all the three stories from AP. Page 15 had ten stories one each from UNI and UPI. Page nos. 16, 17, 20, 21 and 24 were reserved for advertisements. Remaining page nos. 18, 19 and 22 and 23 had a total of 19 stories of which five belonged to PTI, two to UNI and five to various foreign news agencies. Hence, this issue of *Times of* India had 149 stories of which 27 were credited to PTI, 23 to UNI and 36 to other foreign news agencies.

Times of India, Bombay, Thursday, January 3, 1985: Of the total 15 stories appearing on the front page of this issue, six belonged to PTI. These included first column box item with bold headline entitled "*Assembly goes*". This was followed by another story–*Apang sworn-in as Arunachal CM.* While UNI had a two column story entitled–*States poll before March ruled out. Snow freezes life in north, RS to meet on Jan 17, Dhawan Quits*–were other PTI stories. One story each belonged to AP and UPI. Page two, as usual, was reserved for advertisements. Page 3 had a total of eight stories of which just one belonged to PTI. Page 4 had 12 stories of which two were from PTI and four from UNI. Likewise, Page 5 also had 12 stories of which PTI had three and UNI two. Of the total seven stories of Page 6, three belonged to PTI and two each to UNI and TOINS.

Page 8 was the editorial page and Page 9 had 11 stories of which PTI, UNI, AP, UPI, Reuters and AFP all had one each. All the ten stories appearing on Page 10 were credited to

TOINS. Page 11 had 18 stories of which five stories belonged to wire services including one each to PTI and UNI. Page 12 had a total of eight stories of which PTI had two and UNI just one. Page 13 had nine stories of which three stories belonged to PTI, UNI and AP. Page 14 was devoted to advertisements and Page 15 had just three stories of which the lion's share went to PTI with two stories and one story going to TOINS.

Page nos. 16, 17, 18, 20 and 24 were reserved for advertisements while Page 19 had a total of six stories of which two were credited to PTI, one to UNI and remaining three to TOINS. Page 21 had 13 stories of which five each belonged to UNI and AP and one to AFP. The remaining two were from TOI staffers. Page 22 had a total of four stories of which two belonged to PTI and one each to AP and TOINS. Page 23 had nine stories of which two were credited to UNI and one each to AP, UPI and Reuters and the remaining credited to TOINS. Hence, the total number of news stories published in this issue were 160, of which 27 were credited to PTI, 31 to UNI and 23 to other foreign news agencies.

Times of India, Bombay, Friday, January 4, 1985: The front page of this issue carried four stories from PTI namely *Gas struck in AP (Ist column), 23 massacred in UP clash (5 columns), New LS summoned and 10th World Film Festival begins* whereas UNI had three stories including *Rane re-elected Goa CLP leader* and *MGR calls for Nedunchezian* which it shared with TOINS. The remaining five of the total 12 stories belonged to TOINS. Of the total 24 pages of the issue, seven were reserved for advertisements. They included page nos. 2, 3, 6, 14,16, 17, 18, 20 and 24 while Pages 2 and 3, the precursor of present day Page 3 phenomenon, had some entertainment news as well from TOINS.

Page 4 had a total of six stories of UNI's *Independent MP returns to jail* was a box item with a bold headline. The edit page (Page 8) carried an exclusive news feature by AP headlined as *Arms Control Accord in Soviet Interest.* Page 9 had a total of 20 stories of which four were credited to PTI including a two column story entitled *Rajiv's guidelines to ministries* and *BJP to review debacle.* UNI and AP had two stories while Reuters and UPI had one each. Page 10 had commodity news with a total of 17 stories of which one each belonged to PTI, UNI and Reuters. Sports Page 11 had 16 stories of which only two–one each were credited to UNI and Reuters while all the remaining 14 stories belonged to TOINS.

Page 12 had six stories which were shared equally by PTI and TOINS. Page 13 had two stories one each credited to PTI and TOINS. Page 15 had a total of 11 stories of which just one belonged to a wire service namely UNI while the remaining 10 stories were contributed by TOINS. Page 19 had a total of six stories from the states of which one belonged to PTI, three to UNI and two to TOINS. Page 21 had five stories of which two were credited to UNI which included a two column feature entitled *Educative role of museums* and the rest to TOINS. Page 22 had eight foreign news of which one each was credited to UNI and UPI, three to AP and two to Reuters. Page 23 had two stories both credited to UPI. Hence, this issue had a total of 129 stories of which 15 were credited to PTI, 18 to UNI and 17 to others.

Times of India, Bombay, Saturday, January 5, 1985: Of the total 12 stories on the front page, PTI had six and UNI one. The remaining belonged to the TOINS. PTI stories included *Centre ready for early Punjab poll (three columns), BJP reviews poll debacle (two columns) and Russia readies for N-talks.* Page 3 had 14 stories of which one each belonged to PTI and UNI. Page 5 had all 11 the stories from the TOI's staple much the same way as Page 7 that had all the six stories credited to TOINS. The editorial page had only edits. Page 9 had 31 stories of which 10 belonged to PTI, five to UNI and five to foreign news agencies. The remaining stories were credited to TOINS.

Page 10 had eleven stories all belonging to TOINS. Page 12 had 17 stories of which only two were credited to UNI while the rest were in-house production. Page 13 had eight stories of which one each belonged to PTI, Reuters and UPI while two were credited to AP. Page 14 had 16 stories of which three were credited to PTI, seven to UNI and six to TOINS. Page 15 had seven stories of which one was from UNI. Pages 16, 17, 18 and 19 were reserved for advertisements. The remaining pages were missing. The total number of stories found were 133, of which 21 were from PTI, 17 from UNI and 11 from other news agencies.

Times of India, Bombay, Sunday, January 6, 1985: The front page had a total number of 11 stories of which four were credited to PTI, one to UNI and two to Reuters. The major headlines belonged to TOINS that read *Top priority for Punjab/ PM vows to fight communalism. NTR offers Rajiv cooperation (PTI)* and *Free leaders and confer (UNI)* were other major headlines. Page 3 had thirteen stories of which one each belonged to PTI and UNI. Page 5 had 11 stories all from TOINS. Page 6 had five stories of which two were credited to PTI. Page 7 had 20 stories of which two each belonged to PTI and UNI. Page 8 was turned into literary page. Page 9 had 28 news stories of which six were from PTI and three each from UNI, AP and Reuters.

Page 10 had 22 stories about money and banking and all were credited to TOINS. Page 11 had 20 sports stories of which one each belonged to PTI, UNI and AP. Page 12 had eight foreign stories of which one each was credited to PTI and UPI while four were from AP wire service and two from Reuters. Page 13 had six sports stories of which two were from PTI and four from TOINS. Page 14 had one news feature from a staff writer. Page 17 was a Sunday Review while Page 18 carried articles on art and films. Page 19 was entitled *Of men & women* and carried human interest news features. Page 20 was about *Enquiry/Media* while Page 21 was about *International Scene.* Page 22 was about *Nature/Science,* page 23 about *Sports* and the last page featured *Humour, Astrology & Leisure.* The total number of news stories in this Sunday edition were 135 of which 19 were from PTI, eight from UNI and 16 from other foreign news agencies.

Times of India, Bombay, Monday, January 7, 1985: Major headline in the front page of this issue belonged to PTI news story–*4 States agreeable to early polls* spread over three columns. This was among the four stories by PTI published that morning in the daily. Front page had a total of 12 stories of which two belonged to UNI and one each to AP, Reuters and AFP. Page 3 had 12 stories of which only one was taken from a wire service namely UNI and the rest were credited to TOINS. Page 4 had nine stories of which one each belonged to PTI and UNI.

Table 4.1: Number of News Agency Stories Appearing in Times of India in the First Week of January 1985

Date	Total Number of News Stories	News Agency Stories	Stories from PTI and UNI
January 1, 1985	103	39	32
January 2, 1985	149	67	50
January 3, 1985	160	81	58
January 4, 1985	129	50	33
January 5, 1985	133	49	38
January 6, 1985	135	43	27
January 7, 1985	147	51	35

Page 5 had 16 stories of which one story each was shared by PTI and UNI. Page 6 had 13 stories from the states and of which only two belonged to PTI. Page 7 had nine stories from staffers. Page 8 as usual was reserved for editorials. Page 9 had 19 stories of which three each belonged to PTI and UNI and one to Reuters. Page 10 had 12 commodity news items all from TOINS. Page 11 had eleven sports stories of which one each was credited to UNI and AP. Similarly, Page 13 had six sports stories of which two belonged to PTI and one to UNI. Page 18 also carried 13 sports news stories of which two each belonged to PTI and UNI while three were credited to AP.

Page 19 had three news features from TOINS. Page 21 had nine foreign news stories of which one was from PTI, three each from UNI (two from UNI-DPA) and Reuters, two from AP and one from (Pool). Page 23 had three news stories equally shared by UNI, AP and TOINS. Eight pages numbering 2, 12, 14-17, 20 and 24 were reserved for classified and general advertisements. Thus, the total number of news stories published in this issue were 147 of which 17 were credited to PTI, 18 to UNI and 16 to other foreign news agencies.

The Times of India (1990) [2]

Times of India, Bombay, Monday, January 1, 1990: The front page of the *Times of India* dated January 1, 1990 had a total of 12 stories of which five were credited to PTI. The major headline–*Document soon on agricultural policy*– a three column story was credited to TOINS while PTI's *Bomb blast in Srinagar* and *Devi tells Sikhs to cooperate* was also well displayed. One story each was credited DPA and AFP (*Romanian leftists admit guilty).* Page 2 carried classified advertisements and Page 3 had stories emanating from the Bombay city. Of these all six stories were credited to TOINS. The following page entitled City Lights had a huge column on tit-bits by TOINS.

Page 5 carried a total of five stories all credited to UNI that included *Thackeray favours common civil code.* Page 6 had a total of three stories all credited to PTI. These included a six column science feature entitled *Momentous decade for world science.* Page 7 had a total of six stories that included one by PTI and three by UNI that included a four column story headlined as *Council cautions press on castes.* Page 8 had comprehensive Parliament Review by TOINS. Page 9 carried a three column picture of the then Chief of Army Staff Gen. V.N. Sharma chatting with the crew of INSV' 'Samudra'–the first Indian tri-service world sailing expedition, by UNI. It also had a three column story by UNI about *Rare sculptures neglected.*

The remaining two stories were equally credited to PTI and TOINS. Page 10 had a total of seven stories of which two were credited to PTI and three to UNI and two to TOINS. Page 11 had one story by TOINS and Page 12 had four stories of which UNI had one box item entitled *Gujarat Court insulting artists* and two stories were taken from PTI. Page 13 had a total of 11 stories of which two each were credited to PTI and UNI and four were taken from Reuters, DPA, AFP and APN. Page 14 was the editorial page and Page 15 had three syndicated foreign news features. Page 16 had seven stories of which three each were credited to PTI and UNI and two written by TOINS. Page 17 was titled *Market Roundup* and carried 10 stories of which two each were taken from PTI and UNI and remaining were in-house products.

Page 18 too had a total of 10 sports stories of which two were credited to PTI, one each to UNI and AFP and the remaining to TOINS. Page 19 had 11 sports stories of which PTI and AFP had one and UNI two. Page 20 had eight stories of which one belonged to PTI and two to UNI. It also had a three column picture by PIB/PTI on *Assam Accord Talks.* Page 21 entitled Media had three news features by TOINS and page 22 entitled Nature had six stories including a three column picture by PTI and two stories credited to PTI and two to UNI. Page 23 called World had five stories from PTI, UNI, AFP, IPS and AP. Page nos. 24-26 carried tenders and Page 27 advertisements. Page 28 had a total of three stories one each taken from Reuters (*Excerpts from the trial of Ceausescus)*, AFP *(Angola proposes fresh peace plan)* and IPS' *(Decade sees Deng turn back the clock)*.

Times of India, Bombay, Tuesday, January 2, 1990: Front page of this issue carried headlines by both PTI and UNI. It had a three column UNI story headlined as *Legal steps soon on right to work* and *Punjab bandh peaceful* by PTI. It also had a bottom banner headline–*Dalits to seek tie up in state poll* by TOINS. Page 2 carried classified advertisements and Page 3 had 16 stories about the city of which three were credited to PTI and four to UNI. Page 4 had advertisements. Page 5 had 19 stories all credited to TOINS including city briefs and Thane news. Page 6 had three stories including one a two column story by UNI about *Landmark work by ASI.*

Page 7 carried eight stories from the nation that included one story by PTI and four by UNI and a five column KBK graphic on *Major international events of 1989.* Page 8 had three stories including UNI's Moscow datelined *Indo-Soviet trade grows.* Page 9 had six stories from around the world. These included one picture by AP/PTI, one story each by UNI and Reuters and two each from AP and DPA. Page 10 was the editorial page while Page 11 called Agenda carried two news features by arrangement with the Sunday Times. Page 12 called Stocks carried information by TOINS and Page 13 called City Notes had 13 stories of which three were credited to PTI and one to UNI. Page 14 had four sports stories credited one each to PTI, UNI; UPI and TOINS.

Page 15 had six sports stories of which one was taken from PTI and another from AFP. Page 16 called World had 15 stories–seven from Reuters and one each from AP, Tanjug, DPA and UPI. The remaining were credited to TOINS. Page 17 had three news features on Arts from TOINS, Page 18 carried two features sent by DPA and AP separately. Page 22 had a total of six stories of which two were credited to PTI and three to UNI and it included an article entitled *One person of the decade* by Rajdeep Sardesai. Pages 19, 20 and 21 were reserved for advertisements. Thus, it had a total of 115 stories of which 47 were news agency stories.

Times of India, Bombay, Wednesday, January 3, 1990: In this issue, PTI and UNI shared credits for the story–*Mann to attend all party meet* datelined Faridkot. They also shared credits for another story *2 EC members removed.* Of the total 11 stories, seven stories were credited to wire services including three to PTI and two each to UNI and AFP. Page 2 was reserved for classified advertisements while Page 3 had 10 stories of which two were credited to PTI and one to UNI. Page 4 was again reserved for classified advertisements. Page 5 had a total of nine stories, all by TOINS, and included an interview with Dennis Hudson, Professor of World Religions at Smith College, Northampton, U.S. entitled: "*Hinduism finds a niche in U.S.*"

Table 4.2: Number of News Agency Stories Appearing in Times of India in the First Week of January 1990

Date	Total Number of News Stories	News Agency Stories	Stories from PTI and UNI
January 1, 1990	124	69	44
January 2, 1990	115	47	33
January 3, 1990	93	39	30
January 4, 1990	110	63	35
January 5, 1990	131	38	32
January 6, 1990	103	40	30
January 7, 1990	153	38	33

Page 6, eight and 16 carried classified advertisements while Page 7 had eight stories–two from PTI and six from UNI. Page 9 had 12 stories from all across the nation–all by TOINS. Page 10 was editorial and page 11 called Agenda had four stories three features by staffers and one story by PTI. Page 12 carried one huge feature about stocks by TOINS and page 13 carried six City notes stories again by staffers. Page 14 had six sports stories–two each by UNI, AP and TOINS. Similarly, page 15 had ten sports stories of which two each were credited to PTI, UNI and Reuters. Page 17 entitled *The Arts* had no news story as such while Page 18 had seven stories including three foreign news features credited to UNI, AP and AFP each. Page 19 carried tenders while page nos. 20 and 21 carried advertisements. Page 22 had nine stories of which two were credited to PTI and four to UNI. Thus, there were a total of 93 stories of which news agency stories were 39.

Times of India, Bombay, Thursday, January 4, 1990: The front page of the issue carried a three column news on *Govt. will honour Assam accord* credited to TOINS and agencies without mentioning any name. It had a total of 12 stories of which PTI and UNI had three each and one each was credited to AP and INA-Pool. Pages 2, 4, 14 and 21-24 were reserved for advertisements. Page 3 had 12 stories of which PTI had two and the rest TOINS including district news. Page 5 also had 12 stories including city notes of which PTI had two stories.

Page 6 carried three stories from across the nation including two column UNI story on contraband seizure and a three column PTI picture on the same. It also had a story. Page 7 had nine stories from the nation that included four credited to PTI and one to UNI. Page 8 had eight stories–two taken from PTI and four from UNI. Page 9 called World had three foreign features–one by AP i.e. *Single Europe in 90s* datelined Paris and two features by arrangement with the Sunday Times. It also carried a three column picture by AFP/PTI. Page 10 continued with the world stories and carried a total of seven news taken from wire services–two each from PTI and UNI and one each from DPA, AFP and Kyodo.

Page 11 entitled Nation carried three pictures and two news features by UNI entitled: *Army in Sikkim deserves accolades* and *Ashok Kumar retrospective at Film Fest.* Page 12 was devoted to editorials; Page 12 called Agenda carried two news features with arrangement with the Sunday Times. Page 15 carried standard stocks column by TOINS while Page 16 had four stories and two pictures. They included one feature each by AFP and UPI. Page 17 carried 13 sports stories–five from UNI and one from AFP. The rest came from TOINS. Page 18 had six stories from across the world–all credited to wire services. Their break-up is like this–One each from PTI and Tanjug and two each from AP and Reuters. Page 19 carried features on Media while Page 20 again had four international stories one each by PTI, Reuters, AP and TOINS. Page nos. 21-23 carried advertisements. Page 24 had seven stories of which two were credited to PTI and five to TOINS. Thus, it had a total of 110 stories of which 63 were taken from news agencies.

Times of India, Bombay, Friday, January 5, 1990: In

this edition, the two column main story *Noriega gives up; flown to U.S.* was credited to PTI as also *225 killed Pak rail smash.* Of the total 10 stories in this page, three were credited to PTI and four to UNI and one to AFP. Seven pages of this issue (page nos. 2, 4, 6, 8, 14, 16 and 18) were reserved for advertisements. Page 3 carried 17 stories from the city of which three were taken from UNI and the rest were in-house contribution. Page 5 had 19 stories–all by TOINS. Page 7 called Nation had 14 stories–two by PTI and four by UNI and the rest from TOINS. Page 10 was reserved for editorial while page 11 called Agenda had guest write-ups. Page 12 was about stocks. Page 13 had 18 stories from the city called city notes and had just one story by PTI. Page 15 had 20 sports stories–four from PTI and one each from UNI and AP. Page 17 had three stories that included one from PTI. Page 20 had ten stories with the following break-up–one each by UNI, TOINS, Tanjug, Reuters and AP and two by AFP. Hence, it had a total of 131 stories of which 38 were taken from wire services.

Times of India, Bombay, Saturday, January 6, 1990: Front page of this issue had ten news stories of which two were credited to PTI, four to UNI and the rest to TOINS. Page nos. 2, 4,6, 8, 14, 18 and 19 were reserved for advertisements. Page 3 had 14 news items from the city all credited to TOINS. Page 5 had 10 stories including two each from PTI and UNI. Page 9 called Nation had 11 stories including two each from PTI and UNI. Page 10 was the editorial and page 11 was devoted to Agenda and Forum. Page 13 carried three stories on stocks that included one by PTI.

Page 13 again had 21 stories from the city including three from PTI and two from UNI. Page 15 had 13 sports stories of which two were taken from PTI and three from UNI. Page 16 had four stories including AFP story on *Pak rail mishap.* Page 17 had features on arts and page 20 carried seven stories taken from wire services–one each from PTI, UNI, AP, AFP, PL-Pool and two from UPI. It also carried a picture by AP/PTI. It had a total of 103 stories that included 40 from news agencies.

Times of India, Bombay, Sunday, January 7, 1990: New Delhi datelines story on *Indo-Lanka panel to monitor truce* jointly credited to PTI and UNI was the main story of the issue. It had a total of 11 stories of which PTI and UNI had four stories each in addition to the shared aforementioned news item. City page (Page 3) had 14 items of which only one was credited to PTI. Page nos. 2,4,10 and 12 were reserved for advertisements. Page 5 had ten stories including Today's engagements and Weather by PTI. Page 6 called Nation had six stories–all by TOINS. Page 7 had 16 stories including six from PTI and one from UNI.

Page 8 had four features by TOINS. Page 9 had 15 stories including three from PTI, two from UNI and one each from UP, AP and Reuters. Page 11 had 22 stories on Money and Banking from TOINS. Page 13 carried 16 sports stories–four each from PTI and UNI and one from AP. Page 14 called World had three features including one by INA. Page 15 called The Arts had five features by TOINS. Page 16 had nine sports stories including one from PTI and two from AFP. Page nos. 17-24 carried Sunday Review and Features. In all, it had a total of 153 stories including 38 from wire services including national news agencies as well as foreign.

The Times of India (1995): [3]

Times of India, Bombay, Sunday, January 1, 1995: This issue of the *Times of India* had a total number of 36 pages including Sunday review and carried 17 pages of advertisements. The front page had seven stories and all were contributed by TOINS. Page 3 had seven stories from the city by TOINS. Page nos. 5 and 7 had four stories each–all contributed by staffers. Page 9 had one feature by its own staffer while Page 10 had four stories including a two column story by PTI on *WTO has to tackle north-south tiffs.* Page 11 entitled *World* had two features by TOINS, while Pages 12 and 13 were called Marquee and Books respectively. Page 14 was called Sunday Times and carried infotainment news. Page 15 was called Special Report and 16 carried content on Business and Finance. Page 18 had eight sports stories all by TOINS.

Page 19 also had five sports stories credited to its staffers. Page 22 and 27 called Nation had five and two features respectively contributed newspaper's staff. Page 28 carried amidst advertisement a story from Jammu headlined *Forces militants clash in Doda* written by their own staffer. Page 29 was called Review and the subsequent Pages 30-36 were reserved for advertisements. Hence, the total number of news stories in this issue was 35 of which only one story was taken PTI. There was no other story from any other news agency.

Times of India, Bombay, Monday, January 2, 1995: The front page carried 11 stories of which three each were by PTI and UNI while one was from AP. Page 3 had six city stories of which one each were credited to PTI and UNI. Page 4 called City Light had five stories filed by the Times staffers. Page 5 also carried seven stories from the city, all by TOINS. Page 6 called Nation had three stories by TOINS; Page 7 also called Nation had nine stories of which two were taken from PTI and one from UNI and Page 8, also called Nation, had two stories including one three-column feature by UNI headlined *Mercury plummets in North.*

Page 9 had one feature by TOINS and page 10 had four stories including one TOINS feature on Samba spy case. Page 11 had three stories all credited to PTI namely: *TV viewers in for surprise (three columns); Narmada dam to provide one million jobs (five columns);* and *Delhi bans sale of lotteries (three columns).* Page 12 is the editorial page while Page 13 entitled Nation/World had five stories one each credited to PTI, UNI and Reuters. They included PTI's box item Coimbatore datelined story with the headline–*Has Veerappan committed suicide? Patent law amendment angers opposition* by UNI was also well displayed.

Page 14 entitled World in brief had three un-credited stories. Pages 15 and 16 carried one foreign feature each. Page 17 entitled Business Times had 14 stories of which six were from PTI and one each from UNI and Reuters. Page 18 had 13 stories of which one was taken from PTI and three from UNI. Page 19 had two news features from AFP. Page 20 also carried a single feature by Harvey Stockwin from Hong Kong on '*Imminent succession struggle in China may affect region's politics this year*". Page 21 had advertisements while Page 22 carried 10 sports stories of which two were credited to AP and one to Reuters. Page 23 also had nine sports stories by TOINS and Page 24 had one of the six sports stories credited to PTI. Page nos. 25-32 carried the supplement Ascent. Hence, the issue had a total of 116 stories of which 41 were taken from news agencies.

Times of India, Bombay, Tuesday, January 3, 1995: All major political stories appearing on the front page of this issue were taken from PTI such as–*Patna: Laloo Prasad/ warns Seshan/issuing photo identity cards* or *New Delhi, Arjun Singh favours AICC session or New Delhi: Gujarat polls put off to February 20, 25.* Thus of the total 11 stories published on this page, PTI had the credit for five and UNI one. Page 2 carried classified advertisements along with All India Weather report and Doordarshan's list of programmes filed by agencies. Page 3 carried seven stories from Bombay city of which one was taken from UNI and the rest were contributed by newspaper's staffers.

Page 4 carried the column 'Letters to the Editor' along with classified advertisements. Page 5 had five stories of which two were credited to UNI. The stories were: *New Delhi: Centre to review fishing policy* and *Lucknow: UP free of communal violence in '94.* Page 6 called Nation had two stories from PTI and the rest of the page carried advertisements. Page 7 also carried stories from the across the nation and had five news items of which two were taken from UNI. Similarly, Page 8 carried one TOINS story. Page 9 had three stories–one from PTI and two from UNI. Page 10 called World carried one syndicated foreign feature.

Page 11 was full of advertisements only. Page 12 also

called World had eight stories–two from PTI, three from AFP and three features by TOINS. Page 13 also carried one feature credited to TOINS. Page 14 was editorial. Page 15 entitled Nation/World had a total of six stories of three were from PTI and one each from UNI and AFP. Page 16 had two news items –one a PTI story from Washington about cultural war between U.S. and Canada and another, a KBK graphic about *'Major world events during 1994'*. Page 17 had only advertisements while Page 18 also called World had two stories of which one was credited to Pool-Xinhua. Page 19 called Business Times had 11 stories that included two from PTI and one from UNI.

The rest came from Business Times Bureau. Page 20 carried information about stocks and had four stories including two from PTI commercial service. The stories were: *Equity prices move in a narrow Bombay range* and *Silver declines.* Page 21 had five stories including two from PTI. Page nos. 22 to 24 carried news and information about Tenders and Contracts. Page 25 called Nation had three stories of which one was credited to PTI and two to UNI. UNI's story from Jammu-*"Jammu & Kashmir proxy war casualties on rise"* gets seven column display on the upper half while the first column of this page carried UNI's another story–*New Delhi: Electrification of 141 stations planned.*

Page 26 carried seven sports stories including one each from Reuters and AP and two from UNI along with a picture by PTI on DCM Football in New Delhi. Page 27 also carried seven sports stories of which two were taken from PTI and one from Reuters. Page 28 had 10 sports stories and an AP/PTI picture on a cricket match between England and Australia then being played in Sydney. It also had two stories each from UNI and AP. It also carried features like crossword, cartoons and advertisements.

Times of India, Bombay, Wednesday, January 4, 1995: *Bihar polls to be rescheduled; SC refuses to stay Seshan's decision of I-cards* and *EC to postpone state assembly polls* were some of the major headlines of this issue. Of the total 11 stories, PTI had one and UNI four stories to their credit. Page 2, as usual, carried classified advertisements along with All India Weather by PTI. Page 3 had three stories by TOINS focusing on Maharashtra assembly polls. Page nos. 4, 6, 8, 10, 12, 18, 19 and 25 had classified and other advertisements. Page 5 called City/Nation had four stories all filed by TOINS.

Page 6 entitled Nation had two stories one each from PTI and UNI. Page 9 had one feature by TOINS–'*Oxford V-C seeks more Indian scholarships'*. Upper half of Page 11 carried a six column UNI story on *'New Delhi: Satellite TV jolts information sector out of slumber'*. Page nos. 12, 18, 19 and 25 were reserved for advertisements and classifieds. Again Page 13 carried two TOINS stories while Page 14 was editorial. Page 15 called Nation/World had seven stories one each from PTI, UNI and Reuters. Page 16 carried one eight column feature syndicated by New York Times Service on–*Chechen war wounds Yeltsin's image and puts his pol. Future at risk.* Page 17 also carried an NYTS news feature on Haiti with a four column headline.

Page 20 had a column called *World in brief* that had five stories–one from Pool-Kyodo and four from AP. Page 21 also called Business Times had 10 stories of which two were credited to PTI. Page 22 had stocks news from TOINS. Page 23 had three stories of which one on *41 percent growth in cotton textile exports* was taken from UNI. Page 24 called Nation carried just one story from UNI on *Pilgrims throng Vaishno Devi.* Page 26 had two sports items from TOINS. Page 27 again had four sports stories of which one was taken from AP. Page 28 had eight sports stories–one each from AP and Reuters and rest from TOINS. It also carried cartoons. In total, the issue had 82 stories of which 24 were credited to wire services and 21 to PTI and UNI together.

Times of India, Bombay, Thursday, January 5, 1995: The first column of the front page of this issue carried five news capsules credited one each to PTI, UNI, DPA, AP and Reuters in the column called '*In brief*'. However, the main story was-*Calcutta (TOINS): Reforms to go on/reiterates Rao at CII.* Its opening para read: *PM Rao declared categorically that "India is firmly committed to the economic reforms programme" which he said, "rests on solid and stable foundations".* Page 2 carried classified advertisements along with All India Weather by PTI. Page 3 carried five city news stories by TOINS. Page nos. 4, 15, 20 and 21 carried advertisements while Page 5 carried five storied by TOINS.

Page 6 carried two stories that included one PTI story on British foreign secretary Douglas Hurd to address CII centenary celebrations in Calcutta. Page 7, 8 and 9 called Nation had three, two and two stories respectively–all credited to TOINS. They were all political analysis stories filed by the newspaper's own correspondents. Page 10 had review articles by guest writers and special correspondents. Page 11 also called nation had five stories of which one was taken from PTI. Page 12 was editorial page.

Page 13 labelled Nation/World had eight stories including one picture of Russian troops in Grozny by AP/PTI. Page 14 called World had one feature and a news column called 'In brief' that carried five news capsules by AFP, PTI and AP (3). Page 16 had one huge feature by TOINS. Page 17 labelled as Business Times had eight stories of which two were credited to PTI and one five column graphic on state-wise tax collection attributed to UNI. Page 18 had stocks news and page 19 carried 11 corporate news stories including two from PTI. Page 22 had two sports stories by TOINS, Page 23 had eight sports stories of which one was taken from Reuters, Page 24 again had nine sports stories of which one was credited to AFP. Pages 25-32 were reserved for Ascent, an eight page supplement. Thus, it had a total of 93 stories of which 20 stories were credited to various news agencies including PTI and UNI.

Times of India, Bombay, Friday, January 6, 1995: *EC exceeding its powers–charges Bihar (TOINS and Agencies)* and PTI's *Jitendra Prasad is UPCC chief* were among the 10 stories and city weather published in the front page. Of these, three were credited to PTI, two to UNI and one each to AFP and Tanjug. Of the total 28 pages of the issue, eight pages were devoted to advertisements alone. Page 3 and five had six city stories each filed by TOINS while Page nos. 7 to 11 carried stories from across the Nation. Of the total 17 stories under this head, all were attributed to TOINS. No story was taken from any news agency. Page 12 called World had one picture by AP/PTI including one feature by TOINS. Page 14 was the editorial page. Page 15 had seven stories of which two were credited to PTI. Page 16 had one picture by AP/PTI and one two-column PTI feature from Beijing: *Icons of Shiva and Vishnu found in Chinese towns.* Its opening paragraph read thus:

"Beijing: Hindu temples existed in China in the 10 and 11 century A.D. during the Chola period when trade flourished between Indian and China. Evidence of Shiva and Vishnu temples has surfaced following the discovery of icons of Shiva and Vishnu in the old seaport town of Quanzhou in Fujian province of South-East China..."

Page 18 had two foreign features in the World section that included an AP story from Chechnya with the headline: *Several nations urge Russia to end bloodshed in Chechnya.* Page 19 also called Business Times had 12 stories of which three were PTI and two UNI's. A graphic on crude oil and natural gas reserves was also attributed to UNI. Page 20 had five stories about stocks including one UNI story on IDBI sale of shares. Page 21 had eight stories of which two were taken from PTI and one graphic on foreign investment in power sector from UNI. Page 26 had two stories by the Times news bureau while page 27 carried five sports stories also attributed to it. Page 28 had eight sports stories including two credited to AP. In total, the issue had 65 stories of which 21 were credited to various news agencies.

Times of India, Bombay, Saturday, January 7, 1995: This edition of Times of India included a six page supplement called Saturday Times in addition to seven pages of advertisements bringing the total page count to 34.

As usual, the front page had 10 stories of which two each were credited to PTI and UNI and one each to AP and AFP. The major headlines included: *Lucknow(PTI/UNI): UP Congressmen to defy whip* and *New Delhi (UNI): Arjun and Mulayam on CWC agenda.* Page 3 had three stories filed by TOINS; Page 5 had seven stories from the City also filed by TOINS. Three stories each of page nos eight and nine were also filed by TOINS. Page 10 carried seven stories–three each from AFP and AP and one from DPA under the header World in brief. Page 11 had two stories one from PTI and the other from Reuters. The PTI story from Dhaka on *Fatwa leads humiliated teenager to commit suicide* got five columns displayed on the upper half of the page. Page 12 called World had a well-displayed PTI picture of the members of the closed Indian mission in Karachi arriving in IGI airport. It also carried a Beijing dateline Reuters story on *Chinese government blacklisting dissidents.*

Table 4.3: Number of News Agency Stories Appearing in Times of India in the First Week of January 1995

Date	Total Number of News Stories	News Agency Stories	Stories from PTI and UNI
January 1, 1995	35	7	7
January 2, 1995	114	41	27
January 3, 1995	117	51	36
January 4, 1995	82	24	21
January 5, 1995	93	21	10
January 6, 1995	65	21	16
January 7, 1995	120	30	16

Page 13 had two features by NYTS and one AP/PTI picture on a homosexual couple. Page 14 was the editorial page. Page 15 titled Nation/World had 11 stories of which two each were credited to PTI and UNI. Page 16 called Nation had just one story by TOINS. Page 17–Business Times–had 11 stories of which four were credited to PTI. Page 18 had three stocks stories all filed by TOINS. Page 19 had eight stories of which one was credited to UNI. Page 24 had one story by TOINS, Page 25 had two stories including one from PTI. Pages 26-28 had 20 sports stories of which only one each was credited to PTI and Reuters. Page nos. 29-34 were reserved for Saturday Times. Thus, the issue had a total of 120 stories including 30 filed by agencies.

Times of India (2000): [4]

Times of India, Mumbai, Saturday, January 1, 2000: The hostage crisis dominated the front page of the daily with its banner headline saying: *Hostages freed at a heavy cost.* Credited to TOINS, the story accompanied pictures of hostages and dreaded terrorists including Masood Azhar freed in the bargain. The page also carried an editorial on the subject along with nine other stories including a Moscow story from Reuters saying *Russians switch tactics in a bid for Grozny.* The page also carried the regular feature called the *City Weather.* Page 2 carried classified advertisements while Page 3 had five stories from the city credited to TOINS.

Page 4 carried the regular feature called the City Lights while Page 5 had five stories from the city filed by the newspaper correspondents. Page 6 called Nation had three stories including one by PTI with New Delhi dateline saying: *BJP releases second list of candidates* while Page 7 had seven stories credited to TOINS. Page 8 carried advertisements while Page 9 also entitled Nation had three stories including one by PTI. Next two pages were also entitled the Nation and carried three news stories on Page 10 including two credited to PTI and one news feature on Laloo Prasad on Page 11 filed by the Times correspondent. Page 12 carried the editorial content.

Page 13 entitled Nation/World had seven stories of which two each were credited to PTI and UNI while Page 14 called World had three main stories credited two to PTI and one to Reuters along with seven news briefs from foreign locales.

Page 15 again entitled World had two news stories credited one each to PTI and AP while Page 16 had three stories from across the nation including one filed by PTI. Page 17 entitled Business Times had nine news stories of which three each were credited to PTI and UNI while Page 18 had only two news stories and one featured credited to PTI. Page 19 had two national stories credited to TOINS.

Page 20 carried advertisements while page 21 carried only one feature from Patna by TOINS saying *Mishra endorses Tiwari's stand on Mulayam Government.* Page 22 carried seven news stories including one filed by PTI while Page 23 had eight stories including one taken from PTI wires. Page 24 had nine stories from the world of sports of which three i.e. one each were credited to PTI, UNI and Reuters. Thus, it had a total of 92 news stories of which 27 were credited to various news agencies including 23 credited to PTI and UNI.

Times of India, Mumbai, Sunday, January 2, 2000: The front page carried a total of 10 news stories including one each credited to PTI and UNI and two to Reuters. Page 2 had 18 news items from the city filed by TOINS while Page 3 had nine stories from the Nation credited two each to PTI and UNI. Page 4 had a feature called the City Lights. Page 5 had six stories credited to TOINS while Page 6 had nine stories from across the nation of which two stories were credited to PTI and one to UNI. Page 7 had nine stories under the title Nation of which two each were credited to PTI and UNI.

Page 8 had six main news items and eight briefs from around the world. Page 9 and 10 had five international features published by arrangement with international news and features syndicates like The New York Times. Page 11 carried advertisements while page 12 called Business and Finance had seven news stories including two news features along with two columns called Swaminomics and the Contrarian View. Page 13 had five stories from the TOINS staple while 13 was entitled The Sunday Times. Page 5 called R.S.V.P.–Letters carried readers's perspective. Page 16 carried a special report on hostage drama while Page 17 carried entertainment news.

Page 18 carried advertisements while Page 9 carried six sports stories, all filed by TOINs under the title Times Sport. Page 20 called Leisure carried human interest features while page 21 carried 17 sports stories of which two each were credited to PTI and UNI while one each was credited to Reuters, AFP and DPA. Page 22 had six news stories of which 3 were credited to PTI. Page nos. 23-29 were called The Sunday Times Classifieds while page 30 entitled Fortune had numerous human interest features. Page 31and 32 again carried advertisements while Page nos. 33 to 36 were entitled Reviews. Thus, the daily had a total number of 105 news stories including 29 credited to various wire services of which 15 were credited to PTI and UNI.

Times of India, Bombay, Monday, January 3, 2000: The front page carried nine stories of which two were credited to news agencies that included the main headline story displayed over two columns and attributed jointly to UNI and PTI. It read thus: *Islamabad: Pak says it'll deny entry to hijackers.* A New York datelined story: *Gates says there's a future shock beyond Y2K was* also credited to agencies. Page 2 contained Metrofile while Page 3 entitled Mumbai had six stories from TOINS. Page 4 had city brief under the heading City Lights. Page 5 also called Mumbai had six stories including one from PTI. Page nos. 6-8 called Nation carried 16 stories in total of which only two stories were credited to PTI and one to UNI. The PTI story on Page 7 read thus: *Chennai: Hand-over hijackers, BJP tells Pakistan.* Pages 9 and 16 carried advertisements.

Page 10 carried two features and page 11 carried three features by TOINS. Page 12 was the editorial page while page 13 carried four features of which three had foreign datelines. Page 14 had four stories of which two were news features including a news item on the wife of Nipun Katyal who was killed aboard the hijacked Indian plane. It read thus: *Hijackers injected Rachna Katyal with sedatives.* Page 15 carried five international news credited to agencies–two each to Reuters and PTI and one to UNI. Likewise, page 17 had six international news along with a TOINS feature called *Around the World.*

The news stories were credited to news agencies–two to PTI, three to UNI and one to AP. Page 18 also carried four international news–three from Reuters and one from AP. Page 19 also called Business Times had a total of 10 stories of which two were taken from PTI and four from Reuters. Page 20 had five stories of which PTI had a share of one story and Reuters two. Pages 21-24 carried sports news. Of the total 20 sports news stories and news features carried in these four pages, three stories were taken from PTI, two from AFP and one from UNI. Page 24 also displayed an AFP/AP picture of *Sachin Tendulkar at the crease on the third day of the third test between India and Australia* at Sydney. Following eight pages were reserved for Ascent, the special supplement on jobs and placement. Thus, it had a total of 102 stories of which 36 were from wire services including 20 taken from PTI and UNI.

Times of India, Mumbai, Tuesday, January 4, 2000: Like a bouquet of flowers, the front page of this issue carried not just hard news stories, 12 in total, but also market news capsules, city weather, *You Said It* by noted cartoonist R.K. Laxman and a picture of Sydney test match. Similarly, Page 2 named Mumbai carried columns like Metrofile, Readers' Grievances as well as events and engagements along with TV and radio schedules and nationwide weather.

Page 3, also named Mumbai, carried seven news items, all filed by TOINS while Page 5 had three of the five stories from Mumbai city credited to PTI. Page nos. 6-9 called India, carried 26 news stories of which PTI had two stories and UNI just one. Page 10 carried six international news on the hijacking filed by PTI, AFP, DPA, UNI and AP (2). They included a PTI story from Islamabad saying: *Whereabouts of hijackers remain a mystery.* Page 11 also carried seven international news stories including two from Reuters. Page 12 was the editorial while Pages 13-14 again carried 12 international news items of which one was credited to PTI, three to Reuters and two to DPA. One news feature was syndicated by The Sunday Times.

Business Times on Page 15 carried 14 news items including two stories each by PTI and UNI and one by Reuter besides one news picture by AP. Page 16 carried stocks news by TOINS while out of nine stocks stories published on page 17, six were contributed by Reuters. Page nos. 18 to 22 carried news and information on tenders and contracts. Page nos. 23 to 26 carried sports news. Of the 12 news items in page 23, four stories were taken from PTI wires while two from Reuters and AFP besides a picture by AP-PTI. Page 24 had five stories–one each filed by PTI, AFP and DPA. Page 25 had six stories of which two were filed by PTI and other two by Reuters and DPA. Page 26 had six sports news items of which four were credited to PTI along with a picture by AFP of the Sydney Cricket Test. Thus, it had a total of 120 news stories of which 52 were taken from news agencies that included 21 credited to PTI and UNI.

Times of India, Mumbai, Wednesday, January 5, 2000: The front page of the issue carried eight news stories, all filed by TOINS, besides an AFP picture. Page nos. 2, 3 and 5, called Mumbai, carried Metrofile, readers grievances and 10 news stories–all filed by TOINS. It had five pages of advertisements in Page nos. 4, 6, 8, 12 and 13. Page nos. 7 and 9 entitled *India* carried 13 news items of which two were taken from PTI and one from UNI besides one picture by AP on dense fog in Delhi. Page 10 was devoted to the editorial while page 11 carried seven news features of which one was filed by AP and three by Reuters. Three features were syndicated write-ups. Page nos. 14-16 carried 15 news stories, one column named Around the World and two pictures by AFP.

Business Times on Page 14 carried five stories from Reuters, four from PTI and one from UNI. Page 18 had stocks news while Page nos. 19 to22 carried 25 sports news of which only five stories were taken from news agencies–one each from PTI, UNI, Reuters, AFP and AP. These included the Sydney dateline PTI story on: *Team management wants Laxman for triangular series* and Bangalore datelined UNI story on *Bhupathi will miss Davis Cup ties.* Thus, it had a total of 92 stories of which 34 were credited to news agencies of which 14 came from PTI and UNI wires.

Times of India, Mumbai, Thursday, January 6, 2000: Front page of this issue carried seven news stories including a box item saying–*Terrorists release has demoralized forces: RSS Chief.* Page nos. two, three and five carried four news stories from across the Mumbai including the standard columns like the Metrofile–all filed by TOINS. It had five pages–4, 7, 9, 14 and 16 filled with advertisements while page 20 carried news and information concerning tenders and contracts.

Page 6, 8 and 10 called *India* had a total of 22 stories of which one was taken from PTI and two from UNI. These included a PTI story from Meerut on *Security alert in Western U.P. over ISI attack plans.* Page nos. 11 and 13 carried 10 foreign dateline stories including four from Reuters and one each from AFP and DPA.

Page 12 is the editorial page. Page 15 also carried five international news stories along with a column entitled Around the World. Of the five stories, two were credited to Reuters and one each to PTI, AP and AFP. Page 17 carried 12 Business Times news stories of which four were credited to PTI and one to Reuters. Page 18 had stocks news.

Page 19 also called Business Times carried nine news stories of which three were taken from Reuters, two from PTI and one from AFP. Page nos. 21 to 24 carried 24 sports news stories in addition to a column on Sports Watch and Sports Events. They included just one story each from PTI, UNI, AFP and Reuters. In total, it had 99 stories of which 31 were attributed to news agencies including 13 credited to PTI and UNI.

Table 4.4: Number of News Agency Stories Appearing in Times of India in the First Week of January 2000

Date	Total Number of News Stories	News Agency Stories	Stories from PTI and UNI
January 1, 2000	92	27	23
January 2, 2000	105	29	15
January 3, 2000	102	36	20
January 4, 2000	120	52	21
January 5, 2000	92	34	14
January 6, 2000	99	31	13
January 7, 2000	89	22	14

Times of India, Mumbai, Friday, January 7, 2000: Highlight of this issue is an AFP picture of notorious terrorist Maulana Masood Azhar being escorted in Karachi after getting freed in a deal in the Indian plane hijack. Other noteworthy stories published in the front page include *Mumbai arrests reveal Pak hand in hijacking* and *US wants hijackers brought to book.* Page nos. two and three is reserved to Mumbai news and Metrofile. Page 4 carried advertisements. Page nos. five to eight carried 25 news stories from across the country. Of these only two–one each by PTI and UNI were from news agencies, the rest were contributed by TOINS.

These included a Karachi dateline UNI story saying: *Freed terrorists are now in Karachi.* Page 9 carried three foreign news stories along with the column Around the World. Page 10 was the editorial page while Page 11 had a Washington dateline feature on *Crimes against S. Asians on the rise in U.S.* credited to IANS. Page 12 had four international news stories –one from PTI and three from AFP.

Page 13 had nine business stories of which three each were attributed to PTI and UNI and one to Reuters. Page 14 had stocks news while page 15-16 carried news concerning tenders and contracts and a column called News Facts containing five news items from TOINS. Page nos. 17-20 carried 26 sports news stories of which three were credited to PTI and two to AFP. The Leisure section incorporated in these pages carried cartoons and crossword. Thus, it had a total of 89 news stories of which 22 were attributed to news agencies including 14 taken from PTI and UNI.

Times of India (2005): [5]

Times of India, Mumbai, Saturday, January 1, 2005: Following the Tsunami, the front page had five major news items including a six column story by Jug Suraiya with a banner headline–*Its time to pick up the pieces.* It also had a two column box item–*World lends a helping hand* by Times News Network or TNN. Page 2 carried a feature entitled the Best of Bombay Times along with TV, Radio and Today's Engagements column. Page 3 had seven stories from the Mumbai city all by TNN. Page 4 had Times Classifieds.

Page 5, 6 and 7 entitled *Hell and High Water* after Tsunami carried 11 stories including two from PTI, three from AP and one from NYT News Service. AP's Phuket dateline story: *30 languages, one phrase; Let's help* was very well displayed on Page 6. Both PTI stories were from Colombo. They read as: *Discount fear of mines* (box item) and *Tsunami may unite Tamil Tigers and Lankan govt.* Page 8 called India had three stories of which one was taken from PTI and two from TNN including Pune dateline story: *Pitroda suggests ways to reform education system.* Page 10 carried four features under the title Hell and High Water and four Water World Briefs.

The features included: *Nellore: Enough words, give us something concrete; Tirumullaivasal: Nagaptattinam corners biggest slice of relief pie (five columns); New Delhi: They hung in there, fought pain and waves to emerge alive (the story about Jarawas tribals in Car Nicobar Archipelago); and Bangkok: Baby back from the blue (box item).* Page 10 carried three news items including one from PTI and the rest filed by TNN. Page 12 titled International had five brief under the sub-title–Around the World–along with advertisements. Page 13 had two news features on tsunami each filed by AP and

NYTNS (New York Times News Service).

Page 14 was the editorial page. It also carried the feature–The Speaking Tree. Page 15 named Business Times carried eight stories along with executive digest and international briefs of which five were filed by Reuters, two by PTI and one by UNI. They included PTI box item: *Petrol, diesel prices left unchanged.* Page 16 carried stocks news compiled by ET intelligence group and eight stories–three by Reuters and one each by PTI, UNI, AP, AFP and TNN. Page nos. 17-20 carried 13 stories by TNN in addition to the Events calendar for 2005 and three more TNN stories under the title The Sporting World at a Glance. Thus, this issue had a total of 81 stories of which 24 were credited to news agencies.

The Times of India, Mumbai, Sunday, January 2, 2005: Aftermath of the high tide dominated the media all over the world including the Indian media. This issue of TOI was no exception. It had six major headlines including a six column story entitled *Another day, another alarm.* Its credits were shared between Indian news agencies and the TNN. Page 2, as usual, was Mumbai centric and carried features like Movies of the week, Health Check, TV and radio schedules and today's events and engagements. Page nos. three and four also called Mumbai, carried seven stories and two columns–all filed by TNN. Page 6 called India carried two features–a deep focus on stocks and shares and another on fair trade–both credited to TNN. Page 7 and eight entitled Hell and High Water had 11 stories and four features all by TNN. Page 8 called Special Report had 10 news briefs. Page 9 had four news stories including two from PTI.

One of them was a Cuddalore/Keezhputhupattu dateline story on *Animals may have had foreknowledge.* Page 10 had three international features filed by PTI, TNN and NYT-NS along with four un-credited foreign briefs. Page 11 was also entitled Hell and High Water and carried five news features–one each by AP and Reuters and three by NYT-NS. The features were as follows: *AP/Ban Nam Khem/Thailand: Thais complain of bias* and Reuters' *Banda Aceh/Indonesia: Tsunami toll on the rise, aid gushes in*. NYT-NS features included *Crawford/UN: France-US spat over aid* and *London: Europeans craze for beaches turns fatal.* Page 12 was the editorial page.

Page 13 entitled Mind our Matter carried four features by TNN. Page 14 called open space had sponsored features. Page nos.16 to 18 had 19 news items including news stories and news features. Page nos. 19 to 25 were reserved for Times Classified and four pages from Page nos. 25-28 carried Times Life – a special Sunday supplement. Thus, this 28 page Sunday edition of Times of India carried a total of 80 stories of which only 11 news stories were credited to news agencies.

Times of India, Mumbai, Monday, January 3, 2005: International datelined stories and features dominated the front page of this issue. Of the five major headlines, three were credited to NYT-NS and two to TNN for their tsunami stories filed from Thailand and nearby areas. Page 2 carried two features under the banner the Best of Bombay Times. Page 3 called Mumbai had two regular weekly columns and three stories–all filed by TNN.

Pages 4 and 6 carried times classifieds while page nos. five to eight entitled Hell and High Water carried 17 stories of which five were taken from AFP, eight from TNN and one each from UNI, PTI, AP and NYT. Page 9 called India had six stories including one from PTI story on *Pak to release Indian fishermen* and the rest by TNN.

Page 10 had eight international stories of which three were filed by PTI, two by TNN and one each by AFP, AP and Reuters. Page 11 also carried five news stories under the title Around the World. Of these one each was filed by PTI, UNI, AFP, AP and Reuters.

The stories included a story on: *Zardari reunites with family in Dubai after 8 yrs in jail.* The following editorial page focused on Tsunami lessons. Page 13 called Business Times had six stories filed by TNN. Page 14 had six stories by TNN that included two financial news features: *Software takeovers: To buy or be bought* and *Consolidation name of the game for PSU banks.*

Page 15 had five sports stories of which one was taken from AP and the rest filed by TNN. Page nos. 17 and 18 also carried 10 sports stories of which one story was taken from AFP. Page 16 carried news on tenders and contracts.

Page nos. 19 to 28 carried advertisements. Thus, this issue had a total of 75 news stories including features of which 22 were credited to news agencies.

Times of India, Mumbai, Tuesday, January 4, 2005: The front of the issue carried five major news stories–all credited to TNN along with regular features. Page 2 carried the Best of Bombay Times while Page 3 carried three news stories and two standard columns filed by TNN. Page 4 had advertisements.

Page 5 entitled Hell and High Water carried one guest article and four news features while page nos. six and eight were reserved for Times classifieds. Page 7 called India carried a column on India digest along with five TNN stories from across the country. Page 9, also called India, had five stories by TNN.

Page nos. 10 and 11 carried international news under which it published 13 news stories–two each by AP and NYT, one by Reuters and the rest by TNN. Page 12 was the editorial page.

Page 13 carried business news under the banner the Business Times. It had eight news items and an executive digest column. The stories were contributed by NYT, PTI (2), Reuters (2) and TNN (3).

Page 14 carried stocks news including five news stories of which one each was filed by PTI, Reuters and AP and two by TNN. Page nos. 15 to 18 carried 19 sports stories of which two each were filed by UNI and PTI and the rest were contributed by TNN. Page 19 to 22 carried advertisements.

Thus, this issue carried 67 stories of which 17 were taken

from news agencies.

Times of India, Mumbai, Wednesday, January 5, 2005: The front page five news stories of which one each was credited to PTI and AFP and three to TNN. Page 2 carried the column Best of Bombay Times. Page 3 called Mumbai had five news stories filed by TNN along with the Metro Digest. Page nos. four, six and 19 carried advertisements. Page 5 also carried 11 stories from across the Mumbai city–all by TNN.

Page nos. 7 to 11 carried 18 stories from all over India of which two were filed by PTI and one by UNI and the rest by TNN. Page nos. 12 and 13 entitled Hell and High Water carried four features, two in each page.

Of these one each was filed by PTI and NYT. The other two were contributed by TNN. They were: *Port Blair (TNN): 30 years of labour lost in a day* and *Car Nicobar (TNN): Hope floats in ravaged Nicobar.* Page 14 had four international news stories filed by AP, AFP, PTI and UNI. Page 15 also carried two features taken from the Sunday Times and NYT along with the column Around the World.

Page 16 was the editorial page. Business Times on Page 17 had 11 stories of which seven were filed by PTI, two by UNI and one each by Reuters and TNN. Page nos. 18, 20 and 21 carried 17 sports stories all credited to TNN. Page 22 carried advertisements. Thus, the issue had a total of 69 stories of which 15 were credited to news agencies.

Times of India, Mumbai, Thursday, January 6, 2005: The front page carried five major news stories related to Tsunami and its aftermath including New Delhi dateline story on *Disaster management teams set up for the Andamans.* Page 2 carried the Best of Bombay Times while page nos. three and five carried six stories on Mumbai along with the standard column like the Metrofile.

Page nos. 4 and 6 were reserved for advertisements. Page nos. 7 to 11 carried 18 stories from across India of which four were credited to PTI and three to UNI. Page nos.12 and 13 entitled Hell and High Water carried five features–two by

NYT and one each by Reuters and AFP.

Table 4.5: Number of News Agency Stories Appearing in Times of India in the First Week of January 2005

Date	Total Number of News Stories	News Agency Stories	Stories from PTI and UNI
January 1, 2005	81	24	7
January 2, 2005	80	11	6
January 3, 2005	75	22	7
January 4, 2005	67	17	7
January 5, 2005	69	15	13
January 6, 2005	67	14	9
January 7, 2005	60	11	5

Page nos. 14 and 15 carried eight international news stories of which three were filed by TNN, two by Reuters and one each by PTI and UNI. Page 16 was the editorial page while page 17 carried nine business news stories under the banner of Business Times. All these stories were filed by TNN. Page nos. 18 to 20 carried 15 sports news–all but one filed by AFP, the rest by TNN. Page nos. 21-24 carried advertisements. Thus, the issue had a total of 67 news stories of which 15 were filed by news agencies

Times of India, Mumbai, Friday, January 7, 2005: *US may increase HIB visas for professionals* and *Navy on alert for relief efforts, says Natwar Singh* were among the six major headlines on the front page. Page 2, as usual carried the Best of Bombay Times while page nos. three, five and six carried Mumbai news. Of the 17 stories, only one was credited to PTI and two to UNI. Page 4 was reserved for advertisements. Page nos. seven to nine carried news from all over India. They carried 12 news stories all filed by TNN. Page 10 carried advertisements. Page nos. 11 and 12 carried stories related to Tsunami under the title Hell and High Water.

These included four features and two news stories–all filed by TNN. Page 13 was again reserved for advertisements. Page 14 carried the editorial and page nos. 15 and 16 carried nine international news–two each filed by Reuters, AFP and AP and the rest by TNN. Page nos. 17 and 18 carried advertisements. Page nos. 19 to 22 carried 10 sports items–two credited to PTI and UNI each and the rest credited to TNN. Page nos. 23 and 24 were again reserved for advertisements. Thus, the issue carried a total of 60 news stories of which only seven were filed by news agencies.

End Notes

1. Archives, Nehru Memorial Museum and Library, Teen Murti, New Delhi.
2. Archives, Nehru Memorial Museum and Library, Teen Murti, New Delhi.
3. Ibid.
4. Ibid.
5. Ibid.

5

The Tribune

The Tribune, a popular newspaper now published form Chandigarh, New Delhi, Jalandhar, Dehradun and Bathinda, started publication on February 2, 1881, in Lahore (now in Pakistan). It was started by Sardar Dyal Singh Majithia, a public-spirited philanthropist, and is run by a trust comprising five eminent persons as trustees. It is a major Indian newspaper with worldwide circulation.

The English edition apart, the 129-year-old Tribune has two sister publications, *Dainik Tribune* (Hindi) and *Punjabi Tribune.* All the three newspapers are published under the 'The Tribune Trust'.

The Tribune (1985) [1]

The Tribune, Chandigarh, Tuesday, January 1, 1985: *Rajiv team sworn in/Kaushal, Pranab and Ghani Khan out* was the lead story on the front page of the Tribune. Of these, two were credited to PTI and one to UNI. Of the 10 stories published under the title Foreign Briefs, seven were credited to Reuters and one each to PTI, UNI and AP. [2] Page 2 carried advertisements while Page 3 carried regional briefs and district diary. Of the 12 stories on this page, only one was filed by UNI. Page 4 carried the editorial. Page 5 carried nine stories that included one from PTI, two from Reuters and three from UNI along with a KBK graphic on major international events of 1984.

The New Delhi datelined UNI stories were as thus: *A niche in history: Rajiv's memorable poll victory; Eighth Lok Sabha constituted; and Rajiv's win will help solve the Mizo problem.* Page 6 carried four political news stories of which one was credited to PTI and the rest to UNI. UNI stories were: *Patna: Lowest victory margin for Jagjivan Ram; Bhopal: 80 pc of candidates lose deposits; and New Delhi: Big win, big margins.* PTI's New Delhi dateline story: *BJP worst hit* (It contested 226 and won only 2) was also very well displayed. Page 7 carried seven news stories of which three were credited to PTI.

Page 8 had seven stories including three from PTI, Page 9 had 11 stories of which three were taken from PTI and seven from UNI. Page 10 had five stories including one each filed by PTI and UNI. Page 11 had seven stories of which two were credited to PTI and one to UNI. Page 12 had 12 sports news stories and one cartoon. Of these, one story each was taken from PTI and Reuters. Page 13 carried 11 commodities news of which one each was filed by UNI and PTI. Page 14 carried picture diary under the title: The year that was. So, a total of 103 stories appeared in this issue of which 48 were taken from various news agencies and 25 from PTI and UNI specifically.

The Tribune, Chandigarh, Wednesday, January 2, 1985: The front page carried 19 news stories along with foreign briefs and a cartoon by noted cartoonist Rajinder Puri. The break-up was as follows: three news stories were taken from PTI, four from UNI and one each from Reuters, AP, DPA and AFP. The rest were filed by the newspaper staffers. Page 2 carried tender notices while Page 3 was reserved for regional briefs. It had 13 news stories along with a column entitled *Chandigarh Calling*. All the stories were filed by the Tribune News Service or TNS. Page 4 carried the editorial. Page 5 had nine stories–three from PTI, two each from UNI and AFP and one each from AP and Reuters. Page 6 had 12 stories of which three each were filed by PTI and UNI. Page 7 carried 11 news stories and one feature.

Of these, just one story was filed by PTI while seven were credited to UNI. Page 8 had advertisements. Page 9 had 12 stories–five by PTI and seven filed by UNI. Page 10 carried 15 sports stories of which six were taken from UNI and two from AP. All the four sports briefs stories were filed by TNS. Page 11 entitled Stocks/Commodities/Bullion carried 13 news items of which three were taken from UNI. Page 12 had 11 stories of which three each were credited to PTI and UNI. Thus, a total of 118 stories were published in this issue of which 63 were taken from news agencies including 53 from PTI and UNI.

The Tribune, Chandigarh, Thursday, January 3, 1985: The front page carried eight news items plus regular column called Foreign Digest. The regular stories were filed by the Tribune staff while the digest had two stories each from PTI, UNI, Reuters, AP and UPI while three stories from AFP. Page 2 carried tenders and notices.

Page 3 carried regional briefs and district diary. It had 14 news stories of which one each was taken from PTI and UNI. Page 4 was the editorial. Page 5 carried 12 news stories of which three were taken from PTI, four from UNI and one each from UPI, Reuters and AP. Page 6 had 14 stories of which four were attributed to PTI and two to UNI. Page 7 had 10 stories–six from PTI and one from UNI.

Page 9 carried advertisements. Page 10 had 10 sports stories along with sports briefs that included one news from PTI, four from UNI and two from AP. Page 11 had seven stories of which one was from PTI and the rest from TNS. Page 12 had 10 stories of which three were taken from PTI and two from UNI. The issue had a total of 137 stories of which 63 were credited to news agencies while 49 were taken from PTI and UNI.

The Tribune, Chandigarh, Friday, January 4, 1985: The front page had 17 news stories including foreign briefs. Of these, three stories were taken from PTI, four from UNI, two each from AP, Reuters and AFP and one from DPA. The rest were contributed by TNS.

Page 2 carried advertisements. Page 3 had 16 stories including regional briefs and district news—8all by TNS. Page 4 was the editorial page. Page 5 carried 13 news stories that included four stories each from PTI and UNI and one each from AFP, AP, UPI and Reuters. Page 6 had five stories of which one each was credited to PTI and UNI.

Page 7 had eight stories of which two were taken from

PTI, four from UNI and two from INFA (Indian News and Features Alliance). One of the UNI story was: *Lucknow: Tulsi cure for stress-related illnesses.* Another UNI story from New Delhi about *Farm exports to Japan can be raised to 36,000 cr* got a three column display. Page 9 had 10 stories of which two were attributed to UNI. Page 10 had 11 regular sports stories and 12 sports briefs of which two each were taken from PTI and UNI and one from Reuters. Page 11 had 14 news stories of which two each were credited to PTI and UNI and 10 to TNS. Page 12 had 13 stories of which three were attributed to PTI and two to UNI. Thus, it had a total of 123 stories of which 53 were taken from news agencies and 38 were taken from PTI and UNI.

The Tribune, Chandigarh, Saturday, January 5, 1985: The front page carried 21 stories including 10 foreign briefs. The main headline was a two column UNI story: *New Delhi: Centre to pay additional D.A. arrears on Feb 1.* Of the total stories, nine were credited to PTI and six to UNI. Foreign briefs were also credited Reuters (2), AP, AFP, PL-Pool and UN-DPA. Page 2 carried classifieds. Page 3 carried 10 stories from the region and various districts of Punjab and Haryana filed by the TNS. Page 4 called Review carried guest articles and leaders. Page 5 carried 11 foreign news–three each filed by PTI and Reuters and two each filed by UNI and UPI. Page 6 carried tender notices.

Page 7 had 10 news stories–three by PTI and two by UNI and the rest by TNS. The PTI story was as follows: *Ahmedabad (PTI): Gujarat parties gear up for assembly polls* while the UNI story was: *New Delhi (UNI): Cong-I lost in Muslim majority areas.* Page 8 carried nine stories of which six were taken from PTI and two from UNI. Page 9 had 11 stories of which one was credited to PTI and three to UNI. Page 11 had 23 sports news stories including sports briefs. Of these, four each were filed by PTI and UNI and two by AFP. Page 11 had seven news stories of which only two (one each by PTI and UNI) were taken from news agencies. Page 12 had seven news items of which two were credited to PTI and one to UNI. In total, the issue carried 87 stories of which 57 were attributed to news agencies and 52 to PTI and UNI.

The Tribune, Chandigarh, Sunday, January 6, 1985: *'No place for violence/help end Punjab discord: PM'*–this three column stepped headline PTI-UNI story was the main news of the day. Apart from it, the front page carried eight more stories along with eight foreign news briefs filed by agencies–five by PTI and three by UNI. Page 2 carried classified advertisements while Page 3 carried 20 news stories including a feature on Gardening Notes–all filed by TNS. Page 4 carried the Sunday Tribune–the editorial of the day. Page nos. five to seven entitled Sunday Reading carried miscellaneous articles. Page 8 had two news stories including one from PTI. Page 9 had five news items of which two–one each was credited to PTI and UNI. Page 10 and 11 carried classified advertisements. Page 12 carried four news items that included *Washington (AP): PM to visit US in June?*

Table 5.1: Number of News Agency Stories Appearing in The Tribune in the First Week of January 1985

Date	Total Number of News Stories	News Agency Stories	Stories from PTI and UNI
January 1, 1985	103	48	25
January 2, 1985	118	63	53
January 3, 1985	137	63	49
January 4, 1985	123	53	38
January 5, 1985	87	57	52
January 6, 1985	95	46	30
January 7, 1985	116	40	34

Delhi (PTI): Stress on policy of friendship. Page 13 carried 13 news stories of which three each were attributed to PTI and UNI. Page 14 had 20 stories including sports briefs of which four were taken from PTI and one from UNI. Page 15 carried 10 news items on commodities that included one by PTI, two by UNI and seven by NNS. Page 16 carried four news items of which one each was credited to PTI and UNI. Thus, in total the issue carried 95 stories of which 46 were credited to various news agencies and 30 to PTI and UNI.

The Tribune, Chandigarh, Monday, January 7, 1985: *'Army to quit Punjab'* this special news story by the Tribune correspondent hogged the front page headlines. The other news stories in the limelight were: *New Delhi (PTI): Four states agree to early polls (two columns) and Ludhiana (TNS) Dal for direct talks.*

There were a total of 21 (five from PTI) news stories including 11 foreign briefs–all credited to agencies–four to PTI, two each to UNI, Reuters and AP and one to AFP. Page 2 had advertisements. Page 3 carried eight regional briefs and 14 district news items (total 22). Page 4 carried editorial.

Page 5 had nine stories of which six were from news agencies–two each from PTI, UNI and Reuters. Of these, PTI's Moscow story: *Nehru staved off 'shift to right'* was revealing. Its opening paragraph said: "*The real alternative to the course followed by Nehru during his tenure and in the subsequent period was not a revolutionary left-wing but a right-wing government, an authoritative political profile brought out by the Russians say.*"

Page 6 carried five news stories of which three were credited to UNI while Page 7 carried eight of which three news stories were taken from UNI. Page 8 carried 11 news stories and a feature of which one each was credited to PTI and UNI.

Page 9 had advertisements. Page 10 had 11 sports news and 10 sports briefs of which three were credited to PTI, two to AFP and one to UNI.

Page 11 had eight commodity news items of which one was shared between PTI and UNI and three were credited to UNI. Page 12 had 11 news stories of which one each was credited to PTI and UNI. Thus, it had a total of 116 news stories of which 40 were credited to various news agencies and 34 to PTI and UNI together.

The Tribune (1990)

The Tribune, Chandigarh, Monday, January 1, 1990: Of the 10 news stories published in this issue, the main news was the New Delhi datelined story filed by the Tribune Bureau or TB: *Promise to ex-servicemen/One rank one pension scheme soon.* Five of these stories were credited to news agencies–two to PTI and UNI and one to Tanjug. Page 2 carried tender notices. Page 3 carried 16 regional news items of which two–one each was taken from PTI and UNI. Page 4 had advertisements. Page 5 published seven foreign news stories of which two each were taken from AFP and AP and one each from PTI, Reuters and DPA. Of these, the PTI story from Islamabad saying *Pak war games only eyewash* was very well displayed over four columns. Page 6 carried three stories all filed by PTI. They were: *Baroda: Sardar Sarovar Project by 96'97; Jaipur: Drug reactions worry doctors;* and four column displayed story from: *Some where in the Eastern sector: Oxygen scarce but courage aplenty.*

Page 7 carried three news stories of which one from Cuttack by UNI got a four column display. The story was: *Cuttack (UNI) Buddhists sites lie neglected.* Page 8 is the editorial. Page 9 had four stories of which two were credited to UNI. Page 10 had three stories of which one was taken from PTI. Page 11 had four stories of which one was credited to PTI. Page 12 had advertisements. Page 13 had five news stories of which two were credited to PTI and one to UNI. Page 14 had 14 sports news stories of which three were attributed to PTI and two to UNI. They included: *Bangalore (UNI): South zone pile up 665* (box item) and PTI's story from *Jaipur: Railways chug their way to double crown* (three column display). Page 15 carried 15 news stories about stocks and commodities of which five were attributed to PTI and one to UNI. Page 16 had four news items–two by PTI and one each by UNI and DPA. The PTI stories included: *New Delhi: Momentous decade for world science* (four column display on the last page). Thus, it had a total of 82 news stories of which 38 were credited to agencies including PTI and UNI whose total was 32 news stories.

The Tribune, Chandigarh, Tuesday, January 2, 1990: PTI stole the show with five of the 10 major news stories appearing on the front page credited to it. The stories were: *Chandigarh: Punjab bandh near total (three column display); Srinagar: Bomb blasts in valley (two columns); New Delhi: Farm pricing method to change (four columns)* and *Chandigarh: 12 killed in Punjab.* Likewise, UNI's story from Chandigarh–*North India shivers (one column)* was also well-placed. Page 2 published advertisements. Page 3 had 26 news stories from around the region and districts of which two each were credited to PTI and UNI.

Page nos. four and five had seven stories each of which two were from PTI and one from UNI. Page 6 had 10 news stories of which one was credited to PTI and five to UNI. Page 7 had eight stories of PTI, UNI, Kyodo and AP had one each while Reuters and AFP had two each stories attributed to them. Page 8 was editorial. Page 9 carried three features and two stories of which one was credited to PTI. Its first column carried a feature entitled From Here and There. One example of its contents is as follows: *"The English language has become 'impoverished, sloppy and limited', a dismal wasteland of banality, cliché and casual obscenity..."*.

Page nos. 10 and 11 carried 11 regional stories filed by TNS and four stories from the districts of which one each was credited to PTI and UNI. Page 12 carried 14 sports news stories of which five were taken from PTI wires while two from UNI's. Page 13 entitled Market carried 10 market news of which one was taken from PTI and three from UNI. Page 14 carried 10 foreign news items of which four were credited to PTI, AFP, Kyodo and IANS. The rest were contributed by the TNS. In all, the issue under consideration had 97 news stories of which a total of 45 news stories were taken from various news agencies. Of these 45, 36 were taken from PTI and UNI.

The Tribune, Chandigarh, Wednesday, January 3, 1990: *New Delhi (UNI): Govt. drops 2 poll commissioners (three column display); Colombo (PTI): Plot to kill Wizeratne* *(three column box item); Faridkot (PTI/UNI): Mann to attend all party meet (two columns);* and *New Delhi (UNI): Cold wave claims 109 lives* were among the 12 main stories published on the front page. The rest were filed by the Tribune news service and bureau. Page 2 carried tender notices. Page 3 carried 11 regional stories and 11 stories under the banner–Chandigarh Calling. In all, it had 22 news stories all filed by TNS except one which was filed by PTI. Page 4 carried 14 news items of which Reuters and AP one each, PTI and DPA two each, UNI and AFP four each. Page 5 had 11 stories–PTI, UPI and IANS one each, AP two and AFP and Reuters three each. Page 6 carried advertisements.

Page 7 had tender notices. Page 8 was the editorial page. Page 9 carried six news items of which three were news features. Two stories were credited to UNI. Page 11 had two stories of which one was taken from UNI. Page 12 had six stories of which one was credited to PTI. Page 13 had five stories of which two each were credited to PTI and UNI. Page 14 carried 16 sports stories of which three were credited to PTI and one to UNI. Page 15 entitled Market carried five stories of which three were credited to PTI. Page 16 carried 17 news stories of which two each were attributed to PTI and UNI. They included UNI story from Panaji: *Mounted police to check hippies (box item).* Thus, it had a total of 105 stories of which news agencies were 48. The combined tally of PTI and UNI stories stood at 29.

The Tribune, Chandigarh, Thursday, January 4, 1990: The front page carried 12 stories of which six were credited to PTI, three to UNI, one to AFP and two to the Tribune Bureau. Page 2 carried tender notices. Page 3 had a total of nine stories from the region that included two stories by UNI. Page 4 entitled *The Tribune Spectrum,* a weekly survey of development news and issues, carried features. Page 5 had 14 news stories–one each taken from IANS and UNI, two each credited to PTI, AFP, Reuters and Tribune Bureau and four attributed to AP. Page 6 was the editorial page. Page 7 carried five stories and one guest article of which one story was credited to PTI and three to UNI. Page 8 had 14 stories of which one each was credited to PTI and UNI.

The PTI story was: *New Delhi: India, Nepal begin dialogue.* Page 9 carried 10 stories of which two were taken from PTI wires and one from UNI. Page 10 had 18 sports stories of which PTI, Reuters and AFP contributed one each, AP two and UNI six. One of the UNI stories: *New Delhi (UNI): Kanchan seeded 9th in nationals* was very well displayed with a five column bottom split banner headline. Page 11 had 12 stories about stocks–all filed by national news agencies–PTI filed seven while UNI five. Page 12 again had 12 news stories of which two were attributed to PTI and three to UNI and one to IPS. Thus, it had a total of 105 news stories of which 62 were filed by various news agencies. Of these, PTI and UNI's combined tally was 47.

The Tribune, Chandigarh, Friday, January 5, 1990: *Islamabad (PTI): 250 die in worst Pak rail mishap* and AFP's *Miami (Florida): Gen. Noriega flown to USA* were two of the nine main stories carried in the front page. AP, Reuters, AFP and PTI had one story each while UNI had three and the rest were filed by TB. Page 2 carried tender notices. Page 3 carried 21 regional and district news stories filed by TB. Page 4 had 13 stories of which two were filed by PTI and six by UNI. Page 5 carried six foreign news items–two each from PTI, UNI and AFP. Page 6 carried tender notices. Page 8 was the editorial page. Page 9 carried eight stories and a column.

Of the stories, two each were filed by PTI and UNI and one by IANS. Page 10 carried just two stories credited each to UNI and PTI. Page 10 had four stories–two each from PTI and UNI. Page nos. 12 to 14 had a total of 19 stories from all across the country. Of these, 11 were taken from PTI and three from UNI. The PTI stories included the following: *Hyderabad: Srikanth likely to be captain (box item); Hyderabad: Spinners to hold centre-stage;* and *New Delhi: Indian lads let Pak off hook (box item).* Page 15 carried 10 news stories about commodities of which five were taken from PTI and one from UNI. Page 16 had seven stories–one from PTI and AFP and five from UNI. Thus, it had a total of 106 stories of which 58 were taken from various news agencies. The combined tally of PTI and UNI stories stood at 49.

The Tribune, Chandigarh, Saturday, January 6, 1990: PTI news stories and pictures dominated the front page of this issue. Its Faridkot story on Mann–*Mann to attend meeting on Punjab*–was given the banner headline while picture of deposed Gen. Noriega was given a three column display. Likewise, PTI picture of visiting Sri Lankan foreign minister R. Wizeratne was published very prominently. Thus, of the 12 stories in this page, six were credited to PTI, two to UNI and one to UPI. Page 2 carried tender notices. Page 3 carried 22 regional news capsules filed by TB while Page 4 carried advertisements.

Page 5 carried 11 foreign news stories of which one each was filed by PTI, AP, Tanjug, DPA, ADN and AFP, two were filed by Reuters while three were credited to UNI. PTI's story from Islamabad on *'Pak committed to plebiscite in J&K'* was well displayed. Page 6 carried the editorial. Page nos. seven to nine carried weekly supplement Saturday Plus. Page 10 was entitled Entertainment. Page 11 carried 18 stories of which 10 were credited to PTI, seven to UNI and one to AP. It also carried the column–From Here and There. Page 12 carried classifieds. Page 13 carried tender notices. Page 14 carried 15 sports news stories of which three each were credited to PTI and UNI, Page 15 carried 11 news stories about market of which five were attributed to PTI and one to NNS. Page 16 carried 12 news stories of which two were credited to UNI and one to AFP. The rest were attributed to TB. In all, the issue had a total of 101 stories of which 57 were credited to news agencies and from among them, 42 to PTI and UNI.

The Tribune, Chandigarh, Sunday, January 7, 1990: *New Delhi (UNI): Industrial draft by month's end (two column bold headline; New Delhi (UNI): India, Lanka set up group* *on ceasefire;* and *PTI's New York: US terms for deal with Noreiga* were among the major news headlines of this issue. Also, PTI picture of foreign minister I. K. Gujral welcoming Bhutanese king was also well displayed. Page 2 carried tender news. Page 3 carried 10 news stories of which PTI story from Amritsar–*Rs. 1.87 lakh grant for ex-serviceman*–was a box item. Page 4 carried tender news. Page 5 carried 20 news stories.

Table 5.2: Number of News Agency Stories Appearing in The Tribune in the First Week of January 1990

Date	Total Number of News Stories	News Agency Stories	Stories from PTI and UNI
January 1, 1990	82	38	32
January 2, 1990	97	45	36
January 3, 1990	105	48	29
January 4, 1990	105	62	47
January 5, 1990	106	58	49
January 6, 1990	101	57	42
January 7, 1990	101	53	41

Of these, two were taken from PTI and five from UNI. Page 6 also carried tender notices. Page 7 carried classifieds and Page 8 was the editorial page. Page 9 carried three features and a KBK graphic on major international events of 1989. Page nos. 10 and 11 carried tender notices while Page 12 carried 13 news stories along with district diary. Of these, four stories each were credited to PTI and UNI. Page 13 carried 14 news items of which four were taken from PTI, five from UNI and one from AP. Page 14 carried 24 sports stories of which one was taken from DPA, two each from UNI, AFP and Reuters and three from PTI. Page 15 carried 13 business news stories of which two were taken from UNI and four from NNS. Of these, UNI feature on 1989: *Year of Silver* got two column bold display. Page 16 also carried 11 stories concerning business of which two were attributed to PTI and one to AFP. Pages 17 to 24 carried an eight page supplement entitled the Sunday Reading. Thus, it had a total of 101 news stories of which 53 were taken from news agencies. Of these 53 wire stories, 41 were taken from PTI and UNI.

The Tribune (1995): [3]

The Tribune, Chandigarh, Sunday, January 1, 1995: Change is said to be the only constant factor in life and nature and this issue reflected it very well. The first column of the front page sported a headline *Spotlight* and carried six news items credited two each to PTI and UNI and one each to AP and Reuters. In addition, the page carried five main news stories that included *New Delhi (PTI) Tiwari quits as UPCC chief* and *New Delhi (PTI) Cabinet rejects Arjun's charges.* The break-up of stories was as follows: UNI one, PTI three and Tribune Bureau or TB one. Page 2, as usual, carried advertisements along with TV and radio schedules.

Page 3 entitled *Chandigarh and Around* carried 15 news stories all filed by TNS. Page 4 carried 10 regional news stories of which one was credited to UNI–*Jammu: 3,000 stranded on Jammu highway.* Page 5 carried four news analysis filed by TNS. Page 6 had classified advertisements. Page 7 and eight carried tender notices. Page 9 had 21 stories including seven appearing in '*In brief*' column. Of these, seven stories were filed by PTI and 13 by UNI. TNS filed just one story. Page 10 was entitled *Editorial and Focus.* Page 11 called *Perspective* carried three features by TNS. Page 12 called Nation had five stories–three credited to PTI and two to UNI.

Page 13 had advertisements. Page 14 called Business Tribune carried six corporate news items by TNS, one by PTI and two by UNI. UNI's story *Pol. Uncertainty dogs reforms* was a four column box item and *Sugar prices soar during the year* was also very well displayed. Page 16 also called Business Tribune carried six news items one each credited to PTI and UNI and the rest to TNS. Page 16 carried 15 sports news stories of which seven were attributed to PTI. It also carried an AP/PTI picture of Diego Maradona. Page 17 also carried six sports stories of which three were credited to PTI, AP and Reuters. Page 18 carried classified advertisements.

Page 19 called World had 12 stories of which four each were credited to PTI and Reuters, two to AFP and one each to ANI and DPA. It also carried the KBK graphic on major world events during 1994. Page 20 also carried seven news stories from across the world of which one was credited to PTI, three to UNI and one to Reuters. It also had an AP/PTI picture of *Opposition march in Dhaka.* Page nos. 21 to 28 were entitled *Sunday Reading* and carried miscellaneous articles and features. Thus, this issue had 121 news stories of which total news agency stories were 68 and the combined tally of PTI and UNI stories stood at 56.

The Tribune, Chandigarh, Monday, January 2, 1995: The spotlight column had six stories–three taken from PTI and one each from Reuters, AP and TNS. Rest of the front page carried eight stories–two filed by PTI and three each by UNI and TNS. PTI stories included: *New Delhi: PM Rao greets Prez. Sharma on New Year* and *WTO comes into being (three column bold headline).* Page nos. two, six and eight carried advertisements. Page 3 carried 20 news stories from Chandigarh and around. Page 4 carried 11 news stories of which one each was filed by PTI and UNI. Page nos. seven and nine called Nation 15 news stories of which PTI filed seven stories, UNI six and TNS two. Page 9 also included a PTI picture on *Shraddhanjali ceremony of Gianiji.* Page 10 was called *Opinion.* Page 11 entitled *Perspective* carried three news features by TNS and one story by Reuters.

Page nos. 12 and 13 called *Business Tribune* carried eight stories of which PTI contributed three stories. Page 14 carried 17 sports stories of which two were filed by PTI, one each by UNI and Reuters. Page 15 also carried 14 sports news stories of which one was filed by Reuters. Page 16 entitled *World* carried six stories–one each filed by PTI, UNI and AP and three by Reuters. Its *In Brief* column carried four stories credited to PTI, AFP, AP and Reuters. Page 17 carried a sponsored feature called Education Tribune. Page 18 carried 10 news stories of which three each were credited to PTI and UNI. It also included a PTI picture of zoo authorities trying to chain a wild elephant calf. Thus, this edition had 126 news stories of which 60 were taken from news agencies. The number of stories attributed to PTI and UNI stood at 44.

The Tribune, Chandigarh, Tuesday, January 3, 1995: *Madras (UNI) TNCC to boycott Rao's visit* and *New Delhi (UNI) Call AICC session, pleads Arjun* were among the seven UNI stories published on the front page. Of the remaining four stories published, two were credited to PTI and one each to Reuters and AP. Page 2 carried tender notices. Page 3 was full of 22 stories culled from Chandigarh and surrounding areas by TNS. Page 4 carried nine regional news items of which two were filed by UNI. Page 5 carried feature on Tribune Lok Adalat. Page 6 carried tender notices. Page 7 carried 19 stories from all over the nation.

They included seven stories by PTI and nine by UNI. Page 8 called Opinion is the editorial page. Page 9 called Perspective carried the Lahore Diary and column on From Here and There along with two stories filed by PTI. Page nos. 10 and 11 carried 19 market and corporate news items under Business Tribune. Of these six stories were taken from PTI wires while one each was credited to UNI and IPA. Page nos. 12 and 13 carried 20 sports stories of which three each were credited to UNI and Reuters and one to PTI. Page 14 public notice and a column called In Brief. It had 11 stories–one each from PTI, DPA, Reuters, ANI and Kyodo and three each from AP and AFP. Page nos. 15 and 16 entitled Sports Tribune carried 20 news stories including five features credited to guest writers. Of the 15 news stories, three were credited to PTI, four to UNI, one each to Xinhua and DPA. The rest were filed by TNS. Hence, the total number of stories in this issue was 144. Of these, news agency stories stood at 66 that included 48 stories credited to PTI and UNI.

The Tribune, Chandigarh, Wednesday, January 4,

1995: *Seshan defers Bihar poll* and *Pirates hijack Bandit Queen* both filed by TNS were the main news stories. Of the total 15 stories printed on the front page, three were attributed to PTI, six to UNI and one to AP. As usual, Page 2 carried tender notices while Page 3 carried 20 TNS stories from Chandigarh and surrounding areas.

Table 5.3: Number of News Agency Stories Appearing in The Tribune in the First Week of January 1995

Date	Total Number of News Stories	News Agency Stories	Stories from PTI and UNI
January 1, 1995	121	68	56
January 2, 1995	130	55	40
January 3, 1995	144	66	48
January 4, 1995	133	60	48
January 5, 1995	123	65	42
January 6, 1995	120	47	37
January 7, 1995	120	47	30

Page 4 carried 15 regional news stories–all filed by TNS. Page 5 carried six news items. Page 7 called Nation carried 15 news stories–10 filed by PTI and four by UNI. TNS filed just one story. Page 8 was the editorial page and contained column on Letter to the Editor. Page 9 was also an opinion page called Perspective. Page nos. 10 and 11 carried 18 business news stories of which three were attributed to PTI and four to UNI. Page nos. 12 and 13 carried 21 sports news stories of which four were filed by PTI, three each by UNI and AP and two by AFP.

The remaining stories were filed by TNS. Page 14 called World had 10 stories–one each filed by PTI, DPA and AFP, two by Reuters and five by AP. Page 15 carried two features under the banner Health Tribune. The features included *How to survive in this AIDS infected world.* Page 16 carried 10 news stories of which two were filed by PTI and four by UNI. The PTI story included *Rao constitutes Cong poll bodies.* Thus, the issue had a total of 133 news stories of which 60 were attributed to news agencies. The agency stories included 44 stories attributed to PTI and UNI.

The Tribune, Chandigarh, Thursday, January 5, 1995: PTI's Calcutta story: *Govt. committed to reforms: Rao* and a PTI picture showing *PM Rao inaugurating CII session* were the main highlights of the front page that had a total of eleven stories, including three in Spotlight. Of these, three were taken from PTI and four from UNI. Page 2 contained tender notices, TV and radio schedules. Page 3 carried 19 stories from Chandigarh and around. Page 4 carried 12 stories including UNI's *Chandigarh: Another spell of snow* along with one PTI story. Page 5 also carried eight regional news stories. Page 6 had tender notices.

Page 7 called Nation had 12 stories–six from PTI and five from UNI and one from ANI. Page 8 was the Opinion page while Page 9 called Perspective two UNI stories and a cartoon by Newshound. Page 10 called Business Tribune had 12 stories of which one each was taken from PTI, UNI and IPA. Likewise, page 11 had eight stories–four from PTI and two each from UNI and ANI. Page 12 had 10 sports news stories of which one was credited to PTI, three to UNI and four to AP. It also had an AP picture of Maradona. Page nos. 14 and 15 carried 17 sports stories–one each from PTI, Reuters and DPA and three from UNI and five from AP. Page 16 entitled Science Tribune carried four features on: *Mobile phone revolution; Crime busting made easy; Single cell proteins; and Hands off the cane.* It also had a box feature on new products an discoveries. Page 16 had 10 stories of which four were attributed to PTI, five to UNI and one to AP. Thus, it had a total of 125 stories.

The Tribune, Chandigarh, Friday, January 6, 1995: *New Delhi (PTI): Benazir's remarks belligerent* and *New Delhi (UNI): Consulate staff returns* were among the nine main stories that appeared on the front page of this issue. The credit-wise break up of these nine stories was as follows: PTI five, UNI one and the rest TNS. It also carried a picture of

India's Karachi consulate's staff children returning to India. Page 2, along with tender notices, carried five agency stories–two taken from PTI wires and three from UNI. Page 3 carried 22 stories from Chandigarh and around while page nos. four, five and six had 18 regional stories–all contributed by TNS. Page 7 carried 10 stories from across the nation of which three were credited to PTI, six to UNI and the rest to TNS. Page 8 was the Opinion page while Page 9 called Perspective also had opinion pieces. Page nos. 10 and 11 had 10 business news stories of which three were credited to PTI.

Page nos. 12-14 carried 23 sports stories of which six were credited to UNI, three each to AP and Reuters, two to PTI and one to Kyodo. The rest came from TNS. Page 15 called Arts Tribune carried three features while page 16 carried 10 news stories–two each from PTI and UNI and one from AP. Thus, it had 120 news stories of which the news agency stories were 47 that included 37 stories from PTI and UNI wires.

The Tribune, Chandigarh, Saturday, January 7, 1995: UNI's New Delhi dateline story on *UK supports India on Kashmir* was a box item on the front page accompanied by a PTI picture of visiting British foreign secretary Douglas Hurd. Other stories included TNS' *Tactical move by UP rebels* and *Mann arrested from Bassi Pathanan,* a four column story. These were among the 14 stories that appeared on the first page of this issue. Page 2 carried tender notices while Page 3 carried 24 stories from Chandigarh and around–all filed by TNS. Page nos. four and five carried 15 regional news stories filed by TNS while page nos. six and seven carried classified advertisements. Page 8 carried 11 news stories including four briefs. Page 9 again carried 16 regional stories including one UNI story from Ambala. Page 10 and 11 carried the views section under the title Opinion and Perspective. Page 12 also had three regional stories by TNS.

Page 13 carried advertisements. Page 14 entitled Business Tribune had 12 business and corporate news stories of which one was credited to PTI, three to UNI and one to NNS. Page

15 carried three business news stories by PTI. Page nos. 16 and 17 carried 18 sports stories of which four were taken from AP, two each from PTI, UNI and Reuters while one each from AFP and DPA. The rest were filed by TNS. Page nos. 18 and 19 carried sponsored features. Page 20 carried four news stories of which one was taken from PTI and three from UNI. Page nos. 21-24 carried the Saturday Review. Thus, the total stories were 120 of which 47 were attributed to various news agencies that included 30 stories filed by PTI and UNI.

The Tribune (2000): [4]

The Tribune, Chandigarh, Saturday, January 1, 2000: *Jaswant brings hostage home*–an eight column banner headline of a TNS story from New Delhi was the highlight of this first issue of Y2K. The other main stories included *Kandahar (Reuters): Freedom after 8 days of agony; Kandahar (AFP): Hijackers head for Pak; New Delhi (PTI): PM defends release of 3 militants;* and *Moscow (PTI): Yeltsin quits.* The page also carried a signed editorial by The Tribune's editor Hari Jai Singh entitled: *Thanks God, but questions remain.* The total number of this stories in this page were six of which two each were filed by PTI and TNS and one each by Reuters and AFP.

Page 2 carried classifieds while Page 3 and four called Region carried 27 stories including eight news briefs and seven news items from district diary–all filed by TNS. Page 5 entitled Punjab carried eight stories, Page 6 called Haryana carried six stories and Page 7 called Himachal Pradesh carried six stories–all contributed by widening network of the Tribune News Service or TNS. Page 8 entitled Nation carried eight news stories including four news briefs and a column called Focus.

The credits of the stories were evenly divided between PTI and UNI. Page 9 called World carried three features–two by Reuters and one by AP and an in-house column called Window on Pakistan. Page 10 was the opinion cum editorial page while page 11 called Perspective carried two syndicated features and an in-house feature called From Here and There. The syndicated features were: *On the spot* by Tavleen Singh sub-titled *Hijacking takes away New Year cheer* and *Sight and Sound* by Amita Malik sub-titled *Responsibility of the media.* Page nos. 12 and 13 carried advertisements. Page nos. 14 and 16 carried classifieds.

Page 15 carried just one TNS story along with advertisements. Page 17 called Region carried six stories–three taken from PTI an one from UNI. Page 18 called Business Tribune had 15 stories of which two each were taken from PTI and UNI. Page 19 carried five stories of which three were credited to PTI that included a five column news feature on *Investor confidence boosted in 1999.* Page 20 had five sports features filed by TNS. Page 21 carried advertisements. Page 22 had 10 news stories of which one each was filed by AFP and Reuters, two by UNI and four by PTI. PTI's Islamabad story: *Shoaib Akhtar banned for suspect bowling action* got a five column display. Page 23 carried seven stories of which three were credited to PTI. Page 24 had six stories–one each credited to PTI, AFP and Reuters and three to TNS.

They included an AFP story from Hamburg: *Firework ring in new millennium.* The first issue of the new millennium also carried a six page additional supplement named *Chandigarh Tribune* that had 40 stories from Chandigarh, SAS Nagar, Panchkula, Patiala, Ambala, Rajpura, Kalka, Dera Bassi, Kurali, Parwanoo, Kharan, Zirakpur, Baddi, Barotiwala and Ladnu. This special issue also carried an eight page supplement called *The Tribune on Saturday* and a four page supplement called *Yamunanagar Marketing Supplement.* Hence, the total stories in this very special edition were 165 of which the news agency stories were 44 that included 34 stories filed by PTI and UNI.

The Sunday Tribune, Chandigarh, Sunday, January 2, 2000: *Pak engineered hijacking (TNS)*–was the main banner headline spread over six columns of the front page. It also carried a PTI picture of hijackers. The total number of stories including news briefs in this page were 21 of which four were filed by PTI, three by UNI and one by Reuters. Page 2, as usual, carried classified advertisements along with TV and radio schedules. Page 3 and four called Region carried 25 news stories of which one each were credited to PTI and UNI. All other stories were attributed to TNS. Page 5 called Punjab carried 13 TNS stories. Page 6 called Nation had 14 stories from all over India. Page 7 entitled World carried 12 news stories of which one each were credited to PTI and AFP and three each to DPA and Reuters. Page 8 carried *The Tribune Millennium Debate* while page 10 called Perspective had opinion writings. Page nos. 10 to 14 carried classified advertisements.

Page 15 had seven stories under the banner Business Tribune. Of these, one was credited to Reuters, two to TNS and four to PTI including *Low inflation rate keeps govt. happy (five columns).* In addition, it had six features–two guest articles and four regular columns–Grapevine, Check Out by Puspa Girimaji, Tax & You by R. N. Lakhotia and Labour Laws by Praful R. Desai. Page nos. 16 and 17 carried 18 sports stories of which eight were taken from PTI, three from UNI, two from Reuters and one each from AFP and ANI. Page 17 called Backpage carried three stories–two credited to UNI and one to DPA. It also had an AP/PTI picture on *Illumination in Paris.* Eight pages from 19-26 carried *The Sunday Tribune.* The issue also carried six pages of *Chandigarh Calling* that had 56 stories from in around the common capital of Punjab and Haryana. Hence, the issue had 170 stories of which 63 were credited to various news agencies that included 44 stories from PTI and UNI.

The Tribune, Chandigarh, Monday, January 3, 2000: Islamabad (UNI): *Hijackers cross over to Pak* was one of the 17 stories on the front page of this issue. Of these, nine stories were credited to PTI and four to UNI. The remaining four stories were attributed to TNS. The following page had classified advertisements and tender notices. Page 3 carried 22 regional news stories filed by TNS. Page 4 also carried 18 regional news items–all contributed by TNS. Page 5 carried six stories from Punjab of which one each was filed by PTI and UNI. Page 6 to eight carried 25 stories from Haryana of which eight were filed by PTI and seven by UNI.

Page 9 entitled World and Global Monitor had 17 stories of which one story was filed by ANI, two stories each by Reuters and AFP and four by PTI. Page 10 was the opinion page. Page 11 carried three features under the title News Review. Page 12 carried 13 business news stories of which 11 were credited to PTI and one each to UNI and ANI. Page 13 carried three news items–one four column PTI news story *Auto Competition looks up* and two news features.

Page 14 titled Agricultural Tribune carried five TNS stories. Page 15 carried six from all across Punjab filed by TNS. Page 16 and 17 carried 19 sports stories of which 10 were credited to PTI, two each to Reuters and AFP and one each to UNI and AP. Page 18 carried advertisements. Page 19 to 24 carried special supplement called *Chandigarh Tribune* that contained 58 news stories originating from Chandigarh and surrounding areas. Thus, it had a record number of 204 stories of which 68 were taken from various news agencies that included 56 stories attributed to PTI and UNI.

The Tribune, Chandigarh, Tuesday, January 4, 2000: PTI and TNS shared credits for the Srinagar dateline story on *16 killed in Srinagar blast* while UNI stole credit for Chandigarh dateline story *Fog hits rail, road traffic* on the front page of this issue. Thus, of the main seven stories, PTI and UNI had one story each to their credit. Of the seven stories of the Spotlight column, four stories were taken from PTI, two from UNI and one from AFP. The next page carried classified advertisements. Page 3 carried 24 regional news stories–all filed by TNS. Page 4 also had 22 regional stories from TNS. Page 5 had 12 stories from in and around Punjab of which one story from Gurdaspur was filed by UNI. Page 6 called Nation had 23 stories from across the nation including 10 briefs.

Of these, 14 stories werc credited to PTI and six to UNI. Page 7 named World had 18 stories of which one was taken from PTI, two each from UNI and AFP, three each from AP and DPA and seven from Reuters. Page 8 was the opinion page while Page 9 carried news review and a column entitled From Here & There. Page 10 called Business Tribune carried 13 stories of which four stories were taken from PTI, three from UNI and two from DPA. Page 11 had stocks news. Page 12 carried classifieds. Page 13 had sponsored supplement called Education Tribune.

Page 14 and 15 carried 19 sports stories of which eight stories were attributed to PTI, two to Reuters and one each to AFP and UNI. Page 16 called Backpage carried seven news stories of which two were taken from PTI, three from UNI and one each from AP and Reuters. Page 17 to 22 carried a six page supplement called Chandigarh Tribune that had another 39 stories. Hence, the total number of stories in this issue were 191 of which agency stories were 74 that included 53 stories filed by PTI and UNI.

The Tribune, Chandigarh, Wednesday, January 5, 2000: *MLA, family escape militant attack* and *VIPs presence delayed action* were among the 13 stories published in the front page of which two were attributed to PTI, three to UNI, one each to AFP and Reuters and six to TNS. Page 2 had advertisements. Page 3 and four carried 25 regional news items filed by TNS. Page 5 carried 15 stories from Punjab of which only one story was attributed to PTI. Page 6 called Nation had 10 stories of which only two were taken from UNI and PTI. Page 7 had 12 stories from across the globe of which two each were taken from Reuters and UNI and one each from AFP and AP.

Page 8 was the opinion page. Page 9 carried interviews of the week plus the daily column From Here & There. Page 10 carried 16 business news stories of which five each were credited to PTI and UNI. Page 11 carried stocks news. Page 12 carried three stories from Haryana while Page 13 was the Health Tribune. Pages 14 and 15 carried 20 sports stories of which eight were attributed to PTI, three to Reuters and one each to AP and AFP. The rest were filed by TNS. Page 16 called Backpage had seven stories of which two each were taken from PTI and UNI and one from AFP. Page 17 to 22 carried the supplement Chandigarh Tribune that had 53 news stories. Thus, the edition had a total of 175 news stories of which news agency stories were 50 that included 32 stories filed by PTI and UNI.

Table 5.4: Number of News Agency Stories Appearing in The Tribune in the First Week of January 2000

Date	Total Number of News Stories	News Agency Stories	Stories from PTI and UNI
January 1, 2000	163	44	34
January 2, 2000	170	63	44
January 3, 2000	204	68	56
January 4, 2000	191	74	53
January 5, 2000	175	50	32
January 6, 2000	177	51	43
January 7, 2000	180	67	43

The Tribune, Chandigarh, Thusday, January 6, 2000: *New Delhi (TNS) India warns Pak on N-threat* was the main headline of the front page that carried a total of 14 news stories that included four from PTI, two from UNI and one each from AP and Reuters. It also displayed an AP/PTI picture of a blast in Colombo. Page 2 carried entertainment and classified advertisements. Page 3 carried 23 regional news stories filed by TNS while Page 4 carried 18 regional news items of which only one was filed by UNI *Chandigarh: Fifth day of fog in region.* Page 5 had eight stories from Punjab while Page 6 called Nation had 16 stories from all over the country of which seven were taken from PTI and nine from UNI.

Page 7 had 15 stories from across the world of which two each were credited to PTI and UNI. Page 8 and nine were opinion pages. Page 10 carried six business news items of which one was credited to UNI while page 13 was the Science Tribune. Pagc 14 had 19 sports stories of which four were credited to PTI, three each to UNI and AFP and two each to Reuters and AP. Page 15 had advertisements while page 16 named the Backpage had eight stories–two from PTI and one each from UNI, Reuters, AFP and AP. Pages 17-20 were reserved for special supplement called Chandigarh Tribune that had 38 stories filed by TNS. Thus, there were 177 news stories in this issue of which 51 stories were taken from various news agencies that included 39 stories of PTI and UNI.

The Tribune, Chandigarh, Friday, January 7, 2000: The front page had 12 news stories–three attributed to PTI, one to UNI and two to AFP that included New Delhi datelined story *Power failure affects North India* with an accompanying picture. The rest were credited to TNS. Page 2 carried classified advertisements. Page 3 carried 14 regional stories of which one Chandigarh dateline story–*Coldest day of the season*-was credited to UNI. Page 4 had 18 regional stories filed by TNS. Page 5 had advertisements. Page 6 had 18 stories from across the nation of which six each were credited to PTI and UNI and remaining to TNS.

Page 7 had 17 stories from around the world of which two each were credited to PTI, UNI and UPI, seven to Reuters and one each to AP and DPA. Page 8 was the op-ed page that carried signed editorial by the editor Hari Jai Singh on Gaps in Crisis Management–Time for honest port-mortem. Page 9 was also an opinion page that carried columns like the World in Focus and From Here & There. Page 10 carried 13 business stories of which six were credited to PTI and seven to UNI. Page 11 carried stocks and shares. Page 12 had 10 stories from Punjab by TNS.

Page 13 entitled Arts Tribune carried three features. Page 14 and 15 carried 23 sports stories of which eight were attributed to PTI, one each to UNI and ANI and three to Reuters. Backpage carried six news stories of which three were from PTI and one each from UNI, AP and TNS. It also had a scenic picture of Nainital in winters. It also had four pages of Chandigarh Tribune that carried 46 news stories. Thus, it had a total of 180 news stories of which 67 were attributed to news agencies that included 43 stories credited to PTI and UNI.

The Tribune (2005): [5]

The Tribune, Chandigarh, Saturday, January 1, 2005: The front page of this 34-page edition of The Tribune which was now published from Noida and Bathinda as well had its first column reserved for the Tribune Tsunami Relief Fund, Internet poll, Today's Quote and Cast your vote. It also had a sub-title called Inside that named specific pages such as Nation, Punjab, World, Opinion and Sports. It had four main stories–*Port Blair (PTI): After shocks push up water level (three columns); Chennai (PTI): Protest over discrimination in relief distribution (six columns); New Delhi (UNI) Tyagi takes over as Air chief;* and *Chandigarh (TNS) Haryana defies EC.* Page 2 now called Nation had 10 news stories of which three were credited to PTI and the rest to TNS. The PTI story was *Kalapet (Pondicherry): Aid not reaching tsunami-hit people (two columns).*

Page 3 had seven stories by TNS. Page 4 had 19 stories from Punjab of which 10 brief stories concerned Amritsar, Nawanshahr, Phagwara, Phillaur and Tarn Taran. Page 5 also carried nine more stories from Punjab filed by TNS. Page 6 titled Jammu and Kashmir/Haryana had 11 stories including a UNI story from Srinagar. The rest were filed by TNS. Page 7 called Haryana had nine TNS stories from various towns of Haryana state like Rohtak, Karnal, Bhiwani, Fatehabad, Rewari as well as the state capital Chandigarh. Page 8 entitled North India carried classified advertisement along with weather reports. Page 9 called World had nine stories credited to PTI, two each to AP, AFP and Reuters. Two news stories were also taken from the Dawn and The Independent. Page 10 called Opinion was the editorial page while page 11 was the

Oped Page.

It had features like Dateline Washington and Defence Notes. Page nos. 12-15 were taken up by classified advertisements. Page 16 called Nation had three stories from New Delhi, Chennai and Kancheepuram. Page 17 called Himachal Pradesh had six main stories and two news in brief from Bilaspur and Sundarnagar. The main stories originated at Mandi, Shimla and Hamirpur. They were all filed by TNS.

Page 18 carried stocks and entertainment news. Page 19 called Business had 16 news stories of which PTI had six and UNI two. The rest came from TNS. PTI's New Delhi dateline story–*External debt at US$ 113.6 bn*–was a two column box item while another story–*TRAI issues new inter connect regulations*–got a three column display. UNI's story from Manila–*ADB to give US$ 325 mn to tsunami hit*–got a four column display. Page 20 and 21 carried 14 stories of which three were credited to PTI, two to UNI and Reuters and one to AFP. The rest were filed by TNS. Page 22 had two news stories–*Vijayawada (UNI) PM to convene all party meet* and *New Delhi (PTI): Army gets new vice-chief* were well displayed. The rest of the page carried advertisements.

It also had eight pages of Chandigarh Tribune and four pages of Ludhiana Tribune. All the 55 stories in these supplements were filed by TNS. Hence, the total number of news stories including news features in this edition was 176 of which 40 stories were attributed to various news agencies including 25 credited to PTI and UNI.

The Sunday Tribune, Chandigarh, Sunday, January 2, 2005: The 40-page Sunday edition of the Tribune had 24 regular pages, eight pages of Spectrum and another eight pages devoted to Chandigarh Tribune and Ludhiana Tribune. The front page had five main news stories and two briefs credited two each to PTI and UNI. Page 2 had 15 news stories from across the nation of which five were credited to PTI and three to UNI. UNI's story from Chennai about *School boy donates pocket money* was a box item. It also had a four column news feature entitled *Out of the jungle came starving, startled survivors* published by arrangement with The Independent.

Page 3 called Chandigarh Plus had three TNS story. Page 4 had 12 stories from various towns and cities of Punjab namely Ambala, Batala, Hoshiarpur, Moga, Patiala, Phillaur and Phagwara. Similarly, Page 5 also had 10 TNS stories from Punjab. Page 6 entitled Jammu & Kashmir/Haryana had 19 stories filed by TNS. Page 8 had classified advertisements and weather report by TNS. Page 9 and ten also carried classified advertisements. Page 11 called World had eight stories of which three were credited to AFP and four to Reuters along with a Washington dateline Dawn news feature on Pakistan–*Political rights 'casualty' in Pakistan.* Page 12 called Perspective carried guest articles and noted cartoonist Rajinder Puri's cartoons while Page 13 was the Op-ed page.

Page nos. 14-19 carried classified advertisements. Page 20 called North India had three stories by TNS such as: *PM's national relief fund; Cabinet reshuffle soon; and Fire in old subji mandi.* Page 21 carried 11 business news stories of which two were credited to PTI and three to UNI. Tribune's New Delhi datelined story *Product Patent Regime comes into force* had a four-column display. Pages 22 and 23 carried 22 sports stories of which one each was taken from PTI–*Mumbai: Ajay Jadeja pulls Delhi out of trouble*–and Reuters–*Sydney: Inzamam to miss Sydney test.* Page 24 had eight news stories of which one was credited to PTI and two to UNI. The UNI stories were: *Cuddalore: Vivek Oberoi adopts village* and *New Delhi: North shivers as it snows*. Pages 25 to 32 carried entertainment and life-style supplement called Spectrum.

In addition, it had two supplements of four pages each called the Chandigarh Tribune and Ludhiana Tribune. The Chandigarh Tribune had 24 news stories while Ludhiana Tribune had 20 news stories. The total number of news stories in this edition were 184 of which news agency stories are 30 that included 22 stories credited to PTI and UNI.

The Tribune, Chandigarh, Monday, January 3, 2005:

Moderate quake in West Nicobar; Cold wave conditions grip north India; and *Nanavati panel report by month-end* were the three PTI stories from New Delhi that found their place in the front page of this issue. The other two stories came from TNS. Page 2 carried 14 stories from across the nation of which three stories each were credited to PTI and UNI and one to IANS (Indo Asian News Service). IANS' Guwahati story–*Quake warning triggers panic in Assam* got a three column display while PTI's Dehradun story *Roopkund lake drying* was also well displayed. Page 3 had six stories under the banner Chandigarh Plus. Page 4 had 26 stories from all over Punjab while Page 6 carried nine stories from J&K and Haryana.

Of these, one story from Srinagar was credited to UNI and another story from Jammu was attributed to PTI. Page 7 had 12 TNS stories from different places in Haryana namely Panipat, Rewari, Jhajjar, Karnal, Gurgaon etc. Page 8 had three stories from north India including a New Delhi dateline story–all filed by TNS. Pages 9 had 10 stories from all over the world that included one story credited to IANS, two to AFP and three each to PTI and Reuters. AFP's Stockholm story *Mum's heroics save family* got a three column display along with Reuters's story from Crawford (Texas): *Bush orders flag tribute to victims.*

PTI stories were: *Washington: US crackdown on immigrant fugitives; London: Lord Paul gives Rs. 1 crore;* and *London: International donors meet in Geneva* while IANS' story–*London: UK temple raises money* was also well displayed. Page 10 and 11 were opinion pages while Page 12 had nine TNS stories from Himachal Pradesh. Page 13 had nine news stories of which two each were credited to PTI and Reuters and one to UNI. It also had one news feature by Dawn from Islamabad–*Rain, cold dampen rallies against Pervez.* Page 14 carried classified advertisements while page 15 called Forum carried Letters to the editor.

Page 16 entitled Nation had 10 stories–five taken from UNI and one three column box item from IANS–*Port Blair*

(IANS): Prayers, pain & tears. The UNI stories included *Kolkata: Ham radios bring back smiles* and *Tiruchirapally: Similar quake 120 mn years ago.* Page 17 had eight business stories of which one each was credited to PTI and UNI. Pages 18 and 19 had 15 sports stories of which one was attributed to UNI and three each to PTI and Reuters. Page 20 had 10 news stories of which one was credited to UNI, and three each to PTI, Reuters and TNS. It had eight pages of Chandigarh Tribune that carried 32 stories and four pages of Ludhiana Tribune that carried 18 news stories. Thus, the total number of stories in this edition stood at 191 of which 48 were taken from news agencies including 32 filed by PTI and UNI.

The Tribune, Chandigarh, Tuesday, January 4, 2005: Of the six front page news stories only one was credited to PTI *–Chennai: Seer gets bail in assault case.* The rest were filed by TNS. Page 2 had called had 17 stories including three from PTI and four from UNI. The stories included: *Amritpuri (UNI): Amritpuri math offers Rs. 100 cr (box item); Kolkata (PTI): Ancestral warning system saved Andaman tribes (three column-box item)* and *Ahmedabad (UNI): National Rural Healthcare Mission constituted (three column).* Page 3 called Chandigarh Plush had seven TNS stories. Page nos. 4 and 5 both called Punjab carried 23 TNS news stories from across the state while Page 6 called North India had 14 news stories including four from PTI and one from UNI.

Page 7 called Haryana had 19 stories filed by the Tribune staffers. Page 8, also called North India, had three stories by TNS. The World page on Page 9 had 12 stories of which one each was credited to PTI and Reuters, two to AP and four to AFP. The stories included: *London (PTI): India to install warning system; Jakarta (AFP): Tsunami toll crosses 1.44 lakh; Colombo (AP): Looters making most of tragedy; Colombo (AFP): Lankans scared of seafood;* and *Banda Aceh (Reuters): Chaos hampers relief operations (three columns).* Page nos. 10 and 11 carried the editorial and opinion sections while Page 12 named Himachal Pradesh had 11 stories filed by

TNS from all over the state. Page 14 had four TNS stories from north India. Page 14 called News had 12 stories including one by UNI.

Page 15 was the Education Tribune and Page 16 carried stocks and entertainment news. Page 17 had 13 business news stories including one each credited to PTI, UNI and Reuters. Page nos. 18 and 19 had 20 sports stories of which one was credited to AP, two to Reuters, three to UNI and four to AFP. The stories included *Kolkata (AFP): Ganguly to lead Asia XI against ICC XI*. Page 20 carried the full page advertisement of Ford Fusion. The issue included eight pages of Chandigarh Tribune (21 stories) and four pages of Ludhiana Tribune (12 stories). The total stories in this edition were 194 of which the agency stories were 34 including 19 stories credited to PTI and UNI.

The Tribune, Chandigarh, Wednesday, January 5, 2005: Of the six front page stories, PTI story from Jaipur about *Mig crashes near Bikaner, pilot safe* got a prominent display. Page 2 called Nation had 17 stories of which three stories were credited to PTI and one to IANS. IANS story about *Tirunelli: A village of unwed tribal mothers* got a two column central display. Chandigarh Plus on Page 3 had six TNS stories while Page 4 entitled Punjab had 15 stories. Of these, 14 were filed by TNS and one story *New Delhi: Central team leaves for tsunami-hit areas* was filed by PTI. Page 6 called North India had 13 stories filed by the Tribune staffers. Likewise, 10 stories emanating from Haryana were also filed by TNS. Page 8 again called North India had three TNS stories along with classified advertisements.

Page 9 called World had eight stories from all across the globe of which three–one each was filed by PTI, Reuters and AFP. The stories were: *Baghdad (AP): Governor of Baghdad assassinated; Quila Rohtas, Pakistan (AFP): Gurudwara Mata Sahib Kaur reopened;* and *Dubai (PTI): 200 Indians being deported from Iran.* Page 10 was the Opinion page and carried editorials while page 11 was entitled the Op-ed page. Page 12 entitled Himachal Pradesh had nine TNS stories along with classified advertisements while page 13 had 11 stories on tsunami relief of which four stories were filed by agencies including one by PTI. The PTI story was: *Nagapattinam: Fisherman venture out into sea (three column).*

The page also had two Reuters pictures of tsunami relief work. The other agency stories were credited to Reuters, AFP and AP. Page 14 called North India had the list of donors to PM's Relief Fund and two stories including one Chandigarh story by PTI: *Narnaul freezes at 0'c.* Page 15 called Health and Fitness had seven features of which three were credited to ANI. The features were: *London: Detox diet can be even worse than binging (four columns); Washington: Tips for living till 100 years;* and *New York: Migraine–a beautiful visage holds the key.* Tips for long life included the following points: Eat lost of proteins, keep calories down, get enough sleep and get excellent medical facilities. Page 16 had stocks and entertainment news while page 17 carried 13 business stories of which two each were filed by PTI and UNI and one by Reuters.

The rest were TNS news stories. Pages 18 and 19 carried 19 sports stories of which 11 were filed by news agencies–four by UNI and seven by Reuters. Page 20 had seven stories including one Reuters story–*Jerusalem: Israeli firm offers free tsunami alert system (four column).* The issue also had four pages of Jobs and Careers, eight pages of Chandigarh Tribune (23 stories) and Ludhiana Tribune (12 stories). Thus, the total number of news stories in this issue was 181 of which 23 were agency stories that included 16 stories credited to PTI and UNI.

The Tribune, Chandigarh, Thursday, January 6, 2005: *100 aftershocks in Andamans/over 9,000 dead in Katchal alone*–was the main headline of this issue that had six main headlines on the front page credited to TNS and none to any agency. Page 2 had 15 stories from across the nation that included two from PTI and one from UNI. Page 3 called

Chandigarh Plus had six TNS stories while page nos. four and five had 23 TNS stories from all over Punjab. Page 6 had 14 TNS stories from North India while Page 7 had 10 TNS stories from Haryana. Page 8 had classified advertisements and weather forecast. Page 9 called World had 10 news stories of which one was credited to AP and four each were attributed to PTI and Reuters.

The PTI stories included: *Islamabad: Joint survey of Sir Creek begins; Jakarta: Natwar in Jakarta to attend summit of tsunami (four columns);* and *Kathmandu: 150 Maoists killed in Nepal.* As usual, Page nos. 10 and 11 were opinion pages while Page nos. 12 and 13 called Himachal Pradesh had 14 stories from the state filed by TNS. Page 14 had five news stories of which one each was filed by PTI and AFP and two by UNI. They included: *Paris (AFP): How did so many animals escape?* and *New York (PTI): Donations pour in.* Page 15 had eight news stories including two from PTI such as: *Latehar: Two CRPF jawans hit in mine blast* and *UP-Uttaranchal areas rocked.* Page 16 had news about stocks and shares while Page 17 carried 15 business news stories including two filed by PTI and three by UNI. They included: *Mumbai (PTI): SBI donates Rs. 10 cr* and *Mumbai (UNI): RIL ignores Anil's proposal.* Page nos. 18 and 19 had 17 sports news stories including one each from Reuters and AFP, two each from PTI and UNI and three from AP.

They included: *Paris (AFP): Schumacher gifts US$ 10 mn for tsunami hit* and *Zurich (AP) Fifa/AFC gathers US$ 3 mn.* Page 20 had three TNS news stories. The edition also had eight pages of Chandigarh Tribune (28 news stories) and four pages of Ludhiana Tribune (11 news stories). Thus, the total in this issue were 176 of which 28 were taken from various news agencies including 17 from UNI and PTI.

The Tribune, Chandigarh, Friday, January 7, 2005: The front page of this issue carried five main headlines. The one and only news brief was credited to PTI–*Ambanis agree* *on legal split, says Aaj Tak.* All other stories including *Indo-Pak journalists/demand lifting of curbs* was filed by TNS. The Page 2 had 17 national news stories including four each credited to PTI and UNI. They included: *Ayodhya (UNI): Rickshaw puller donate Rs. 50,000; Ahmedabad (PTI): Kalam for tsunami prediction mechanism;* and *Car Nicobar (PTI): On tree for 10 days without food (box item).* Page 3 called Chandigarh Plus had eight TNS stories from in and around the city while page nos. four and five 21 news stories from Punjab credited to TNS. Likewise, Page 6 had 14 news stories from Himachal Pradesh filed by TNS and Page 7 carried 13 news items from Haryana also filed by TNS.

Table 5.5: Number of News Agency Stories Appearing in The Tribune in the First Week of January, 2005

Date	Total Number of News Stories	News Agency Stories	Stories from PTI and UNI
January 1, 2005	76	42	25
January 2, 2005	184	30	22
January 3, 2005	191	48	32
January 4, 2005	194	34	32
January 5, 2005	181	23	16
January 6, 2005	176	28	17
January 7, 2005	177	38	22

Page 8 carried six news stories along with classified advertisements. Page 9 called World had 11 news stories of which two were filed by PTI, three by Reuters and four by AP. The stories included: *Jakarta (PTI): India for effective relief distribution system (four columns); United Nations (PTI): UN fears diversion of aid from other disasters (three columns);* and *Capitol Hill (AP): Bush donates US$ 10,000.* Page 10 and 11 were reserved for editorial and opinion sections respectively. Page 12 had advertisements about appointments. Page 13 called North India had seven stories including three stories from Srinagar–including three stories from Srinagar–two from PTI and one from UNI. Page 14 had five news stories filed by TNS. Page 15 was dedicated to Science and Technology while page 16 carried stocks and entertainment news.

Page 17 carried 15 business news stories including an AP/PTI picture of Bill Gates and an AFP story from Paris on *Tsunami fund–Corporate benevolence at its best.* The other stories included three by PTI and one each credited to UNI and AP. Page nos. 18 and 19 carried 19 sports stories of which one each was filed by AP and AFP and four each by PTI and Reuters. The stories included: *Kolkata (PTI): Ganguly to raise funds; Colombo (AP): Muralitharan leads tsunami relief work; Colombo (PTI): South Asia games postponed;* and *Melbourne (Reuters): Agassi ready for assault.* Page 20 had three news stories including one from AP thus: *Hong Kong: Strong quake strikes off Indonesian coast.* The issue had eight pages of Chandigarh Tribune (24 stories) and four pages of Ludhiana Tribune (12 stories). Thus, total stories in this edition were 177 of which 38 stories were filed by various agencies including 22 credited to PTI and UNI.

End Notes

1. Archives, Nehru Memorial Museum and Library, Teen Murti, New Delhi.
2. Ibid.
3. Ibid.
4. Ibid.
5. Archives, The Tribune, Chandigarh.

6

The Statesman

The Statesman is one of India's oldest English newspapers. It was founded in Kolkata in 1875 and has directly descended from *The Friend of India* (founded 1818). *The Englishman* (founded 1821) was merged with *The Statesman* in 1934. The Delhi edition of The Statesman began publication in 1931. The Statesman Weekly is a compendium of news and views from the Kolkata and Delhi editions. Printed on airmail paper, it is popular with readers outside India. With its average weekly circulation of approximately 180,000, it is a leading English newspaper in eastern India, particularly West Bengal. The Sunday Statesman has circulation of about 2,30,000.

The Statesman is also published from Siliguri and Bhubaneshwar to cater to readers in North Bengal, Lower Assam, Sikkim and remaining North-East. It is a founding member of the Asia News Network, a group of 15 Asian newspapers that have joined hands to cover Asian events through Asian eyes and with an Asian perspective.

The Statesman (1985) [1]

The Statesman, Delhi, Tuesday, January 1, 1985: *New Union Ministry sworn-in* was the eight column banner headline on the front page of this edition of The Statesman. Of the total nine stories published on this page, only one was credited to any news agency and that was–*Shillong (UNI): Earthquake kills 16 in Assam.* Page 2 had three news items along with TV, radio and film schedules. Page 3 carried a full page feature entitled–*Looking back in anger and joy.* Page 4 had 10 news stories including one from UNI. Page 5 had three stories of which two were credited to PTI and one to UNI along with a

KBK graphic on the *events of 1984.* Page 6 carried the editorials while Page 7 had 10 news stories of which two each were credited to PTI and UNI and one to Reuters.

Likewise, Page 8 carried 10 news stories of which three were taken from PTI and five from UNI. Page 9 carried three news features published by arrangement with Reuters and AP. Page 10 had eight stories from all over the world. They included one from AP, two each from PTI and UNI and three from Reuters. Page 11 carried city notes along with commodity news and nine stories under economic news in brief of which two were credited to PTI and one to UNI. Page 12 carried 13 sports news stories including one from AP, two from Reuters and three each from PTI and UNI. The stories included: *Dhaka (PTI): Bihari muslims protest in Dhaka* and Reuters' *50 guerillas killed near Thai border.* Thus, this small 12-page issue of the Statesman carried 78 news stories of which 37 were credited to various news agencies including 27 attributed to PTI and UNI.

The Statesman, Delhi, Wednesday, January 2, 1985: Of the six main stories, two were credited to PTI and one to UNI on Karnataka political imbroglio. Page 2 had entertainment news while Page 3 seven stories of which one each was credited to PTI and UNI. Page 4 had five news stories and a column. Page 5 had seven stories of which one was credited to Reuters. Page 6 carried the editorial while Page 7 had 12 news stories. Page 8 had 11 news items while Page 9 had four foreign news features. Page 10 had 11 news stories from across the globe contributed by Reuters (three), AP and AFP two each and one by DPA. Page 11 carried city notes plus commodity news and four economic news briefs of which two each were taken by PTI and Reuters. Page 12 carried 16 sports news stories including four credited to PTI, three to UNI, one each to AP and Reuters. The stories included *Calcutta (UNI): 3rd test heading for a draw.* Thus, this issue had total 83 news stories of which 32 were taken from news agencies including 14 from PTI and UNI.

The Statesman, Delhi, Thursday, January 3, 1985: *Bangalore (PTI): Karnataka assembly dissolved: President's Rule likely soon* and *Krishinagar (UNI) Bangla rifles exchange fire with BSF* were the two main stories of the 11 news items on the front page of this issue. They included two stories each from PTI and UNI and one from AFP. Page 2 had eight news stories of which two were from PTI and five from UNI. Page 3 had six stories and a feature on *Don't chew your life away* and news briefs. Page 4 had 16 news stories including three by PTI and two by UNI of which one was– *5,000 families hit by quake in Assam.* Page 5 had three features including one by UNI on *3-D answer to video piracy (three columns).* Page 7 had 23 news stories including 10 news briefs. Of these, four were filed by PTI, five by UNI, three by Reuters and one each by AFP and UPI.

Page 8 had 18 news items that included four by Reuters, two by AP and one each by UNI, AFP and UPI. Page 9 carried news on stocks and shares and four stories attributed two each to PTI and UNI. Page 10 had 12 sports news of which two each were credited to PTI and UPI, three to Reuters and five to UNI. The UNI stories included *Punjab women beat Kerala (two columns).* This issue had total 101 news stories of which 49 were taken from news agencies including 41 credited to PTI and UNI.

The Statesman, Delhi, Friday, January 4, 1985: Noted film critic and columnist Amita Malik's write-up entitled *French star of the evening* on the inauguration of the Indian Film Festival at New Delhi's Vigyan Bhawan was prominently display on the front page of this issue along with nine other stories that included *New Delhi (PTI): Ministerial panel formed to go into Punjab issue* and *Imphal (UNI): Rishag Keishing CLP (I) leader.* Page 2 had 12 news stories including two from PTI and eight from UNI along with weather forecast and TV and radio schedules. Page 3 had nine stories and one feature on *Policing the police.* Page 4 had 10 news stories including one credited to PTI and three to UNI. Page 5 had six stories on the film festival including one by UNI. Page 6 was the editorial page. Page 7 carried 24 news stories including three each credited to PTI and Reuters, six to UNI and one each to AP and AFP.

Page 8 carried five news stories–two by PTI and three by UNI and one Statesman feature on The Soviet Revolution. Page 9 had sponsored advertisement on the Festival of Soviet Books while page 10 had 11 news stories credited three each to PTI and Reuters and two each to UNI and UPI. Page 11 had three stories–two from PTI and one from UNI along with stocks and commodity news. Page 12 called the sports page had 12 sports stories including two from PTI and four from UNI. Thus, the total stories in this issue were 104 of which 56 were taken from various news agencies that included 42 stories from PTI and UNI.

The Statesman, Delhi, Saturday, January 5, 1985: *Lok Sabha elections in Assam may be held in March; Power crisis in Punjab and Haryana (Chandigarh/PTI);* and *Manipur Assembly/ Cong (I) majority absolute* were among the 18 news stories that appeared on the front page of this issue. Of these, five stories were by PTI and two by UNI. Page 2 had six news stories of which two were taken from PTI and three from UNI. Page 3 had six stories including Delhi news in brief by Statesman. Page 4 had 13 news stories including three from PTI. Page 5 had seven stories–six by PTI and one by UNI and a feature. Page 6 was the editorial page. Page 7 had 22 news stories including UNI's *New Delhi: Cong (I) got bulk of new votes.*

Of the total stories, two were credited to PTI, 10 to UNI and one each to AP and Reuters. Page 8 also had 22 news stories of which three each were credited to PTI and Reuters, one to UPI, four to AP and eight to UNI. Page 9 had four stories–one from PTI and three from UNI while Page 10 had 12 sports news stories including one each from AP and UPI, two from Reuters, three from PTI and four from UNI. Hence, the total news stories in this issue were 103 of which 70 were taken from various news agencies that included 56 news stories credited to PTI and UNI.

Table 6.1: Number of News Agency Stories Appearing in The Statesman in the First Week of January 1985

Date	Total Number of News Stories	News Agency Stories	Stories from PTI and UNI
January 1, 1985	78	37	27
January 2, 1985	83	32	14
January 3, 1985	98	54	47
January 4, 1985	104	56	42
January 5, 1985	103	70	56
January 6, 1985	108	82	60
January 7, 1985	102	57	47

The Sunday Statesman, Delhi, Sunday, January 6, 1985: Of the 18 news stories on the front page of the Sunday edition, the top slot was allotted to New Delhi datelined Statesman story on *PM pledges to give top priority to Punjab problem* while *A privilege to be an Indian* was the PTI box item. Of these, two each were credited to PTI and Reuters and seven to UNI. Page 2 had 10 stories filed by the daily staffers while Page 3 also had 10 stories of which three were credited to UNI. Page 4 had nine stories of which seven were features on the film festival while the remaining two stories were filed by PTI. Likewise, Page 5 also had three news features and three stories–two credited to PTI and one to UNI.

Page 6, as usual, carried the editorials and also had six news stories of which two each were credited to PTI and UNI and one each to Reuters and AP. Page 7 had 16 stories–two each taken from AP and Reuters, five from PTI and seven from UNI wires. Page 8 had 13 foreign stories of which one each was credited to AFP and UNI, two to AP, four to PTI and five to Reuters. The AFP story on Hong Kong–*Leak in Hong Kong could be radioactive* was a box item. Page 9 had six stories of which two each were credited to PTI and UNI and one each to AP and Reuters. Page 10 had 14 news stories of two each were taken from PTI, AP, AFP and Reuters and three from UNI. The issue also had four pages of literary supplement. Overall, it had 108 news stories of which 82 were attributed to different wire services that included 60 from PTI and UNI.

The Statesman, Delhi, Monday, January 7, 1985: The front page had two main headlines out of 14 stories published. They were Statesman's Washington correspondent Warren Unna's story *Geneva talks to seek starting point* and *Colombo (UNI): Priest among 9 Tamils killed by Lankan troops.* In total, five stories were credited to PTI and three to UNI. Page 2 had 10 stories of which three were taken from PTI wires and six from UNI. Page 4 had five stories filed by staffers. Page 6 was the editorial page. Page 7 had 15 news stories of which two each were credited t o PTI, AP and Reuters and three to UNI. Page 8 had eight stories of which six–three each were taken from PTI and UNI. Page 9 had six stories of which one each was taken from AP and Reuters. Page 10 had nine stories –two each from AP and Reuters and three each from PTI and UNI.

Page 11 carried seven business news stories of which two were credited to PTI. Page 12 had 10 sports stories of which two were credited to PTI and two to UNI. Hence, the total stories in this issue were 102 of which 57 were taken from news agencies that included 47 stories from PTI and UNI.

The Statesman (1990): [2]

The Statesman, Delhi, Monday, January 1, 1990: *Chandigarh (PTI): 12 killed, 5 kidnapped in Punjab (three columns)* and Statesman's Bhubaneshwar dateline story–*Administrative reshuffle in Orissa* were two of the 13 news stories published on the front page. Of these, seven were credited to PTI, one each to UNI, DPA and Reuters and rest to the newspaper staffers. Page 2 had four stories two each taken from PTI and UNI that included *Calcutta (UNI): Basu to discuss Haldia with PM* while Page 3 had the *New Delhi*

Notebook by Observer–a Statesman feature on the national capital. Page 4 had 14 stories from eastern India including four –two each credited to PTI and UNI. Page 5 had three PTI stories and one news features by the newspaper.

Page 6 had editorial while Page 9 had 15 stories–four credited to PTI and eight to UNI. They included: *Gangtok (PTI): Sikkim crucial for Indian army.* Page 8 had nine stories of which seven came from PTI wires while Page 9 had three news features filed by the Statesman correspondents from the north-eastern states. Page 10 had seven foreign news stories of which three were credited to PTI and two to AFP. They included *Islamabad (PTI): Changes in Pak army strategy needed* and *Brussels (AFP): ILO's concern over jobless.* Page 11 had seven corporate news stories from news agencies– three from PTI and four from UNI. It included *Calcutta (UNI): Tea institute being neglected.* Page 12 had 12 sports news of which one each was credited to UNI and Reuters, two to AP and six to PTI. It also had amusing cartoon *Hagar the Horrible* by noted cartoonist Dik Browne. In all, the newspaper had 88 news stories of which 63 were credited to various news agencies including 55 taken from PTI and UNI wire services.

The Statesman, Delhi, Tuesday, January 2, 1990: PTI's Chandigarh dateline story on *Punjab bandh partial, peaceful (three columns)* and *Govt. proposes new Exim policy* by UNI were two of the nine main headline stories published on the front page. Of these, two each were credited to PTI and UNI. Page 2 had eight news stories of which three were credited to PTI and two to UNI. Page 3 carried city news totalling 13 while Page 4 had 11 news items from eastern India all filed by the Statesman correspondents. Page 4 had 11 news stories from all over India of which three each were filed by PTI and UNI. Page 5 had two news features by the Statesman while Page 6 was the editorial page. Page 7 had six news stories of which one was credited to PTI and two to UNI.

Page 8 had five stories by the newspaper staffers. Page 9 had 10 news stories of which three were credited to PTI and one to UNI. Page 10 had 12 foreign news stories credited two each to AP, PTI, UNI, AFP and Reuters and one each to UPI and DPA. Page 11 had seven corporate news stories of which two each were credited to UNI and PTI. Page 12 had 18 sports news stories of which five were credited to PTI, four to UNI and one each to AP and Reuters. Thus, the issue had 95 news stories of which 47 were attributed to various news agencies including 39 credited to PTI and UNI.

The Statesman, Delhi, Wednesday, January 3, 1990: *Poll panel to have single member/Two commissioners dropped*–a special report by Statesman bureau and *New Delhi: PM announces package for Assam* were two of the 14 main news stories appearing on the front page of this issue. Of these, 10 stories were credited various news agencies including two each taken from PTI and UNI. Page 2 had 20 news stories from the eastern India including *Agartala (PTI): Tripura poised to leap forward* and Statesman's *Bhubaneshwar: Mrs. Satpathy calls for Panchayat polls.*

Of these, eight stories were credited to PTI and six to UNI. Page 3 had six city news stories filed by the newspaper staffers. Page 4 had 16 news stories of which seven were filed by PTI. Page 5 had nine news stories of which two were credited to PTI and six to UNI. Page 6 was the editorial page while Page 7 carried 18 foreign news stories of which two each were credited to PTI, AP and AFP and three each to UNI and Reuters. Likewise, Page 9 also had nine foreign news items credited two each to PTI, UNI and Reuters and one each to AFP and APN. Page 9 had advertisements. Page 10 had 18 sports stories of which two each were credited to AP and Reuters, four to PTI and five to UNI. In all, the issue had 110 news stories of which 72 were credited to various news agencies including 51 attributed to PTI and UNI.

The Statesman, Delhi, Thursday, January 4, 1990: The front page had 17 news stories of which the main headlines were: *New Delhi (Statesman): Assam accord to be implemented/ No compromise with the rebels: PM (four columns); New Delhi*

(Statesman): Hopeful start to talks with Nepal (three columns); and *Lahore (AP): 40 killed in Lahore bridge collapse.* Of these, two stories were credited to PTI and one each to UNI and AP. Page 2 had seven stories of which three were credited to PTI and one to UNI. The stories were: *New Delhi (UNI): Seminar on workers' participation plan; Cochin (PTI): Rajiv criticizes NF Govt; Nainital (PTI): Industries in Kumaon neglected* and *Nainital (PTI): Planning panel to review mega-projects.* Page 3 had seven Delhi news plus one feature.

Page 4 had 10 news stories of which two were taken from PTI and three from UNI. Page 5 had five stories alongside the mid-week review. Of these, three were credited to PTI and two to UNI. Page 6 was the editorial page. Page 7 had 15 news stories of which eight were credited to PTI and one to UNI. Page 8 had nine foreign news stories credited one each to PTI, UNI and AFP, two to AP and three to Reuters. Page 9 had four news stories of which one each was credited to PTI and UNI. Page 10 had 12 sports news of which three each were credited to PTI, UNI and AFP. In total, it had 87 news stories of which 46 were credited to various news agencies that included 40 taken from PTI and UNI.

Table 6.2: Number of News Agency Stories Appearing in The Statesman in the First Week of January 1990

Date	Total Number of News Stories	News Agency Stories	Stories from PTI and UNI
January 1, 1990	88	62	55
January 2, 1990	95	47	39
January 3, 1990	110	72	51
January 4, 1990	87	46	40
January 5, 1990	93	41	30
January 6, 1990	67	38	27
January 7, 1990	92	38	33

The Statesman, Delhi, Friday, January 5, 1990: *Delhi to come very close to statehood* and *Accord on Haldia project* were the two special reports by Statesman on the front page of this issue alongside *Miami (Fl) AFP: Noriega surrenders; flown to Miami/ Trial for drug trafficking.* Of the total 11 stories, one each was credited to AFP, PTI and UNI. Page 2 also had 11 stories taken from news agencies–nine from PTI and two from UNI. Page 3 had 12 stories all credited to Statesman. Page 4 had 10 stories of which two were taken from PTI and one from UNI. Page 5 called Market Corner had 11 commercial news stories filed by the newspaper.

Page 6 was the editorial. Page 7 had 16 news stories of which one was credited to AP, two to AFP, three each to UNI and Reuters and five to PTI. Page 8 had three news features filed by AP, DPA and PTI and six news stories credited one each to PTI and UNI along with city notes. Page 9 had two business stories including one credited to PTI. Page 10 had 11 sports news stories of which one each was credited to PTI, UNI, AFP and AP. Thus, it had 93 news stories in total of which 41 were credited to various news agencies including 30 taken from PTI and UNI.

The Statesman, Delhi, Saturday, January 6, 1990: *Next round in Kathmandu/ Talks with Nepal conclude on optimistic note* was the New Delhi datelined special report by the Statesman and a PTI box news–*Azharuddin to lead India* that appeared on the front page along with 12 other news stories. Of these, two stories each were filed by PTI and UNI and one each was credited to AP and Reuters. Page 2 had seven new stories of which two were credited to UNI and three to PTI. Page 3 had nine stories filed by staffers. Page 4 had 14 news stories again filed by staffers. Page 5 had three stories–two by PTI and one by UNI along with three news features filed by the Statesman. Page 6 was the editorial page and had column on quotes called On Record.

Page 7 had five news stories of which one each was credited to PTI, UNI and DPA. Page 8 had nine foreign news items–one each from Reuters and UPI and two each from AP, PTI and UNI. Page 9 had two PTI stories while page 10 had 11 sports news stories of which two each were credited to UNI,

AFP and Reuters and four to PTI. In all, it had 67 news stories including 38 news stories taken from various news agencies that included 27 credited to PTI and UNI.

The Statesman, Delhi, Sunday, January 7, 1990: The main headline of this issue was–*Indian and Sri Lanka/agree to finalize/ friendship treaty*–filed by the Statesman bureau. The front page had 12 news stories including five taken from PTI and four from UNI. Page 2 had 10 stories of which seven were credited to PTI and two to UNI. Page 3 had five stories and two features namely the Listening Post and Telewatch that consumed three-fourth space of the page. Page 4 had 13 news stories of which one each was credited to PTI and UNI. Page 5 had five news features filed by the Statesman correspondents including: *Bhubaneshwar: Local elections in Orissa likely; Agartala: CPI (M)'s call to TUJS; Guwahati: Bird sanctuary area leased; Bhubaneshwar: Tussle over sharing of seats in Orissa.* Page 6 was the editorial page and carried the Minoo Masani column called 'As I see It.'

Page 7 had 19 news stories of which three each were filed by UNI, PTI and Reuters, two by AFP and one each by AP and UPI. Page 8 carried nine stories of which three were attributed to UNI and one each to Reuters and AFP. Page 9 had five stories of which four were credited to UNI and one to PTI. Page 10 had 12 sports news of which two each were credited to PTI and UNI. In all, it had 92 news stories of which agency stories were 38 that included 33 stories taken from PTI and UNI.

The Statesman (1995): [3]

The Sunday Statesman, Delhi, Sunday, January 1995: The 32-page Sunday edition of the Statesman had a 16-page *The Sunday Statesman Miscellany* apart from regular 16 pages of the newspaper. It carried human interest stories, articles and features. However, the front page of this issue had six main stories of which just one was credited to a news agency. It was a PTI story: *New Delhi: India fulfils WTO terms.* Other stories included a Statesman special–*Tiwari quits as UPCC chief* and *100 killed in Myanmar train accident.* The highlight of this page was an eight column *Happy New Year* cartoon by Rajinder Puri. Page 2 called City had three stories of which two were credited to UNI. These stories were interspersed with columns like At the Cinema and Helpline. Page thee also carried 11 city stories of which three were taken from PTI wires.

Page 4 called Region/Court had three stories of which one each was credited to PTI, UNI and the Statesman. Page 5 entitled Features/Nation had Television/Listening Post and Film Notebook. Page 6 was the editorial page while page nos. 7 to10 were reserved for advertisements while Page 11 had seven stories of which five were attributed to UNI while two were filed by the staffers such as: *Third front formed in Orissa* and *Orissa resists CEC's order.* Page 12 called Nation had five stories–one credited to PTI and three to UNI. They were: *Ahmedabad (PTI): Crime rate falls in Ahmedabad; Chandigarh: Akalis on a suicidal warpath; Madras (UNI): Swamy out to prove Jayalalitha guilty* and *Agartala (UNI): CRPF jawans killed by Tripura rebels.* Page 13 entitled World had 14 news stories from across the globe including five news briefs.

Of these, three each were filed by AFP and Reuters, two by DPA and one by AP. Page 14 had 11 sports stories of which one was credited to PTI and three to UNI. Page 15 called Business & Finance had six news stories of which two were features while four stories were credited to PTI. They included a three-column box news by PTI–*Fiscal discipline, stabilization mainstay of reforms* and *World awaits birth of WTO in 1995.* In all, it had 77 stories of which 33 stories were taken from various news agencies that included 24 stories credited to PTI and UNI.

The Statesman, Delhi, Monday, January 2, 1995: The front page had eight news items including hard news stories, political analysis and a caveat by the editor C.R. Irani. The news stories included the Statesman special report on *Bihar poll may be put off, says CEC* and *ISRO spy case: no clinching evidence against suspects.* It had two analytical stories by the newspaper staffers such as: *Lucknow: Rao's time-tested weapon does it again* and *New Delhi: Arjun, Rai meet Tiwari/Bid to create anti-Rao nexus.* The two UNI stories were: *Rao urged to nominate new PCC chief* and *Opposition criticizes ordinances.* Page 2 had four stories plus a feature on Delhi Mail. Of these, one story each was credited to UNI and PTI. The PTI news feature on *NDMC drive in elite areas* got a three column display.

Page 3 called City had the New Delhi Notebook along with Delhi news in brief and two news stories that included one news feature by PTI on *More TV channels in 1995 likely.* Page 4 had four stories and a column called Job Watch. The stories were credited two each to PTI and UNI. The UNI stories were: *Demonstration to end child labour* and *Subdued welcome to New Year* while PTI stories were: *DPEP to focus on girl's education* and *Schemes to curb pollution.* Page 5 called the Arts had three features of which two were contributed by UNI. They were: *Thanjavur: A pilgrim's progress* and *Aurangabad: Unscientific research spoilt Ajanta, Ellora.* Page 6 was a supplement on Infotech while Page 7 called Nation/Region had 10 news stories of which five were from the regions.

They were three from Jaipur and two from Dehradun. Of these, five stories were taken from PTI, four from UNI and one was filed by the daily staffer entitled: *Akali unity still a long way off.* Page 8 was the editorial page while Page 9 had nine stories–three from PTI and six from UNI and a feature called Political Diary. Page 10 called Nation had seven news stories of which two were credited to PTI and five to UNI. The stories included: *Calcutta (UNI): Rao to open 82nd Science Congress* and *Bangalore (PTI): ISRO attains many heights, new lows during year.* Page 11 called World plus World File had nine stories including a feature on *Beirut: Paris of West Asia* published by arrangement with The Times, London.

The other stories were credited one each to PTI and UNI and six to AP. Page 12 also called World had 10 news stories–one each by PTI, DPA, AFP and Reuters and two by UNI. It also had a column called World View by Jonathan Power. The UNI stories included *Karachi: Amnesty seeks Pak probe.* Page 13 called Business and Finance had eight stories–one each taken from PTI, DPA and AP and four from UNI. The AP story was: *US-China trade: sanctions on Chinese goods likely.* Pages 14 and 15 carried 19 sports news of which five each were credited to PTI and UNI, four to Reuters and two to AP. Page 16 had seven news stories of which two were taken from PTI, three from Reuters and two were in-house contribution. The Reuters stories included: *IPR dispute: US-China on collision course* while PTI stories included: *New York: Hasina to intensify stir.* Thus, it had a total of 109 news stories of which 81 stories were taken from various news agencies that included 58 from PTI and UNI.

The Statesman, Delhi, Tuesday, January 3, 1995: *Madras (UNI): TN Congress to boycott Rao's visit in protest* and *Bangalore (PTI): Govt. to take over Roerich's estate* were two of the 10 main stories on the front page of this issue. The other stories included political analysis like *Arjun calls for response* and *JD to challenge CEC order.* Page 2 had five city stories of which one each was credited to PTI and UNI. Page 3 also had seven city stories of which one was credited to PTI and two to UNI apart from Grievances column. The UNI story –*Improvement mark India's media year* read thus:

New Delhi: 1994 marked the onslaught of satellite TV channels forcing the government to upgrade Doordarshan technology and promulgating an Ordinance to regulate cable operators. In fact, 1994 seemed to be a repetition of 1984 when Doordarshan in order to expand its reach, set up 300 transmitters in just one year.

In 1994, Ministry of Information and Broadcasting realized that the only way to beat satellite channels is to join them. Apart from increasing the number of its own satellite TV channels to 13 including the still-suspended Doordarshan-3, Doordarshan also announced plans to acquire 60 channels from the beginning of 1995.

Added to this was the high-level study for establishing an ISH (information super highway) and the approval to the Broadcasts Engineering Consultants India Ltd., a company under the ministry's control for providing engineering and management services to the electronic media within and outside the country.

AIR also saw some growth last year when 20 Sky Radio channels were started from April 1 and he FM channels at Delhi, Bombay, Calcutta, Panaji and Madras were thrown open to private broadcasters. Plans were also afoot for FM stations in Kanpur, Nagpur, Cuttack, Ahmedabad, Bangalore, Hyderabad and other state capitals in a phased manner. Twenty-eight radio stations are scheduled to be commissioned soon.

Arrangements were also finalized for launching the radio paging services in 17 cities from January 15.

Page 4 entitled City/Court had six stories apart from Noida Newsletter. The stories included two from PTI and one from UNI. Page 5 entitled Features/Nation had three features including a travelogue by Bill Aitken and a news feature by PTI. Page 6 called Nation had six stories–two from PTI, three from UNI and one by the Statesman. Likewise, Page 7 had nine stories from across the nation while Page 8 was the editorial page. Page 9 had 14 news stories including three from PTI and six from UNI. Page 10 entitled *World* had four stories of which two were credited to AP. It also had a UNI/AFP picture of Chechens in Grozny. Page 11 also had 10 stories of which two each were taken from Reuters and PTI while one each was credited to AP, AFP, DPA and IANS. These included: *New York (IANS): Protest over racist attacks on Indians.* Page 12 had three features of business and finances of which one each was credited to PTI and UNI. Page 13 also had

14 business stories of which three each were taken from PTI and UNI.

The stories included: *New Delhi (UNI): Financial reforms to continue, RBI Governor* and *New Delhi (PTI): Reforms may slow down: Industry.* Page nos. 14 and 15 had 20 sports news of which one was taken from PTI, two each from AP and AFP, three from UNI and four from Reuters. Page 16 had 10 news stories including a four column PTI story from London on *Hurd may press India for jet deal.* The other stories included one each from AP, AFP, DPA and Reuters and two from UNI. Thus, it had 120 news stories of which 72 were credited to various news agencies including 51 to PTI and UNI.

The Statesman, Delhi, Wednesday, January 4, 1995: *Bihar polls put off by a fortnight* by the Statesman and PTI's Colombo datelined story on *Lanka accord on truce* were among the nine stories on the front page of this issue. Page 2 had five city stories including one by PTI. Page 3 had 19 city stories including two by UNI while Page 4 had 12 stories including four stories under the heading *Gurgaon Newsletter.* Of these, two each were credited to PTI and UNI. Page 5 entitled Features/Nation had five stories of which one each was taken from UNI and PTI. PTI story from Thanjavur on *The magnificent Tamil Haiku* was given a four column bottom split display. Page 6 entitled Nation/Region had nine stories–credited two each to PTI and UNI–under the nation column and five stories–one from PTI and three from UNI- from the region.

The regional stories emanated from places like Lucknow, Mussorie, Moradabad and Varanasi. Page 7 had advertisements while Page 8 was the editorial page. Page 9 had 11 stories of which four were taken from PTI and two from UNI. Page 10 had five stories from across the globe credited one each to PTI, UNI, Reuters, AP and AFP. Page 11 also had nine stories from around the world of which four were taken from AP and one each from AFP and Reuters. Page 12 had seven business and financial stories of which four were attributed to PTI and two to UNI. Page 13 had information about Bombay Stock Exchange while Page nos. 14 and 15 carried 21 sports stories credited five each to AP and Reuters, four each to PTI and UNI and two to AFP. Page 16 had one Reuters story along with one analytical story on *Khaleda may impose emergency* by the Statesman. Thus, this issue had some 125 news stories and features of which 60 were credited to news agencies including 40 from PTI and UNI.

The Statesman, Delhi, Thursday, January 5, 1995: PTI's London story *War cry by Benazir* and a special report by newspaper on *Elections in Orissa deferred by a month* were two main news stories among eight published on the front page of this issue. Of them, two stories were credited to AFP. The opening paragraph of Benazir story read thus: *London: "Third Indo-Pak war may break-out if India continues to ignore the Kashmiris' right to self-determination"–Benazir Bhutto told Al Wasat, a London publication. "Kashmir had never been a part of India, and it has been a disputed land since 1947", she said.* Page 2 had two stories by the daily staffers while Page 3 had 13 stories including seven Delhi news briefs. Of these, two were filed by UNI such as: *Ex-servicemen's welfare sought* and *Call to protect employment level.*

Page 4 had seven stories of which four were filed by PTI. Page 5 had six stories of which two were credited to PTI. Page 6 had 14 stories of which five were credited to PTI and four to UNI. UNI's Jammu story on *Pak training camps shifted* was well displayed. Page 7 called Nation had seven stories of which one was taken from PTI and four from UNI. Page 8 was the editorial page while Page 9 had 12 stories of which three each were credited to PTI and UNI. Page 10 had five stories from around the world including one from AFP and another from UNI i.e. *Colombo: Cautious response to Lankan truce.* Page 11 also had 12 foreign datelined news stories of which five were taken from AP, three from DPA and two from AFP. Page 12 had 11 business news stories while Page 13 had four features by arrangement.

Page 14 and 15 had 20 sports news stories of which three each were credited to PTI and Reuters, two each to UNI and AP. Page 16 had 11 news stories of which one was credited to PTI, two each to AFP and Reuters and three to UNI. The edition also had a four-page supplement called Voices–The Statesman in schools. In total, the issue had 132 stories of which 67 were credited to agencies that included 44 stories from PTI and UNI.

Table 6.3: Number of News Agency Stories Appearing in The Statesman in the First Week of January 1995

Date	Total Number of News Stories	News Agency Stories	Stories from PTI and UNI
January 1, 1995	75	33	24
January 2, 1995	103	81	58
January 3, 1995	120	72	51
January 4, 1995	125	60	40
January 5, 1995	132	67	44
January 6, 1995	129	65	43
January 7, 1995	128	65	58

The Statesman, Delhi, Friday, January 6, 1995: The front page of this issue had 10 news stories including two UNI stories and an IANS feature spread across six columns in the bottom half. Written by Ela Dutt from Washington its headline was *Indian airliner the second most hazardous in Asia.* Page 2 had three stories one each from PTI and UNI while Page 3 had 15 city stories including a four column PTI feature on *Comfortable grain position.* Page 4 called City/Court had nine stories–five from PTI and one from UNI while Page 5 called Features/Nation had three news features including one UNI feature on the *Eighth World Tamil Conference at Thanjavur.* Page 6 was the editorial page while Page 7 had 14 news stories including one each from PTI, UNI and Reuters.

Page 8 had 14 business news stories of which three were credited to PTI, four to UNI and one to Reuters. Page 9 had information about Bombay Stock Exchange while page 10 had

11 sports stories–three each from Reuters and AP and one each from AFP and DPA. Page 11 had eight news stories of which one was credited to PTI, two to UNI and three to AP. Page 12 had 13 stories from the region that included four from PTI and three from UNI. Page 13 had seven stories of which four were taken from PTI and one from UNI. Page 14 had four stories of which one was taken from AP and the rest by arrangement by foreign news syndicates like The Times, London, and the New York Times. Page 15 had 13 news stories from across the globe of which one each was taken from PTI and IANS, two from UNI and six from AP. Page 16 had five stories including one each from PTI, AFP and DPA. The PTI story from Imphal had the following headline: *Military violence on rise in Manipur.* Hence, it had 129 stories of which 65 were credited to various news agencies that included 43 from PTI and UNI.

The Statesman, Delhi, Saturday, January 7, 1995: *Cable TV regulation: registration date extended till April 1st* and *Ex. Dy. CM of Maharashtra backs dissidents* were among 11 main news stories published on the front page of this edition. Of these, one was taken from PTI wires while two from UNI. Page 2 had four stories from the city of which one each was credited to PTI and UNI. Page 3 had 19 news stories of which three were taken from PTI and five from UNI. Page 4 had 13 stories–five each from PTI and UNI. PTI stories included a box item entitled as: *Appealing to the better side of man.* Page 5 had three features including the 'Quaint Corner' and two stories by PTI. Page 6 had 12 regional news stories of which seven were taken from PTI and one from UNI.

Page 7 had 10 stories from around the world of one was taken from PTI, two from AFP and three from AP. It also had four features including one called the World View by Jonathan Power. The other features included *Moscow: West renews pressure on Yeltsin.* Page 8 was the editorial page while Page 9 had seven stories including three from UNI. Page nos. 10 and 11 were literary supplements while Page 12 had four stories concerning business and finance of which one was taken from

PTI and IANS and two from UNI. The IANS story regarding *US company set up unit to invest in India* was give a five column banner headline at the bottom split. Page 13 had 10 stories from business and finance of which one each was taken from PTI and IANS and two from UNI.

It also had a special story filed by the newspaper correspondent on *Economic deregulation no longer a matter of choice.* Page nos. 14 and 15 had 27 sports stories of which five were taken from PTI wires, four from Reuters and one each from UNI and AFP. Page 16 had eight news stories of which one each were taken from AP, DPA and Reuters and two from UNI. The issue also had eight pages of The Saturday Statesman. Thus, the total number of storied in this edition were 128 including 65 filed by various news agencies that included 55 from PTI and UNI.

The Statesman (2000): [4]

The Statesman, New Delhi, Saturday, January 1, 2000: Hostages freed, back in India was the eight column banner headline of the main story filed by the Statesman News Service or SNS. It was accompanied by two big pictures of the hijacked airliner and the released hostages at the centre. The story also had a chronology of the hijack. Another special story entitled *The price we paid* by the Statesman was prominently displayed. Another prominent story by SNS was on *Trade-off splits cabinet, Advani offers to resign.* In all, it had five stories including one each from PTI, UNI and AP.

Page 2 to four had 16 local news stories by SNS. Page 5 carried an advertisement of Samsung Electronics. Page 6 was the editorial page while Page 7 called Perspective carried four news features. Page 8 and nine entitled Nation had 11 stories by SNS. Page nos. 10 had 11 sports news stories including two each taken from UNI and AFP and three from PTI. Page 11 called Leisure had news of entertainment. Page 12 had three sports stories including one by Reuters. Page 13 had 15 news stories of 11 were credited to PTI. Page 14 had four business news stories including one credited to PTI. Page nos. 15 and 16 had 11 foreign news stories and an AP/PTI photo. The stories included one each from PTI, UNI, IANS and AFP and three from Reuters. The issue also had four pages of The Saturday Statesman on Life Style. Hence, the issue had 79 news stories including 35 taken from various news agencies of which 27 came from PTI and UNI.

The Sunday Statesman, New Delhi, January 2, 2000: *Hijackers releases terrorists on way to Quetta*–was the main story on the front page of this issue along with *Jaswant points to Pak hand/vows retribution.* Both the stories were filed by SNS along with a *Caveat* by the editor C.R. Irani entitled: "*...in ourselves that we are underlings*" that went on to say: "*As Cassius says to Brutus: 'The fault, dear Brutus, is not in our stars but in ourselves that we are underlings'-He says it all, doesn't he!*". In all, it had eight news stories. Page 2 and four carried classified advertisements while Page 3 had six local news stories by SNS. Page nos. five and six also carried 12 local news stories by SNS including a survey on *Delhiites divided on the release of militants.* Page 7 called National had six stories by SNS. Page 8 was the editorial page while Page 9 called National plus India Digest had 17 news stories of which 10 were taken from PTI and three from UNI.

PTI story from Katchal Island in the Bay of Bengal entitled *Katchal keeps date with millennium dawn* had a six column banner headline. The story was accompanied by an AP/PTI picture of the dawn displayed prominently. Page 10 called International had three news stories–one each filed by PTI, AP and AFP and a news feature by The Times. Likewise, page 11 had six news stories including two Times features. The stories were filed by PTI, Reuters, AP and AFP. Page 12 had 15 business news stories of which six were credited to PTI and one each to UNI and IANS. It also had a market review. Page nos. 13 and 14 had 18 sports stories that included one story by AFP, three by UNI and four by PTI. Page 16 had 16 sports news stories that included three features of which one was taken from PTI and two from UNI. It also had a 16 page supplement called The Statesman Impressions. In all, it had 110 news stories that included 38 news stories credited to various news agencies of which 30 were taken from PTI and UNI.

The Statesman, New Delhi, Monday, January 3, 2000: The front page of this issue had 13 stories of which six were news brief. *New Delhi (SNS): Fog bogs down Delhi* and *Islamabad (PTI): Pak pledges to block hijackers* were two of the seven main headlines. Of the total, three stories were credited to PTI and four to UNI. Page 2 had nine regional stories including two by PTI and one by UNI along with classified advertisements. Page nos. 3 and 4 carried seven local SNS stories including Delhi Mail. Page 5 had five national news stories filed by SNS. Page 6 was the editorial page while Page 7 called Perspectives had two features and net news. Page 8 carried 11 national news stories along with eight news briefs.

Of these, eight were filed by PTI and five by UNI. PTI's Bangalore story about *Violent mob vent ire against newspaper* was a box item. Page 9 had seven foreign news stories–one from IANS, two from AP and four from Reuters. Page 10 called Asia had seven news stories from the region–three credited to Reuters (Beijing, Colombo and Tokyo), one each to AFP (Islamabad), IANS (Jakarta) and DPA (Colombo). Page 11 had 14 business and financial news stories of which six were credited to PTI. Page 12 had 12 sports stories of which one each was attributed to DPA and Reuters, and three each to PTI and AFP. Page 13 was the Leisure page while Page 14 carried the column New Delhi Notebook. Page nos. 15 to 18 carried special supplement called the Literary Review. Thus, the issue had 95 news stories including 47 stories from news agencies that had 29 stories from PTI and UNI.

The Statesman, New Delhi, Tuesday, January 4, 2000: *Pune (UNI): Declare Pak a rogue state: PM; Calcutta (SNS) Overhaul of party programmes needed: Basu* and *Srinagar*

(UNI): 16 killed in Kashmir blast, 30 hurt were among 12 news stories including five news briefs that appeared on the front page of this edition. Of the seven main stories, three were credited to UNI and four to SNS. It also had a caveat by the editor C.R. Irani entitled *A time for action.* Page 2 had four regional stories by SNS that included *Punjab BJP men raise revolt flag.* Page 3 had seven local news stories by SNS while Page 4 had 10 local news stories by SNS along with a column on Grievances.

Page 5 had eight national news stories including one each from PTI and UNI. Page nos. six and seven also carried 25 news stories from across the nation that included three taken from PTI and 11 from UNI. The stories were mainly filed from places like Imphal, Cuttack and Behrampur in eastern India. Page 8 carried the editorial content along with the column on Letters to the editor.

Page 9 called Perspectives had three news features and net news. Page 10 carried tender notices while Page 11 had 15 world news stories including two AP/PTI pictures.

The credit wise break-up of stories was thus: four credited to AFP, three to Reuters and two each to AP, IANS and DPA. Page 12 had 16 business news stories including five taken from PTI wires and three from UNI.

The UNI stories included a five column box story *New Delhi: Steel production up 1.9 percent in 1999.* Page 13 carried stocks and shares news from Delhi and National Stock Exchange. Page 14 had 13 sports news–three taken from AFP, two each from PTI and UNI and one each from AP and Reuters.

Page 15 was the leisure page that had entertainment news while page 16 carried six news stories–two from PTI and one from AFP and two AP/PTI news pictures. In all, it had 115 news stories that included 53 taken from various news agencies of which 33 were credited to PTI and UNI.

The Statesman, New Delhi, Wednesday, January 5, 2000: Of the total 13 stories on the front page, two were credited to PTI and three to UNI. PTI box story was the Washington's reaction to Indian demand of a rogue state status for Pakistan following the release of dreaded terrorists as: *US no to rogue tag* and the UNI story on the then RSS chief Rajju Bhaiyya's telling comment on the hostage crisis: *Crisis has highlighted the 'Hindu samaj mein vyapt bhiruta'*. Another box item was the UNI story about: *Damage to BJP, says Advani.*

Table 6.4: Number of News Agency Stories Appearing in The Statesman in the First Week of January 2000

Date	Total Number of News Stories	News Agency Stories	Stories from PTI and UNI
January 1, 2000	79	35	27
January 2, 2000	110	38	30
January 3, 2000	95	47	29
January 4, 2000	115	53	33
January 5, 2000	111	45	24
January 6, 2000	100	52	25
January 7, 2000	128	65	58

Page 2 had four regional stories from Jammu, Jaipur, Agra and Bhopal filed by SNS. Likewise, Page nos. 3 and 4 had 13 local stories by SNS. It included a four column PTI news feature on corruption.

Page 5 had nine international news stories of which one each was credited to PTI, UNI and SNS and two each to AP, Reuters and DPA. Page 6 carried the editorial while Page 7 called Perspective had two news features and a Rajasthan newsletter along with four news stories credited one each to PTI and UNI and two to SNS. Page 8 had 10 national news items of which three were credited to PTI and one to UNI while India Digest on the same page had nine stories of which four were attributed to PTI, three to UNI and two to SNS. Page 9 had 10 stories credited three each to AP and Reuters and one each to DPA, PTI and UNI.

Page 10 had 18 stories from the world business and

finance of which five were credited to PTI and one to UNI. The rest were filed by SNS. Page 11 also had three business stories of which one was taken from PTI. Page 12 had 11 sports news of which three each were taken from PTI and AFP and two from AP. The rest came from SNS. Page 13 called Leisure had the entertainment news. Page 13 also had 10 sports news stories of which three were taken from PTI, two from AP and one from Reuters. Page nos. 15 to 18 contained a four-page supplement on Midweek Sports. In total, the issue had 117 stories including 58 taken from various news agencies of which 34 were credited to PTI and UNI.

The Statesman, New Delhi, Thursday, January 6, 2000: *India says no to Clinton mediation* by SNS and PTI's *Masood seen in Karachi* along with AFP's *Pak clerk expelled from Kathmandu* were among the seven main headlines while the first column of the front page had six news briefs taken two from UNI and SNS and one each from Reuters and PTI. Page 2 had four regional stories filed by SNS from Bhopal, Hardwar, Jammu and Shimla. Page 3 and four had 15 local news stories also filed by SNS. Page 5 had 17 news stories from across the nation. Of these, four were filed by PTI, three by UNI and the rest by SNS.

Page 6 carried the editorial while Page 7 had two SNS news features and four news stories of which two were credited to PTI and one each to AP and SNS. Page 8 had 10 sports stories of which three were credited to PTI, two each to UNI, Reuters and AFP and one to SNS. Page 9 had columns called City Watch and Leisure. Page 10 had four sports features of which one was credited to AFP and the rest to SNS. Page 11 had 18 foreign news including nine news briefs. Of these, eight were credited to AP, three to Reuters, two each to PTI and The Times News Service and one to AFP. The rest were filed by SNS. Page 12 had 10 business and financial news stories of which one was credited to PTI. In total, it had 111 news stories of which 45 were credited to various news agencies including 24 credited to PTI and UNI.

The Statesman, New Delhi, Friday, January 7, 2000: AP's Karachi datelined story–*'We are in Pak'–said freed militants*–was the box item while *Mumbai arrests rip mask off hijackers* and *22 hurt in Old Delhi Station blast* were among eight main headlines on the front page of this issue. It also had six news briefs on the first column. Of the total, one was credited to AFP, two to PTI and one to IANS. The rest were attributed to SNS including *Janata Dal fails to reunite.* Page nos. two to four had 16 local stories filed by SNS. Page 5 called Asia had six stories of which three were taken from AP, two from AFP and one from IANS. Page 6 carried the editorial while Page 7 called Perspective had two regular columns namely Net.

News and World View along with five news stories of which one each was credited to PTI and Reuters and the rest to SNS. Page 8 had eight national news stories of which one was taken from PTI, Bangalore while India Digest had six news briefs including four from PTI and one each from UNI and SNS. Page 9 had 11 foreign news stories of which five were taken from Reuters, four from AP and one each from AFP and DPA. Page 10 had 12 business news stories of which four were credited to PTI, seven to SNS and one to AP.

Page 11 had two business news stories taken from PTI wires. Page 12 had 12 sports news stories of which three were taken from PTI, four from UNI and two each from AP and AFP while one came from SNS. Page 13 was the Leisure page –the precursor of today's Page 3. Page 14 had six stories of which one was credited to PTI, two to SNS and three to Reuters. The issue had a six page supplement on University scene, Art & Review and Teen World. In total, the edition had 100 stories of which 52 were taken from various news agencies that included 25 credited to PTI and UNI.

The Statesman (2005): [5]

The Statesman, New Delhi, Saturday, January 1, 2005: This issue of *The Statesman* had 14 regular pages and four pages of the *World Focus* along with four pages of *Life Style and Entertainment.* For a change, it also had coloured advertisements below the mast and printed coloured photographs. The front page had six main stories of which two were credited to PTI and one to UNI. However, the main stories came from SNS that included *Worldwide toll crosses 1 lakh and still rising; Sonia summons Sibal over tsunami spat* and a box news entitled *Incompetent scientists.* It also had the editor in chief C.R. Irani's *Appeal for help.*

The PTI stories were: *Manmohan to call all party meet* and *Animals and tsunami.* Page nos. 2-4 called Capital had 10 stories from across the city filed by SNS. Page 5 called Nature's Fury had 12 news stories of which one each was credited to PTI and AFP. It also had an AFP picture of a relief camp in Port Blair. Page 6 had seven news stories from SNS. Page 7 called India had three stories including a three column PTI story on *Film stars, politicians make most recalled league.* Page 8 was the editorial page and included columns like On Record and Letters to the editor.

It also had a news feature by The Times, London. Page 9 called the North-East Page had a column by Sanjoy Hazarika and four stories all filed by SNS. Page 10 called India had 10 news stories from across the country. Page 11 had nine business news stories including two by PTI one of them being a five column story headlined as *Chinese economy to grow slower in 2005.* Page 12 had 13 news stories that included one credited to the CNBC-TV18 Market Team. Page 13 had 12 sports news stories of which three each came from PTI and AFP and two from UNI. Page 14 had two stories on tsunami taken one each from PTI and SNS. Page nos. 15 to 18 formed a four page supplement entitled *The Statesman World Focus.* It first page had 10 stories including five un-credited news briefs under the heading–*It's a mad, mad, mad world.*

The other stories came from AP, AFP and ANN in association with The Star and The Jakarta Post. The stories were as follows: *Banda Aceh (AP): World pours aid for Asia;*

London (AFP): London parties on; Bali (The Jakarta Post/ANN): After tsunami, Bali saved the day for Indonesia and *UN (The Star/ANN and Agencies): Lankan brewery switches to water.* Page 2 called 'What's on today' had a schedule of TV, radio, dance, theatre, films, meetings and other programmes. Page 3 called Asian Voices had seven news stories of which four came from ANN (Asian News Network).

It also had a news feature taken from The Nature plus an Opinion column. Page 4 called the World Focus had nine stories and eight un-credited world briefs. The main stories were credited one to AP, two each to UNI, AFP and Reuters and three to PTI. The PTI stories included a box item headlined as *US daily condemns Musharraf, flays Bush* and *Black day for Pakistan opposition.* Page nos. 19 to 22 carried four page supplement on Life Style and Entertainment. In total, it had 122 stories including 41 credited to various news agencies of which 20 were from PTI and UNI.

The Sunday Statesman, New Delhi, January 2, 2005: The front page had three stories–two by SNS and one by ANN and other agencies along with the newspaper's *Appeal for help* and a caveat by the editor. The main headline was *Wave of orphans* accompanied by an AFP pictured displayed over three columns. Page 2 carried classified advertisements while Page 3 had five local stories by SNS. Page 4 again had classified advertisements while Page 5 had eight local stories filed by SNS. Page 6 called Nature's Fury had 13 stories of which six were taken from AFP, two from AP, one each from the ANN, The Nation and The Times and two from PTI. The PTI story included the box item news from *Washington: Donate, urges Bush.* Page 7 also called Nautre's Fury had eight news stories of three were taken from PTI and five from SNS. The PTI stories were: *Ahmedabad: Modi's gesture; Car Nicobar: Thousands still missing* and *India PT Lighthouse (*box item).

Page 8 carried the editorial while Page 9 called Perspectives had two guest articles and three stories under the banner People & Places. It had two stories from AP and one from PTI. Page 10 had 15 stories from across the nation including eight from PTI and seven from SNS. It also had one picture by PTI. Page 11 had 14 foreign news stories of which four were taken from AP, three from AFP, one from PTI and two news features from The Times, London. The stories included: *Baghdad (AP): Troops under terror attack* and *Dubai (PTI): Zardari vows to return.* Page 12 had 13 news stories from the world of business and finance.

Of these, three were credited to PTI and the rest to SNS. The PTI stories were: *Stock market markedly buoyant (five columns); Weekly stock movement* and *Steel prices hiked.* Page 13 and 14 had 11 sports stories of which four were taken from PTI, three from AFP and two from AP while one was taken from The Times, London. Page 15 called Leisure/Sport had six sports stories of which two were taken from PTI, three from UNI and one from SNS. The PTI stories were: *Bhopal: MP win national softball title* and *New Delhi: Railways, Delhi clash in final.* Page 16 had three sports stories of which one was taken from PTI and the other two credited to SNS. The edition had eight page supplement called *The Sunday Statesman Magazine.* Thus, the issue had a total of 107 news stories including 52 taken from various news agencies of which 22 were credited to PTI and UNI.

The Statesman, New Delhi, Monday, January 3, 2005: PTI's New Delhi story on *Central team to assess damage* got the four column display on the front page of this issue. The front page had four more stories credited two each to AFP and SNS. Page 2 had two SNS stories from the capital while Page 3 had six city stories. Page 4 called Capital/India had nine stories by SNS while Page 5 had nine stories including three by PTI and one by UNI. Page 6 had 12 stories under the banner Nature's Fury of which 10 were taken from PTI wires. Page 7 called Science had two features by SNS. Page 8 and nine were the op-ed pages. Page 9 had a column called People and Places and two features published by arrangement with The Times. Page 10 had a full-page technology column while page 11 had 13 business news stories of which eight were credited to PTI and one to CNBC-TV18.

The story was: *ONGC Tripura power plant to be ready in 3 yrs.* Page 12 had 15 sports news stories of which five were credited to AP, three to AFP, two each to UNI, PTI and Reuters and one to SNS. Page 13 also had six sports news stories credited two to AP and one each to PTI, UNI, AFP and SNS. Page 14 carried the regular feature Notebook along with a picture. Page nos. 15 to 18 were devoted to World Focus. Its first page had six news stories. The stories included AP's *Aid flows but survivors still waiting;* PTI's *AQ Khan's N-network much wider than thought;* and Reuters' *Elephants save tourists.* It also had a feature called *It's a mad mad mad world.* Page 2 had schedule of today's engagements while Page 3 had eight news stories and an opinion column featuring articles by The Star, Yomiuri Shimbum, The Chinese Daily and The Strait Times. Page 4 called World Focus had seven stories plus 11 world briefs of which four each were credited to Reuters and AP, two each to AFP, UNI and PTI and one each to ANN and DPA. In total, it had 117 news stories of which 65 were credited to various agencies including 35 from PTI and UNI.

The Statesman, New Delhi, Tuesday, January 4, 2005: The front page had five stories credited one each to PTI and AP and three to SNS. The PTI story was: *PM's 6-pt science programme/ scientists put on notice.* Page 2 to four had 15 local news stories filed by SNS. Page 5 called India had 12 stories from all over the country including five briefs of which three were taken from PTI wires and two from SNS. Of the seven main stories on this page, two came from PTI. Page 6 called Nature's Fury had 16 stories of which eight were taken from PTI wires.

Page 7 called Campus had news about university. Page 8 was devoted to editorial while Page 9 had four stories–three by AP and one by AFP–under the banner People & Places. Page 10 had career news while page 11 had 18 business stories of which eight were credited to PTI, five to CNBC TV18 and four to SNS. Page 12 had a news feature on *Markets hit new high* by CNBC TV18 Market Team. Pages 13 and 14 had 15 sports news stories of which three came from PTI, seven from AP and the rest from SNS. The four-page supplement World Focus had 11 stories on its first page while Page 2 carried engagement schedules of various media. Page 3 called Asian Voices had eight news stories and two opinion pieces from The Jakarta Post and The Daily Star.

Of the eight news stories, three came from The Nation/ANN, two from The China Daily/ANN and one each from The Star/ANN and The Philippines Daily/Enquirer. Page 4 called The World Focus had seven news stories of three were taken from PTI, two from AP and one each from Reuters and The Times. It also had eight un-credited world news briefs along with an AFP picture. Thus, this issue had a total of 113 news stories including 44 taken from various news agencies of which 26 were credited to PTI and UNI.

The Statesman, New Delhi, Wednesday, January 5, 2005: The front page had five stories including PTI box story on *Runway cracks hamper relief work.* The other four stories were filed by SNS including *Bumps on road to reconstruction.* Page 2 to four had 18 news stories under the banner Capital filed by SNS. Page 5 had 12 stories from across the country of which six were credited to PTI and one to UNI. Likewise, Page 6 also had eight news stories of which two were taken from PTI and one from UNI. Page 7 had a column called Getaway. Page 8 was the dedicated editorial page and Page 9 had three syndicated features and four news stories credited three to AP and one to AFP. Page 10 had eight stories under the title Nature's Fury and seven quake briefs.

Of these, six were taken from PTI wires, two from ANN and one each from AP and AFP. Page 11 had 11 business news stories credited three to PTI, two to CNBC TV18 and one to The Jakarta Post/ANN and the rest to SNS. Page 12 had market survey by CNBC TV18. Page 13 and 14 carried 18 sports news of which five were taken from PTI, two from

AFP, one from The Times and the rest were credited to SNS. Page one of the World Focus had nine stories of which four were taken from Reuters, AP, AFP and ANN. Page 2 had the engagement schedule column while Page 3 called Asian Voices had seven news stories and two opinion pieces taken from The Korean Herald and The Strait Times. All the seven stories were filed by ANN and its associates. Page 4 called World Focus had 14 news stories including seven un-credited news briefs. Of the seven stories, two were taken from PTI, three from AP and one each from Reuters and AFP. Thus, it had a total of 124 news stories of which 57 were credited to various news agencies that included 31 taken from PTI and UNI.

Table 6.5: Number of News Agency Stories Appearing in The Statesman in the First Week of January 2005

Date	Total Number of News Stories	News Agency Stories	Stories from PTI and UNI
January 1, 2005	122	41	20
January 2, 2005	107	52	28
January 3, 2005	117	65	35
January 4, 2005	113	44	26
January 5, 2005	124	57	31
January 6, 2005	130	52	24
January 7, 2005	100	53	22

The Statesman, New Delhi, Thursday, January 6, 2005: The front page had eight news stories including an exclusive SNS story on *Swiss bank cash flooding bourses (five columns).* Of these, only one story was credited to PTI. Page 2 to four had 18 SNS news stories from in around the capital. Page 5 called India had 12 news stories and four India briefs of which four were credited to PTI. The PTI box story was: *IPR: Time on, game up.* Page 6 was the editorial page while Page 7 called Perspectives had five AP and one AFP story along with a picture. Page 8 had 14 quake related stories under the title Nature's Fury and Quake Briefs. Of these, five were credited to PTI, three to AP, one to The Jakarta Post/ANN and the rest to SNS.

Pages 9 and 10 had 16 business news stories that included seven stories taken from PTI and market watch by CNBC TV18. PTI stories included a five column story on *Sensex records biggest crash in a day.* Pages 11 and 12 carried 22 sports news stories of which three each were taken from UNI and AFP, two each from PTI and AP while the rest came from SNS. The Statesman World Focus had five un-credited news briefs and four news stories–one each from PTI, Reuters, AP and The Times–on its first page. Page 2 had news schedule while Page 3 called the Asian Voices had seven news stories culled from various Asian newspapers along with two opinion write-ups taken from The Jakarta Post and The Nation.

The news stories were credited to the following: Yomiuri Shimbun/ANN, The Korea Herald/ANN, The Star/ANN, The Nation/ANN, The Stait Times/ANN and The China Daily/ANN. Page 4 called the World Focus had five news stories–two from Reuters, one each from AFP, AP and The Times and seven un-credited news briefs under the title It's a mad mad mad world. Plus, it had a four page supplement called Section II on education and career development. Thus, the issue 130 news stories of which 52 were taken from various news agencies that included 24 from PTI and UNI.

The Statesman, New Delhi, Friday, January 7, 2005: *Ambani empire to be divided* was one of the seven main headlines on the front page of this issue that included two stories taken from PTI. Page 2 called City Life had one feature along with classified advertisements. Page 3 and four had 21 news stories including five news briefs all taken from PTI wires. Of the main stories, two each were credited to PTI and UNI. Page 5 had three stories of which one was credited to ANN and the rest to SNS. It also had four quake briefs credited one each to PTI and AP. Page 6 also had eight quake related stories credited one each to PTI and UNI and two each to Reuters, AP and AFP.

Page 7 had entertainment news while Page 8 carried the

editorial content. Page 9 had three syndicated features along with three news stories credited to SNS. Page 10 contained Art and Review. Page 11 and 12 had 14 business stories including information about stocks and shares by CNBC TV18. Page 13 and 14 had 19 sports stories credited three each to AP, PTI and UNI, two each to AFP and IANS. The rest came from SNS. First page of World Focus had five news stories of which three were credited to Reuters and one each to AP and The Island and the Strait Times/ANN.

Page 2 had the column entitled *What's on today* while Page 3 named Asian Voices had seven news stories and two opinion pieces from ANN and its associates. Page 4 called the World Focus had six news stories of which three were credited to Reuters, one each to PTI, UNI and AP. It also had five un-credited world briefs related to tsunami. Thus, the issue had a total of 100 news stories of which 53 have been taken from various news agencies including 22 from PTI and UNI.

End Notes

1. Archives, Nehru Memorial Museum and Library, Teen Murti, New Delhi.
2. Ibid.
3. Ibid.
4. Ibid.
5. Ibid.

7

The Hindu

The Hindu is an English-language Indian daily newspaper. With a circulation of 1.45 million, *The Hindu* is the second largest circulated daily English newspaper in India after *Times of India* and slightly ahead of *The Economic Times.* According to the Indian Readership Survey, 2008, *The Hindu* is the third most-widely read English newspaper in India after the *Times of India* and *Hindustan Times.* It has its largest base of circulation in South India, especially Tamil Nadu. Headquartered at Chennai, *The Hindu* was published weekly when it was launched in 1878, and started publishing daily in 1889. In 1995, it became the first Indian newspaper to offer an online edition.

It is published from 13 locations–Bengaluru, Chennai, Coimbatore, Delhi, Hyderabad, Kochi, Kolkata, Madurai, Mangalore, Thiruvananthapuram, Tiruchirapalli, Vijayawada and Visakhapatnam.

The Hindu (1985): [1]

The Hindu, Madras, Tuesday, January 1, 1985: The 32-page issue of the Madras edition of The Hindu priced at 90 paisa only had 12 of the 32 pages devoted to advertisements alone. The front page 10 stories of including three credited to news agencies–one each to PTI, UNI and Reuters. The main headlines were *New Delhi: 40 member team at centre and Madras: MGR re-elected leader of legislative party* both filed by the staff correspondents. Page 2 to four carried advertisements. Page 5 had nine foreign news stories credited two each to AP, Reuters and PTI and the rest to Hindu staffers. Page 6 had the list of candidates re-elected to the Lok Sabha. Page 7 had advertisements. Page 8 was reserved for editorial and letters to the editor. Page 9 had 17 stories from state capitals and metro cities including Madras, Bombay, Delhi, Calcutta as well as Colombo.

Of these five were credited to PTI, two to UNI and one each to AP and Reuters. Page 10 had five stories including one three column feature by PTI entitled *In the hallowed chambers of power.* Page nos. 11, 18, 19, 24, 25, 29, 31 and 32 had advertisements. Page 12 carried nine Madras dateline stories by Hindu. Page 13 had 13 stories from the world of finance, commerce and business filed by Hindu except one which was credited to PTI. Page 14 had 12 sports stories of which four were filed by staffers while the rest were un-credited. Page 15 carried TV and radio schedule while Page 16 had two stories of which one was credited to PTI. Page 17 carried two signed features on education while Pages 20 and 21 carried book reviews. Page nos. 22, 23, 26, 27, 28 and 30 carried a feature on *1984 in retrospect.* Thus, the issue had 80 news stories of which 22 were credited to various news agencies including 14 taken from PTI and UNI wires.

The Hindu, Madras, Wednesday, January 2, 1985: *New Delhi: Exclusion of Pranab from cabinet baffling; New Delhi: Swearing in of MGR will wait* and *Imphal: Cong (I) leading in Manipur assembly poll* were three of the 14 main headlines on the front page of the issue. Of these, three each were credited to PTI and UNI and one each to AFP and UPI. Page nos. 2 to 4, 15 and 21 to 27 had advertisements. Page 5 had six foreign news stories of which one each was credited to PTI, UNI, UPI and UNI-DPA while two were taken from Reuters. Page 6 had the list of candidates elected to the Lok Sabha. Page 7 had four stories of which one each was credited to PTI and UNI. Page 8 carried the editorial while Page 9 23 foreign news stories of which six each were credited to PTI and UNI and one each to Xinhua, AP, Reuters and DPA.

Page 10 had two stories credited to PTI including one feature on *Slight fall in Cong (I) vote in Gujarat (three columns).* Page 11 had two stories including one three column news feature from Bombay: *IAEA study to avoid fertilizer use.* Page 12 had 17 news stories from the south filed by Hindu staffers (HS). Page 13 had five business news stories by HS while page 14 carried 20 sports stories by HS. Page 16 had three stories of which one was credited to UNI. Page 17 had six entitled Science/Engineering/Technology had two news features and four stories by HS. Page 18 also had three science features including one story and one feature both credited to PTI Science Service.

Page 19 had six stories including one by PTI. Page 20 called Agriculture had four features under the banner For the Farmers' Notebook. Page 28 had two science features by HS. Thus, this 28 page issue had 11 pages devoted to advertisements and the remaining space carried 116 news stories of which 38 were credited to various news agencies including 28 taken from PTI and UNI wires.

The Hindu, Madras, Thursday, January 3, 1985: Of the 18 news stories printed on the front page of this issue, PTI and UNI shared the credit for the box item news about *Supreme court judge/heads legal aid panel/for gas victims.* However, two stories that found display over this one were both filed by HS. They were: *Bangalore: Karnataka assembly dissolved* and *Madras: AIADMK team to meet MGR.* The other stories on the page were: *Rajiv briefs ministers* and *Iran claims OPEC/ sanctions to undersell*–filed from Bahrain by HS. Thus, the news agency wise break-up of stories was as follows: PTI got credit for two stories while UNI, Reuters and UPI for one each. Page nos. 2 to 4 were reserved for advertisements while Page 5 had 10 foreign news stories of which two each were credited to PTI, AFP and Reuters and one to UPI. Page 6 carried the list of candidates elected to the Lok Sabha along with advertisements.

Page 7 had six stories of which three were taken from PTI and one from UNI. The PTI stories included: *Calcutta: Cong (I) got more votes, fewer seats in Bengal.* Page 8 was reserved for the editorial content. Page 9 had 13 stories including two from PTI and one each from UNI and UPI. UNI's Ahmedabad story on *Alimony is linked to price index* was a four-column box item. Page 10 had one feature on film festival filed by HS while Page 12 had 20 stories from the south credited to HS. Page 13 had one news feature and four stories on business and finance filed by HS while Page 14 had 17 sports stories credited to each to PTI and UNI and one to Reuters. The rest were in-house contribution. Page 15 had four stories by HS while page 16 carried three news stories including one credited to UNI. Thus, this 16 page issue had 95 news stories of which 26 were credited to various news agencies including 17 taken from PTI and UNI wires.

The Hindu, Madras, Friday, January 4, 1985: Of the 15 main stories published on the front page of this issue, four were credited to PTI, two to UNI and one each to AFP and Reuters. The PTI stories included a box item from New Delhi saying *Gas struck at Kaikalur* and *Luknow: 23 die in UP village clash. PM sets up ministerial/group for Punjab issue* was the main story by HS. The other stories filed by HS included *Madras: Nedunchezhian leaving for U.S. today* and *Bangalore: Hegde decides to stay on till poll.* Page 5 had 10 foreign news stories credited four each to Reuters and AP and one each to PTI and UNI. Page 6 carried the list of candidates elected to the Lok Sabha along with advertisements. Page 7 had six stories including one by UNI while Page 8 was devoted to editorial content.

Page 9 had 14 stories of which one was credited to PTI and two to UNI. Page 10 had three in-house features on cinema while Page 11 carried a feature on Carnatic music along with advertisements. Page 12 had 14 stories from the south filed by the Hindu staffers. Page 13 had 10 stories concerning business and finance filed by HS and page 14 had 17 sports stories including PTI's *Volleyball: Kurukhetra retains title.* Likewise, page 15 also carried six sports stories filed by HS along with schedules of Radio and TV. Page 16 had three stories including UNI's *Exemplary conduct in times of adversity.* Thus, this issue had a total of 109 news stories of which 23 were taken from various news agencies including 13 from PTI and UNI.

Table 7.1: Number of News Agency Stories Appearing in The Hindu in the First Week of January 1985

Date	Total Number of News Stories	News Agency Stories	Stories from PTI and UNI
January 1, 1985	80	22	14
January 2, 1985	116	38	28
January 3, 1985	95	26	17
January 4, 1985	109	23	13
January 5, 1985	85	17	10
January 6, 1985	85	12	5
January 7, 1985	74	20	12

The Hindu, Madras, Saturday, January 5, 1985: India's UNI and Sri Lankan Lankapuvath shared the credit for the Colombo dateline story–*Sri Lanka seeks T. Nadu police assistance*–that appeared on the front page of this issue. *Lucknow: Water had set off the fatal reaction a* box item story credited to PTI was among the 10 other news stories published on this page. The other news stories included *New Delhi (HS): Govt. awaiting Colombo's move* and *New Delhi (HS): New Lok Sabha session may be brief.* Page nos. 2 to 4 had advertisements while Page 5 had seven foreign news stories of which three were credited to Reuters and one each to UNI and DPA. Page 6 had three stories including one by PTI while Page 7 had four news stories including one each by PTI and UNI.

Page 8 carried the editorial. Page 9 had 17 stories originating from different places as far off as Chandigarh and Helsinki. Of these, two were credited to Reuters while one each came from AP, PTI and UNI. Page 10 named the Saturday Sports Special contained one in-house sports feature while page 11 had two political news analysis along with the column Letters to the editor. Page 12 had 15 stories under the banner Southern Slice while Page 13 had one news feature, share price movement index and five stories under the title Finance/Commerce/Business. Page 14 had 20 sports stories including two credited to PTI and one to AFP. Page 15 had race track results along with seven news stories and radio and TV schedules filed by HS. Page 16 had crossword, spiritual column and advertisements. In total, this issue had 85 news stories of which 17 were credited to various news agencies that included 10 taken from PTI and UNI wires.

The Hindu, Madras, Sunday, January 6, 1985: The first column of the front page had eight news briefs credited one each to PTI, UNI, AP, AFP, UNI-DPA and Hindu while two were taken from Reuters. Apart from this, it had other main headlines such as *Rajiv declares war on poverty, communalism (HS); Steps to tone up administration (PTI/UNI); NTR adds decency clause to poll pact (HS);* and *Casual railway employees in Bengal retrenched (PTI/UNI).* Of the six such stories, credits for two were shared between PTI and UNI.

Page nos. 2 to 4 called Nation had nine news stories by HS while Page 5 named The Foreign Scene had two stories–one from Harare filed by HS and the other published by arrangement with The New York Times. Page 6 called Business & Foreign Exchange had 11 stories by HS while Page 7 to eleven carried advertisements. Page 12 had six HS stories while page 13 called Southern Slice had 12 news stories from the south. Page 14 carried 18 sports news including one by PTI and two by Reuters while page 15 had the race results along with radio and TV schedules. Page 16 entitled In the News had four features while page 17 had a sponsored UNICEF feature.

Page 18 called Finance and Family had one human interest feature by the Hindu correspondent. Page 19 carried cartoons, bridge and the World that was–from the pages of the Hindu. Page 20 had a feature entitled Life Style Abroad published with collaboration with the New York Times. It also had additional eight pages of Sunday supplement. In total, the issue had 85 news stories of which 12 were credited to agencies including five from PTI and UNI.

The Hindu, Madras, Monday, January 7, 1985: Six of the 10 main stories on the front page of this edition were credited to news agencies–three to PTI, two to UNI and one to Reuters. The rest were filed by newspaper staffers. Pages 2 to 4 were reserved for advertisements while Page 9 had nine foreign news stories of which two each were credited to PTI, UNI and AFP while one each was taken from Tanjug and DPA wires. The PTI story from New York-*TV programmes in U.S. pour scorn on India, Hinduism*–read thus:

An American evangelical organization "Dayspring International' poured venom against India and described it as a land of 'division, despair and death' in dire need of message of Christ. It plans to reach all of India in 10 years while duplicating the strategy of other third world countries.

Page 6 had two stories including one PTI story while Page 7 had two features on management. Page 8 carried the editorial content while Page 9 had 16 stories including UNI's box item from Lucknow saying *Antarctica has immense oil reserves.* Page 10 had two stories both filed by PTI while Page 11 had two features credited each to PTI and UNI. Page 12 carried 19 stories under the banner Southern Slice while page 13 had six business news stories along with commodity review filed by HS. Page 14 had 23 sports stories including two by PTI. Page 15 had racing results and radio and TV schedules while Page 16 had three stories filed by the daily staffers. Thus, this issue had 74 news stories of which 20 were credited to various news agencies including 12 from PTI and UNI.

The Hindu (1990): [2]

The Hindu, Madras, Monday, January 1, 1990: PTI's *New council to deal with farm prices; 4th Commission–same rank/same pension* and *Wijeratne coming for pull-out talks* were among the 11 news stories on the front page of this issue. Of these, four were credited to PTI and one each to DPA, AFP and AP. Page 2 carried advertisements while Page 3 entitled Madras City had five stories. Page 4 had 10 stories from the southern region. Page 5 had seven foreign news stories including one each from Reuters, Kyodo and UPI and two from AP. Page 6 had eight stories of which two each were credited to PTI and UNI. Page 7 carried advertisements while Page 8 was the editorial page.

Page 9 had 15 news stories of which three were credited to PTI, one each to AP, Reuters and DPA. Page 10 to 12 carried advertisements while page 13 had three business features by HS. Page 14 had 11 sports news stories including two by PTI. Page 15 had four stories and race track results while Page 16 carried the article on the Vedic origin of democracy. In total, the issue had 77 news stories of which 28 were credited to various news agencies that included 17 from PTI and UNI files.

The Hindu, Madras, Tuesday, January 2, 1990: *New fiscal, export policies proposed* and *Warming up a cold morning* were among five stories on the front page filed by the Hindu staffers. Page nos. 2,6,18, 20, 21 and 24 carried classified advertisements. Page 3 had 17 Madras dateline stories while Page 4 carried three stories from the Madras region–all filed by HS. Page 5 had seven foreign news stories –two taken from Reuters and one each from UNI, UPI, AP, AFP and PTI. Page 7 had a medley of four stories originating from Washington to Bhubaneshwar. Page 8 was the editorial page while Page 9 carried 17 stories including a four column box item by AFP from Tokyo: *Let's bring down this wall too, says Kim II Sung.* The other stories included three from PTI and two each from UNI, DPA, Reuters and AP.

Page 10 had two UNI stories while page 11 had five stories including a science feature by UNI. Page 12 had three financial stories by HS while Page 13 had two film features filed by the Hindu staffers. Page 14 had 15 news stories all credited to HS while Page 15 had nine sports stories by HS. Page 16 had one PTI story, crossword and the Hindu spiritual column entitled *Course of action in dilemma.* Page 17 called Open Page had three news features by PTI while page 19 named Education had three features on education including one on Know your English. Page nos. 22 and 23 called Books had book reviews. Thus, in total, the issue had 96 news stories including 23 credited to various news agencies of which 11 were taken from PTI and UNI.

The Hindu, Madras, Wednesday, January 3, 1990: Front page of this issue displayed a two column box story by UNI as *Passengers stage dharna in plane* along with another UNI story from Faridadkot saying *Mann to attend meet on Punjab.* It also had two stories by PTI. However, the other main headlines including *Guwahati: PM's package for Assam* and *New Delhi: Election panel is one-member body again* came from HS. Thus, of the 13 stories on this page, two each were taken from PTI and UNI wires. Four pages (pp. 2,7,10 and 11) of this 20-page issue were reserved for advertisements.

Page 3 had 10 Madras dateline stories by HS while Page 4 had six such stories including two by UNI. Page 5 had eight foreign news stories including three from AFP, two from AP and one from UNI. Page 6 had 11 foreign news stories of which three were from PTI, two from UNI and one each from Reuters, AP, AFP and DPA. Page 8 carried the editorial content while Page 9 had 17 stories of which three were taken PTI, four from UNI and one each from AP and AFP. The PTI stories including a box item from Washington saying *Women led US troops in Panama.*

Page 12 had three in-house stories about commodity rates, stocks and shares and business affairs. Page 13 had two corporate news stories along with share price movement. Page 14 had 14 stories including two taken from PTI. Page 15 had 11 sports stories along with radio and TV schedules while page 16 carried crossword and spiritual column entitled Forebearance in the face of crisis. Page 17 called Science/Engineering/Technical had two features while Page nos. 18 and 19 entitled Health had 12 health related news features while page 20 had four features on Agriculture including the column For the farmers' notebook. Thus, this issue had 117 news stories including 30 taken from various news agencies of which 21 were from PTI and UNI.

The Hindu, Madras, Thursday, January 4, 1990: Of the 12 main headlines on the front page of this edition, three were credited to PTI and two to UNI. The rest were filed by HS. The main stories included: *Chandigarh (PTI/UNI): Missing MP'd body found* and *New Delhi(HS): Indo-Nepal talks off to good start.* Page nos. 2, 10, 12, and 19-22 were reserved for advertisements. Page 3 had 16 Madras dateline stories while Page 4 had two out of five stories credited to PTI and UNI. Page 5 had eight foreign news stories including three taken from AP and two from Reuters. Page 6 had two stories including a Jammu dateline story from UNI saying *More pilgrims last year.*

Page 7 had five stories credited two each to PTI and UNI while Page 8 was the editorial page. Page 9 had a medley of 18 national and international stories credited four to PTI and one each to AP, Reuters and DPA. Page 13 had three business stories along with commodity news and share price movement index. Page 14 had 23 sports stories while Page 15 had five sports news stories along with race track results. Page 16 carried the Hindu crossword and the Hindu spiritual space entitled 'To realize soul is the purpose of birth'. Page 17 entitled Business Review had four news features while page 18 called Management had three features. Page 23 entitled Finance and Family had two features while Page 24 had four features along with commodity prices, bullion and output trends. Thus, it had total of 101 news stories and features of which 28 were credited to various news agencies including 16 taken from PTI and UNI wires.

The Hindu, Madras, Friday, January 5, 1990: *Washington(HS): Noreiga flown to US for trial; New Delhi: India Nepal move closer by Hindu's KK Katyal; Khudian (PTI): Orders to Punjab government/Army defectors to be* *rehabilitated;* and *Karachi (AP/Reuters): 250 die in Pak accident* were among the eight main headlines on the front page of this issue. Page nos. 2, 22, 24 and 26 carried advertisements while Page 3 had 14 Madras datelined news stories. Page 4 had six stories by HS while Page 5 had six foreign news stories credited one each to PTI, UNI, Tanjug, DPA, AP and AFP. Page 6 had four stories of which two were taken from PTI and one from UNI.

The stories included *Dhaka (PTI): Ershad assures free polls* and *Washington (UNI): US keen on good ties.* Page 7 had four stories of which one each was credited to PTI, UNI and AP while the rest came from HS. Page 8 carried the editorial content while Page 9 had a medley of 12 stories originating from within India and abroad. They included two stories each credited to PTI and UNI. Page 10 had four stories including two taken from UNI wires while Page 11 had seven stories credited one each to PTI and UNI. Page 12 had one business news and a column on stocks and shares. Page 13 also had two business news stories while Pages 14 had 17 sports stories of which one each was credited to PTI and AP while Page 15 had race track results and five sports stories by HS.

Page 16 carried the crossword and the spiritual column entitled Divine commands of conduct. Its opening paragraph reads as: *Saints are deputed by God to awaken the dormant spiritual power in man to enjoy peace and bliss. Do the vocation befitting your station in life. Avoid dealing with the wicked. Supplement devotion with righteous conduct. Avoid company of hypocrites. To undo sins committed by mistake, adopt expiatory measures as per the scriptural directives.* Page 17-20 was a four page supplement entitled Friday Features carrying news and information about cinema, arts and entertainment.

Page 21 had 15 stories originating from Madras about arts and music. Page 23 had two features while Page 25 carried the column Letters to the Editor. Page 25 had five news features on science and technology while Page 28 contained a medley of 11 Madras dateline stories. Page nos. 29 to 32 carried a supplement on Special Shopping Guide. Thus, this 32-page issue had 137 news stories of which 23 were taken from various news agencies including 16 credited to PTI and UNI.

The Hindu, Madras, Saturday, January 6, 1990: Of the ten stories appearing on the front page of this issue, two were credited to PTI and one each to UNI, Kyodo and AFP. The PTI stories included *Srinagar: Shoot at sight orders at Kashmiri towns* and *Washington: Noriega produced in Miami court.* The other main headlines included *New Delhi (HS): Colombo wants Feb.4 deadline; Karnataka's no to T. Nadu plea for water* and *Tokyo (Kyodo): Gorbachev cancels all meetings.* Page 2 carried classified advertisements while Page 3 contained 18 Madras dateline stories by HS.

Likewise, Page 4 had 12 stories from the Southern region that included two stories by PTI and one by UNI. The UNI story was: *Summons to Kerala MLA in 'defection' case.* Page 5 had six foreign stories including two from Reuters and one each from AFP, AP and TNA or Thai News Agency story from Bangkok saying: *Politically active governors must be recalled.* Page 7 had two features by HS and one UNI story while Page 8 contained the editorial space. Page 9 had 13 stories including three each from PTI and UNI and one from AP. Page nos. 10 to 11 carried advertisements while page 12 had one financial news feature along with RBI rates and select shares in Dalal Street.

Page 13 contained a column on share price movement. Page 14 had 18 sports stories including two taken from PTI wires, the rest were credited to HS. Page 15 had four sports news stories by HS and race track results. Page 16 contained the Hindu crossword and spiritual column entitled Human incarnation to help devotees. Page 17 called Saturday Sports Special contained one sports feature while page 18 had four news features by HS and page 19 had just one news story. Page 20 had two news stories along with the column Letters to the editor. Thus, the issue had 97 news stories and features of which 27 were credited to various news agencies including 20 taken from PTI and UNI wires.

The Hindu, Madras, Sunday, January 7, 1990: *New Delhi (HS): Radical industrial policy hinted at* was the main headline story of this edition while stories like *Madras: Ceasefire to end Tamil groups fighting* and *Srinagar (PTI): 31 hurt in J&K incidents* also were well displayed. Of the 13 total stories on this page, two were credited to PTI and one each to UNI, Reuters and AP. The rest were in-house contribution by newspaper staffers. Page 2 had seven stories including one from PTI. The majority of stories related to Sri Lanka for example *New Delhi (HS): Indo-Sri Lanka accord to end internecine violence.* Page 3 had 16 stories from the Madras region while Page 4 had eight stories from the Asian region including *Sangi, Pakistan (AP): Switchman held for Pak train accident.* The page also had one story from AFP and three stories from PTI. Page 5 called The Nation had three political news analysis from the Hindu special correspondents from Kerala, Goa and Manipur.

Table 7.2: Number of News Agency Stories Appearing in The Hindu in the First Week of January 1990

Date	Total Number of News Stories	News Agency Stories	Stories from PTI and UNI
January 1, 1990	77	28	17
January 2, 1990	96	23	11
January 3, 1990	117	30	21
January 4, 1990	101	28	16
January 5, 1990	137	23	16
January 6, 1990	97	12	20
January 7, 1990	90	12	8

Likewise, Page 6 had four news analysis from Tamil Nadu, Andhra Pradesh, Maharashtra and Karnataka. Page 7 had one news feature from Kabul under the title The Foreign Scene and another news feature on commodities under the title Finance/Commerce/Business. Page 14 had 15 sports stories by HS while page 15 had race track results and five sports stories including one by PTI. Page 16 had four news features under the title In the News while page 17 had one feature from Reuters. Page 18 had two news features. Page 19 had one human interest on Life Style while page 20 had two news features on television and one human interest feature.

Page 21 had a column on spotlight along with regular features on bridge, camera, crossword and spirituality. Page 22 called Health had two news features on the following: *Can cholesterol reduction prolong life* and *Malaria drug can cause mental disorder.* Page 23 entitled Children had content for kids while page 24 called Conservation had two features on the related topics. Page nos. 25 to 28 contained Sunday Weekly Edition of The Hindu. In total, the issue had 90 stories of which 12 were credited to various news agencies including eight taken from PTI and UNI wires.

The Hindu (1995): [3]

The Hindu, Madras, Sunday, January 1, 1995: The massive 80-page edition of The Hindu, priced at ₹ 3 only, had just 16 pages of news content while the rest were reserved for advertisements, shopping guide and the Sunday magazine. Its front page had eight main news stories including *Thanjavur (HS): World Tamil conference opens* and *New Delhi: Cabinet rejects Arjun's charges.* Page 2 and 13-22 contained advertisements while three had seven city/regional news stories by HS. Similarly, Page 4 also had five southern stories. Page 5 had 10 foreign news stories of which two were taken from Reuters and DPA while one each was credited to PTI and AFP. Page 6 had 15 news stories of which two were credited to PTI, three to UNI and one to Reuters.

The UNI stories originated from New Delhi and Bhubaneshwar. Page nos. 7-9 called the Nation had six features credited to HS while page 10 entitled the World had one foreign feature from Tokyo credited to Kyodo while page 11 had two stories from London and Bahrain by HS. Page 12 called the Economy had again two features by staffers while

Page 22 had 10 sports stories by Hindu correspondents. Page 23 also had eight sports stories along with race track result. Page 24 had two features at the centre of the page while Page nos. 25 to 32 had an eight-page special shopping feature. Page nos. 33 to 48 contained advertisements. Page 49 had three features while page 50 had one news feature. Page nos. 51 to 80 contained the Hindu Magazine. Thus, in total, the issue had only 88 news stories and features of which 14 were credited to various news agencies that included eight stories taken from PTI and UNI wires.

The Hindu, Madras, Monday, January 2, 1995: PTI's New Delhi story on *WTO begins work with support* was among the nine main headlines on the front page of this issue. The other stories included *Hyderabad (HS): AP to call off power project.* Of the three news agency stories on this page, two were from PTI and one from UNI. Page nos. 2, 7, 8 and 22 were reserved for advertisements. Page 3 had three stories from the Madras city along with the Reporters' Diary while Page nos. 4 -5 had 10 stories from the southern region filed by HS. Page 6 had nine stories from the states that included four news features. Page 9 also had five stories including two from PTI from Darbhanga and Jamshedpur. Page 10 had 10 foreign news stories of which four were credited to AP, two to Reuters and one each to AP, DPA and PTI.

Two stories were filed by HS from Moscow and Colombo. Page 11 also had five foreign news stories of which two each were taken from Reuters and AP and one from PTI. The PTI story was: *United Nations: Re-think likely on future role of U.N.* Page 12 was the editorial page while page 13 had 11 news stories including eight from PTI and one from UNI. The PTI stories were from Guwahati, Coimbatore, Calcutta, London and Jamshedpur while the UNI's New Delhi story was about *Opposition resents patents law move.* Page 14 had 12 stories from across the globe including *Karachi (HS): Tension still prevails in Karachi.* Page 15 had three news features emanating from Guwahati and Bombay.

Page nos. 16 and 17 called State View had eight news analysis from different states like Andhra Pradesh, Bihar, Goa, Uttar Pradesh, Delhi, Haryana, Gujarat and Tamil Nadu. Page 18 had two business news stories taken one each from PTI and UNI and a column called the Corporate Scene. Page 19 had three stories including an in-house feature called the Financial Scene. Page 20 carried two interviews with business interviews. Pages 22 and 23 carried 27 sports stories including one each from PTI, UNI and AP. Page 24 carried the Hindu crossword and spiritual column entitled God bound to His devotees. In total, the issue had 120 news stories and features that included 41 taken from various news agencies of which 29 were credited to PTI and UNI.

The Hindu, Madras, Thursday, January 3, 1995: Of the seven main headlines on the front page of this issue, PTI had just one column, one paragraph story from Bhubaneshwar saying *Seshan cancels visit.* The rest of the stories including *India-Iran discuss economic issues, Laloo wants polls on schedule* and *TNCC(I) to boycott PM's visit* were filed by the daily staffers. Page nos. 2, 7, 8, 21 and 28 were reserved for advertisements. Page 3 had 15 stories from the Madras city and the surrounding region by HS.

Likewise, page nos. four and five too carried 12 regional stories including PTI's *Thanjavur: Scholars disallowed from attending meet.* Page nos. six and nine had 11 stories from the states. Page 10 had 10 stories from across the globe of which three each came from Reuters and AFP while one each was credited to PTI and TNA. Likewise, page 11 had three foreign news stories including two from PTI, Beijing on *Campaign to spread Deng's doctrine* and *New law to ensure orderly labour market.* Page 12 contained the editorial contents and an interview with the visiting Singapore prime minister. Page 13 had eight news stories of which two were taken from PTI and one from UNI while page 14 had nine news stories including one by UNI.

It carried an extensive coverage of the CII's Calcutta session by the Hindu correspondents. Page 15 had five stories from across the nation including two from PTI while Page 16 had two news stories along with the Night Sky. Page 17 had one HS story from Bombay while page 18 and 19 had seven news stories. Page 21 had information about stock exchanges by HS while Pages 22 and 23 carried 27 sports stories including two each from AP and UNI. Page 24 carried crossword and spiritual column entitled Humility, hallmark of a true devotee. Page 25 called the Open Page had two features while Page 26 carried three write-ups on education. Page 27 carried book review while Page 28 was full of advertisements. The issue had 117 stories of which 23 were taken from various news agencies including 14 taken from UNI and PTI wires.

The Hindu, Madras, Wednesday, January 4, 1995: Of the 11 main headlines on the front page of this issue, two were credited to UNI such as: *Bombay: Bomb blast accused arrested* and *Calcutta: Singapore PM in Calcutta.* The rest of the stories were credited to the Hindu staffers or HS. Page nos. 2, 7, 8, 21 and 26 carried advertisements. Page 3 had five stories from the Madras city while Page 4 had eight stories from the southern region. Page 5 had a feature on *Pollution threat to marine life.* Page 6 and nine had eight stories from various states by HS. Page 10 had 12 stories from around the world of which three were credited to Reuters, two each to AFP and AP while one was taken from UNI and NYT.

Likewise, page 11 had three foreign news stories of which two were taken from AP and one from NYT along with an AP/PTI picture of North Korean president. Page 12 was the editorial page. Page 13 had 10 news stories from across the country including one each from PTI and UNI. Page 14 had three news features and four stories of which three were taken from PTI and one from UNI. The PTI stories included: *Raipur: PM delaying decisions; Calcutta: EC extends date;* and *Basu's advice to Laloo.* Pages 15 to 17 had 11 stories from across the nation including one by PTI. Page 18 had 18 corporate stories from HS while Page 19 had two business news stories. Page 20 also called Business had information about stocks and shares.

Pages 22 and 23 carried 24 sports news stories including one from AP. Page 24 carried the crossword and the spiritual column entitled Introspection essential in life. Page 25 named Science & Technology had seven news stories including two news features while page 27 had five features by HS and one story by PTI entitled *Value addition chemicals from IC.* Page 28 entitled Agriculture had seven news stories including a feature on 'For the farmers' notebook'. Thus, this issue had 127 news stories of which 22 were taken from various news agencies that included 11 from PTI and UNI wires.

The Hindu, Madras, Thursday, January 5, 1995: All the main headlines on the front page of this issue were contributed the Hindu staffers be it the Calcutta stories on *Reforms will have special schemes for the poor* or *States agree on reforms, Rao tells Goh Chok Tong.* Of the eight stories on this page, two were credited to AFP for its stories from Khartoum and Moscow. Page 2 had classifieds while Page 3 to five had 28 stories from the Madras city and southern region including a feature on Kancheepuram. Page 6 had eight stories from the states while page nos. seven and eight had advertisements. Page 9 had again five political analysis stories from the states by Hindu correspondents posted there.

Page 10 had 11 stories from around the world of which two each were credited to AFP, AP and DPA while one each was credited to Reuters and PTI. One story was published by arrangement with NYT while two stories were credited to HS. Likewise, Page 11 had five foreign news stories of which two were credited to AP and one to Kyodo. Page 12 carried the editorial content and page 13 had nine stories including one from UNI. Page 14 also had six stories including two by UNI.

Page 15 had five stories of which two were credited to PTI while of the four stories on Page 16 one was credited to UNI. Page 17 had advertisements. Page nos. 18 and 19 had six business news stories while page 20 had information about various stock exchanges like Bombay, Madras, Coimbatore, Kochi, Delhi and NSE. Page 21 had advertisements and Pages

22 and 23 had 31 sports stories including two from AFP and one each from AFP and UNI. Page 24 had crossword and the spiritual column entitled: God's grace alone can transform man. It read thus: *In the realm of spiritual life, it is God Himself who seeks out a devotee/disciple.*

Table 7.3: Number of News Agency Stories Appearing in The Hindu in the First Week of January 1995

Date	Total Number of News Stories	News Agency Stories	Stories from PTI and UNI
January 1, 1995	88	14	8
January 2, 1995	120	41	29
January 3, 1995	117	23	14
January 4, 1995	127	22	11
January 5, 1995	137	23	8
January 6, 1995	108	18	9
January 7, 1995	135	25	9

This is a fact established in the lives of God realized souls. It is God Himself, who often comes to claim his disciple in human form when a particular soul has achieved spiritual maturity necessary for the grace of God to descend on the soul. This is called the intercession of the Divine Grace. Page 25 had four business features while Page 28 had seven stories from the Hindu corporate desk. Page nos. 26 and 27 were advertisement pages. Thus, this issue had 137 news stories of which 23 were credited to various news agencies including eight taken from PTI and UNI wires.

The Hindu, Madras, Friday, January 6, 1995: *PM highlights the glory of Tamil, World Tamil Sangam to be revived, Jitendra Prasad is UPCC chief* and *CBI to close espionage case* were among seven stories by HS that appeared on the front page of this 36-page issue. As usual, eight pages of this edition–Page nos. 2, 7, 8, 21, 28, 30, 32 and 34–were devoted to commercial advertisements. Page nos. 3 to 5 had 25 stories from Madras city and southern region. Page nos. 6 and 9 had seven stories from the states including two from PTI on snowfall in Mussorrie and Ardha Kumbha in Allahabad. Page 10 and 11 had 16 stories from around the world including four from AP, two each from Reuters and DPA and one each from PTI, UNI and Kyodo. The stories also included to taken from NYT.

The rest came from HS. Page nos. 15 to 17 had 18 news stories of which three came from PTI and two from UNI. The PTI stories included *New York: Indian markets best bet for investors* and UNI stories included *Washington: Perry not to focus on NPT.* Pages 18 and 19 had 15 business stories along with corporate results while Page 20 had news about various bourses. Pages 22 and 23 had 20 sports stories including race track results. Page 24 carried the Hindu crossword and spiritual column. Page 25 was called Friday Review and had film analysis while Page nos. 26, 27, 29, 31 and 33 were devoted to music and related news and information. Page 35 entitled Music and Cinema had more news from the world of entertainment. Page 36 carried the column 'What's on this week' that had schedules of TV, radio and satellite TV as well as TV highlights. Thus, the issue had 108 news stories including 18 from various news agencies of which nine were credited to PTI and UNI.

The Hindu, Madras, Saturday, January 7, 1995: The front page of the 34-page issue had 14 main news stories including Colombo datelined story on *Key suspect held (key suspect in the bomb blast that killed the Sri Lankan opposition leader Gamini Dissanayake and 53 others last October, has been held in Colombo).* Interestingly, this story's credits were shared between four news agencies namely, PTI, UNI, AFP and Xinhua. However, the other stories were credited to HS. They included *Lucknow: Tiwari supporters plan satyagraha; New Delhi: Reforms benefit poor too, says Hurd; New Delhi: Japan minister offers US$ 1 bn credit;* and *Madras: Govt. soft-pedalling on tax reforms.* Page nos. 2, 7, 8, 21 and 26 were reserved for advertisements.

Page nos. 3 to 5 had 23 stories from Madras city and

southern region. Page nos. 6 and 9 had 11 stories from various states by HS. Page nos. 10 and 11 had 16 foreign news stories credited five to AP, four to Reuters and one each to AFP and DPA. The rest including a five column Colombo datelined story on '*Foreign observers to monitor ceasefire in Sri Lanka*' were contributed by daily staffers posted at various foreign destinations. Page 12 was the editorial page while Page 13 had 11 news stories of which two were credited to PTI such as: *New Delhi: Open up or get sidelined, Goh cautions India* and a box story on democracy in Singapore entitled '*A different democracy*' reading thus:

According to Goh, PM's salary is fixed on the basis that political leaders had an even more responsible role than CEOs of MNCs. Political leaders were chosen from five or six professions, subjected to psychological tests and then trained to meet the country's requirements. Only subsequently would they be allowed to stand for elections by their parties.

Page nos. 14 and 15 had 14 news stories from across the nation including two each by PTI and UNI. The stories included *Lucknow (UNI): Centre refuses to be party to Ayodhya title case.* Similarly, Page nos. 16 and 17 also had seven national news stories of which one each was credited to PTI and UNI. Page nos. 18 to 20 carried 13 news stories on business, finance and various stock exchanges. Page nos. 22 and 23 carried 26 sports news stories including two credited to Reuters and one each to UNI, AFP and AP. Page 24 carried the Hindu crossword and the spiritual column entitled *Tolerance essential for freedom.* Page nos. 25, 27 and 28 carried special sports feature called Sports Special. Page nos. 29 to 34 carried a five-page Saturday supplement called the Young World. Thus, the issue had a 135 of which 25 were credited to various news agencies that included five from PTI and four from UNI.

The Hindu (2000): [4]

The Hindu, Chennai, Saturday, January 1, 2000: This 72-page mega edition priced at two rupees eighty paisa only had 39 pages of news content that included 12 pages of commercial advertisements. The remaining 33 pages were again full of advertisements and special supplements like shopping guide etc. No wonder the Hindu is one of the richest Indian newspapers and its staffers are also very well paid. Now coming to the news content, its front page had only five news stories filed by its staffers along with the front page editorial on the hijack and hostage crisis with the following headline: *Great relief but a heavy price.* Page nos. 2 and 3 had six stories under the banner Chennai/Life.

Page nos. four to six had 18 stories 'From the South'. Page 9 had two stories from other states. Page nos. 7, 8, 11, 12, 14, 15, 20, 21, 25, 26, 28 and 29 were full of advertisements. Page nos. 10 and 13 had 11 stories from across the nation while page 16 was the editorial page. Page 17 had nine news stories of which two were credited to PTI while page 18 had eight news stories including three from PTI and one from AFP. Page 19 had three stories by HS. Page nos. 22 and 23 had 11 foreign news stories including two from AFP and one each from PTI and DPA. The rest were news features including two taken from NYT and the rest filed by HS staffers. Page nos. 24 and 27 had nine sports stories including one by PTI.

Page nos. 30 to 32 had 14 sports stories along with race track results. Page nos. 33 to 36 was a four-page supplement called Sports Special while Page nos. 37 to 39 entitled Millennium Mosaic carried six human interest features. The remaining 33 pages were reserved for advertisements and other special supplements like the shopping guide. Thus, the issue had 96 news stories including 12 stories taken from various news agencies that included seven stories taken from PTI and UNI wires.

The Hindu, Chennai, Sunday, January 2, 2000: *There was a threat to blow up the plane* and *Hijack footprints lead to Pakistan, says Jaswant* were among the five news stories on the front page of this 40 page issue. Page nos. 2 and 3 had 26 news stories from the Chennai city and surrounding areas.

Page nos. 4 to 6 had 20 stories from the southern region. Page nos. 7 and 8 had 10 stories from other states. Page 9 had advertisements. Page nos. 10 and 11 had 20 stories from across the nation including three from PTI and one from UNI. The other stories filed by HS included *Hijackers, militants Quetta-bound, US for prosecution of those involved in hijack* and *We'll meet again, said one hijacker.*

Page 12 had 14 foreign news stories credited three to Reuters, two to AP and one each to AFP, PTI and DPA. It also included two pictures by AP. Page 13 had four business news stories including one filed by PTI. Page nos. 14 and 15 called The Nation had four news features by HS. Page nos. 16 and 17 had four foreign news features from Ivory Coast, Chechen, Cambodia and Bangladesh published by arrangement. Page 18 to 20 had 21 sports stories along with race track results. Page nos. 21 to 24 were meant for classified advertisements while page nos. 25 to 40 carried a 16-page supplement called The Hindu Magazine. Thus, the issue had 128 news stories including 12 stories taken from various news agencies of which eight were credited to PTI and UNI.

The Hindu, Chennai, Monday, January 3, 2000: *New Delhi's India ready to back claim on Pak role, Islamabad's Taliban disowns statement* and *Harkat behind hijack* and *Tirunelveli's Education programme for prisoners* were among 10 news stories including three news briefs on the front page of this issue. Of the total, one news brief each was credited to PTI and UNI. All other stories were contributed by HS. Page nos. 2 and 3 had 12 news stories from the Madras city plus the weekly column on Readers' Mail. Page nos. 4 and 5 had 15 news stories from the southern region while Page nos. 6 and 9 carried seven news stories from other states.

It included one UNI story from Patna. Page nos. 10 and 11 had 12 news stories from across the nation that included five stories from PTI and three from UNI. Page 12 was the editorial page. Page 13 to 15 had 23 news stories from various parts of the country of which six were credited to PTI and one to UNI.

Page nos. 16 and 17 had 13 foreign news stories that included a Reuter story on *Anti-Castro leaflets dropped over Havana.* Of the total, three were credited to Reuters, two to PTI and one each to AP and AFP. The rest were filed by HS. Page nos. 18 to 20 had 10 business news stories including two PTI stories one of which read as–*NSE conducts second mock trading.* Page nos. 22 to 24 carried 28 sports stories along with race track results. Of these, one each was credited to PTI and DPA. Page nos. 25 to 28 carried a supplement called The Hindu Metro Plus. Thus, the issue had 118 news stories of which 28 stories were taken from various news agencies that included 22 from PTI and UNI.

The Hindu, Chennai, Tuesday, January 4, 2000: *India wants Pak declared a terrorist state, Released terrorists likely to enter POK* and *Overstaying foreigners to be deported* were among nine stories that appeared on the front page of this issue. Of these, three news capsules under the title News Digest in the first column were credited to PTI. Page nos. 2 and 3 had 14 stories from the city and around Page nos. 4 and 5 carried 20 stories from the southern region. Page 6 had three news features on Andhra Pradesh, Karnataka and Kerala under the banner From the States while Page 8 had 10 news stories from across the nation of which two each were credited to PTI and UNI. Page nos. 7 and 9 were reserved for advertisements. Page 10 was the editorial page.

Page nos. 11 and 12 had 25 stories from across the nation including a PTI box story from Amritsar on *'Airport did not have a ladder'* and *New Delhi: Govt. under fire for 'mishandling' the hijack issue.* It also had a special report entitled *Time for frontal attack on terrorism* by senior journalist K. K. Katyal. Page 13 also had 11 national news stories including two single column PTI stories–*Behrampur: Terrorism continues in Orissa villages* and *Mumbai: Blast accused seeks bail.* Page nos. 14 and 15 had 13 foreign news stories of which four were credited to AFP, three to Reuters, two to DPA and one each to Kyodo and PTI.

The rest were filed by HS staffers. Page nos. 16 carried seven business news stories including one by PTI while page 17 carried the stocks news by HS. Page nos. 18-20 carried 30 sports news stories of which one was credited to AFP. Page nos. 21 to 24 called the Open Page carried readers' views and features on education, career and book reviews. Thus, the issue had 139 news stories of which 28 were credited to various news agencies including 17 from PTI and UNI wires.

The Hindu, Chennai, Wednesday, January 5, 2000: Of the eight news stories on the front page of this issue, two small single column news items were credited to PTI. The other stories came from HS and included *Islamabad: Masood can come to Pak* and *Hijackers in Pak military base.* As usual, page nos. two and three carried 20 stories from in around the Chennai city along with guide to radio and TV. Page nos. 4 and 5 had 15 regional news stories while Page nos. 6 and 9 carried seven analytical stories from various state capitals. Page nos. 7 and 8 were reserved for commercial advertisements. Page nos. 10 and 11 carried 12 national news stories of which six were credited to PTI and one to UNI.

The PTI stories were as follows: *Guwahati: Tight security at ONGC units* and *Two ULFA militants killed in encounter; Itanagar: NLFA militant dies in police custody; New Delhi: Two mega museums to be set up;* and *Mumbai: Maharashtra warns transporters.* The UNI story was *New Delhi: Govt. to tone up services for visually handicapped.* The editorial on page 12 entitled *Bungling that proved costly* came heavily on the government for its handling of the sensitive hijack issue. It said: "*The bargain struck with the hijackers goes against the spirit of the declaration adopted at the all-party meeting that whatever the government decided must be based on two factors–the safety of the passengers and the overall interest of the nation...*"

Page nos. 13 to 15 carried 31 news stories from all over the country of which 10 were credited to PTI and four to UNI. Page nos. 16 and 17 carried 16 news stories including two each credited to Reuters and AFP. Of these, two news features were attributed to NYT. Page nos. 18 to 20 carried 15 business news stories including four filed by PTI. Page 21 carried advertisements while Page nos. 22 to 24 carried 25 sports stories of which two were credited to AFP and one each to Reuters and AP. Page 25 carried a four page supplement called the Business Review and Page nos. 29 to 36 carried another eight-page supplement named Opportunities. The issue had 148 news stories of which 35 were credited to various news agencies including 27 taken from PTI and UNI wires.

The Hindu, Chennai, Thursday, January 6, 2000: Islamabad datelined story by a Hindu staffer about *Masood, Zargar see in Karachi, POK* and *A Swiss.*

Table 7.4: Number of News Agency Stories Appearing in The Hindu in the First Week of January 2000

Date	Total Number of News Stories	News Agency Stories	Stories from PTI and UNI
January 1, 2000	96	12	7
January 2, 2000	128	12	8
January 3, 2000	118	28	22
January 4, 2000	139	28	17
January 5, 2000	148	35	27
January 6, 2000	154	34	24
January 7, 2000	173	35	25

VIP was aboard IC-814 from Paris were among 10 news stories on the front page of this issue. Of these, one each was credited to AFP and DPA and the rest were contributed by the daily correspondents. Page nos. 2 and 3 had 11 stories from the Chennai city and around while Page nos. 4 to 6 had 22 stories from the southern region. Page nos. 7 and 8 had advertisements while Page 9 four news stories under the title from other states of which one story from Patna was credited to PTI. Page nos. 10 and 11 had 15 stories from across the nation of which five stories were credited to PTI and one to UNI.

Page 12 was the editorial page that carried two articles on *Engaging the Islamic World* by C. Raja Mohan and *Amending the Constitution* by Rajinder Sachar. Page nos. 13 to 15 carried 31 news stories from various parts of the country. Of these, four were credited to PTI and two to UNI and one to Reuters. The PTI stories included *Islamabad: Musharraf calls for restraint;* and *Washington: Time to declare Pak a terrorist state-Pollock.* Page nos. 16 and 17 carried 18 foreign news stories of which four stories were credited to International Telegraph Group Ltd., London, and one each to Reuters and New York Times (NYT). Page nos. 18 to 20 carried 24 business news stories apart from detailed information about stocks and shares and a column on economic outlook.

Of these stories, nine were credited to PTI, one each to UNI and AFP and two to Reuters. Page 21 again had advertisements. Page nos. 22 to 24 had 30 sports stories and race track results. Of these, just four stories were credited to news agencies that included two from AP and one each from PTI and AFP. Page nos. 15-27 entitled Science and Technology and page 28 entitled Agriculture carried sponsored features. Thus, the issue carried 154 news stories of which 34 were taken from various news agencies that included 24 credited to PTI and UNI.

The Hindu, Chennai, Friday, January 7, 2000: There were eight main news headlines on the front page of this issue that included *Four accomplices held in Mumbai* and *Win Chadha ready for trial.* Of these, just two small news capsules on the first column entitled News Digest were credited to PTI. The rest were contributed by HS. Page nos. two and three carried 24 stories from the Chennai city and around while Page 4 and six carried 21 stories from the south. Page nos. 5, 7, 8 and 21 carried commercial and classified advertisements. Page nos. 9 to 11 carried 19 stories from across the nation of which two each were credited to PTI and UNI. Page 12 carried the editorial content. Page nos. 13 to 15 carried 31 major news stories of which 11 were taken from PTI wires and one each from UNI and AP.

They included a three column UNI story on *Pak hand exposed in hijack episode.* Page nos. 16 and 17 carried 18 foreign news stories of which four were attributed to Reuters, two to AFP and one each to DPA and PTI. Page nos. 18 to 20 carried 22 business news stories and columns on stocks and shares. Of these, five stories were credited to PTI. Page nos. 22 to 24 carried 30 sports news stories of which three stories–one each was taken from AP, AFP and Reuters. Page nos. 25 to 32 carried the eight-page weekly supplement Friday Review. Thus, the issue had 173 total news stories of which 35 were credited to various news agencies that included 25 taken from PTI and UNI.

The Hindu (2005): [5]

The Hindu, Delhi, Saturday, January 1, 2005: Of the 14 main news headlines on the front page of this issue, two news briefs in the first column were credited to PTI while AP got the credit for the story on tsunami toll. The rest were in-house contribution. They included *New Delhi: All party meeting to tackle tsunami challenges: Manmohan* and *Integrated relief command for Andamans set up.* Page 2 called Life had two features by Hindu staffers while Page 3 entitled Around the City had nine in-house stories from in and around the national capital. Page nos. four and five called the States had 19 stories of which one each was credited to PTI and UNI while one was shared by the two. The shared story was *Mumbai: Sunil Dutt appears in court.*

The other stories were: *Lucknow (UNI): Gonda SP suspended* and *Shimla (PTI): Himachal reels under cold wave.* Page nos. six and seven entitled From the South carried eight special stories from the southern region while Page 8 had television and radio schedules along with other engagements column. Page 9 called Variety had three news features including the one entitled *Enquiry commissions a waste of time: Lahoti* along with regular features on religion, the day that age and the Hindu crossword. Page 10 was the edit page while page 11 had 11 news stories by Hindu staffers. Page 12 carried the details about the Hindu Relief Fund set up for tsunami victims while page 13 had nine stories by Hindu correspondents.

Page 14 carried 13 international news stories of which one each was credited to UNI, AFP and Reuters and three to AP. Page 15 called Business had four news briefs shared equally between UNI and PTI and six main stories of which five were credited to PTI. It also had a market column. The PTI stories from Mumbai included: *Slower rise in forex reserves* and *Current A/C deficit put at US$ 3.25 bn in first half.* Page 16 carried eight business news stories including five news snippets. Of the three main stories, two were credited to PTI. Page nos. 17 to 19 carried 25 sports news stories all filed by Hindu staffers. Page 20 entitled Newscape had three news features of which two were credited to Reuters and one to AP.

They were: *Phuket (AP): United by a single phrase–Let's help; Phuket (Reuters) Mother makes agonizing choice* and *Paraliya (Reuters): They owe it to their military training.* Page nos. 21 to 24 carried special Saturday supplement called the Metroplus and Page nos. 25 to 28 carried another weekly supplement for children called Young World. Thus, the issue had a total of 134 news stories of which 23 were credited to various news agencies including 17 taken from PTI and UNI wires.

The Hindu, Delhi, Sunday, January 2, 2005: As usual, the four main stories on the front page were credited to the daily staffers while the three news capsules were attributed to PTI. Page 2 called Life had news about cinema while Page 3 called City had 12 stories from in and around the city. Page 4 had 10 stories from the states while Page 5 carried classified advertisements. Page 6 had eight news stories from the southern states while Page 7 had 10 news items including KBK graphic on India 2004 highlights. Of these, two stories–one each was credited to UNI and PTI. The stories were:

Srinagar (UNI): Valley cut off (thee columns) and *New Delhi (PTI): Centre mulls new norms for FDI in township development (four columns).*

Page 8 had nine news stories while Page 9 had 11 of which one story was credited to UNI. The story was: *Patna (UNI): FIR against Mayawati for violating model code.* Page 10 had three news features by Hindu staffers. They included: *An eventful year for Supreme Court* and *A 'desi' chip maker preferred worldwide.* Page 12 had 11 foreign news stories of which five were credited to AP, two each to AFP and Reuters and one to UNI. One Phuket datelined news feature was published with arrangement with the Guardian. It read as: *Frantic search for relatives from Khao lake.* Page 13 had six business stories of which three were credited to PTI and one to UNI. The UNI story on *Price cuts revive FMCG sector fortunes* with New Delhi dateline got a four column display.

The PTI stories included *New Delhi: Forbes honour Ratan Tata* and *Mumbai: Forex reserves up to US$ 394 mn.* Page 14 entitled Insight had four news features and a guest article. Page nos. 15 to 17 had 27 sports news stories of which four stories were credited to AP. Page 18 called Newscape had five news features on tsunami.

Of these, one was picked up from the Guardian while one each was credited to UNI, AP, Reuters and AFP. The issue also included an eight page supplement called The Hindu Magazine along with six pages of Literary Review and four pages of classified advertisements. Thus, this 36-page Sunday edition of the Hindu carried 109 news stories and features of which 30 were picked from various news agencies that included 14 credited to PTI and UNI.

The Hindu, Delhi, Monday, January 3, 2005: The 28-page issue priced at ₹ 2.50 only with eight news briefs credited two each to AFP, PTI, Reuters and Hindu staffers and six main stories including one credited to AP on its front page. The stories included AP's *Asian toll estimated at 1,50,000* and Hindu's *Operation Andamans in full flow, Master Plan 2021* *has grand plans for Delhi* and *Dense fog blinds capital.* Page 2 called Life had two profile features on Naomi Ackerman, the Israeli theatre artist and Aparna Caur, the Delhi-based painter. Page 3 had nine stories from in and around the city while Page 4 had nine stories from the states.

Page 5 also had six stories from other states including two taken from UNI wires. Page nos. 6 and 7 had eight analytical stories from the southern states filed by Hindu staffers.

Page 8 had television and radio schedules while Page 9 called Variety had four news stories including one by PTI. Page 10 was the edit page while Page 11 had six news stories of which one each was picked up from PTI and AP wires.

The PTI story was *London: Swaraj Paul donates Rs. One crore* and AP story was *Banda Aceh: Indonesian survivor found after a week.* Page 12 had three news stories by HS while Page 13 had seven such stories. Page 14 had 10 foreign datelined news stories of which two each were credited to AP and Reuters while one was credited to PTI.

Page 15 and 16 had seven business news stories along with regular features like Tax Forum, Market, Question and Answer. Page nos. 17 to 19 had 29 sports stories of which three each were credited to AP and AFP.

Page 20 called the Newscape had five stories–two credited to ANI and one each to PTI, UNI and AP. The issue also had four pages of sponsored supplement and four pages of Metroplus. The total news stories were 120 of which 29 were credited to various news agencies including 10 taken from PTI and UNI wires.

The Hindu, Delhi, Tuesday, January 4, 2005: The front page displayed a huge (8x10) picture by AP with a caption–*Back to the sea*–along with seven news briefs and four main stories. Of these, three news briefs were credited to PTI and two to UNI.

Page 2 entitled Life had two news features while Page 3 had 12 news stories from in around the city. Page nos. 4 and 5 entitled States had 18 news stories including one by UNI.

Table 7.5: Number of News Agency Stories Appearing in The Hindu in the First Week of January 2005

Date	Total Number of News Stories	News Agency Stories	Stories from PTI and UNI
January 1, 2005	134	23	17
January 2, 2005	109	30	14
January 3, 2005	120	29	10
January 4, 2005	129	24	16
January 5, 2005	134	31	15
January 6, 2005	139	19	12
January 7, 2005	147	33	20

Page nos. 6 and 7 carried nine stories from the southern region while Page 8 had television and radio schedules and Page 9 called variety had advertisements. Page 10 was the edit page. Page nos. 11 and 12 had 16 news stories while Page 13 had 11 foreign news stories. Of these, two each were credited to AP, the Guardian while one each was picked up from New York Times News Service (NYTNS) and Reuters. Page 14 had book reviews while Page 15 too had book reviews besides three guest articles under the banner the Open Page.

Page 16 had 10 business news stories along with regular feature on markets. Of these, six stories were credited to PTI and two to UNI. The stories included–*Mumbai (PTI): Bourses start New Year with a bang* and *New Delhi (UNI): LML promoters not to sell stakes.* Likewise, Page 17 had 11 business news stories including one by PTI and five sports stories by HS. Page 18 also had 13 sports stories while Page 19 had seven sports stories including one by PTI. Page 20 called Newscape had six news stories of which one each was credited to Reuters, NYTNS, AP, AFP and the Guardian News Pvt. Ltd. Thus, the 20-page issue had 129 news stories of which 24 were taken from various news agencies including 16 credited to PTI and UNI.

The Hindu, Delhi, Wednesday, January 5, 2005: *New Delhi: Focus now on repair of infrastructure; Nagapattinam: Where the Danish fort stood like a rock;* and *New Delhi:*

Capital caught in endless jam were among the 15 stories on the front page of this issue. Of the 10 news briefs, one each was taken from AP, PTI and UNI and rest of the stories were credited to HS. Page 2 called Life had the column entitled Talk of the town. Page 3 had 14 news stories from in and around the city while Page 4 had 11 stories from the states and Page 5 had 10 more such stories. Page nos. 6 and 7 had 12 analytical news stories from the southern states filed by HS. Page 8 had television and radio schedules while Page 9 had today's engagements along with commercial advertisements. Page 10 was the edit page and Page 11 had 10 news stories by HS.

Likewise, Page nos. 12 and 13 had nine news stories by HS including *Cabinet nod for rural health mission.* Page 14 had eight foreign news stories of which three were credited to AP and one each to Reuters and the Guardian. Page 15 had 11 business news stories of which four were credited to PTI. They included *New Delhi: Pantaloon to take up majority stake in Indus League* and *Mumbai: Sensex hits new intra-day peak.* Page 16 also had nine business news stories of which one each was credited to PTI and UNI. Page nos. 17 to 19 had 28 sports news stories of which two each were credited to PTI, UNI, Reuters and AP while was taken from AFP wires. Page 19 had five news stories by HS while page 20 had six news stories of which three were credited to AP and one to Reuters. It also had an AFP picture of tsunami victims. The issue included a four-page supplement entitled Opportunities. In total, it had 134 news stories of which 31 were credited to various news agencies including 15 taken from PTI and UNI.

The Hindu, Delhi, Thursday, January 6, 2005: Of the 12 news stories on the front page of this issue, the main headlines by HS were: *Jakarta: India to offer expertise to tsunami-hit countries* and *New Delhi: Disaster management teams set-up in the Andamans.* Of the eight news briefs, five were credited to PTI and the rest were credited to the Hindu. Page 2 called Life had two human interest features while Page 3 had 10 stories from in and around the national capital. Page 4 and five had 16 stories from the states while Page nos. 6 and 7 had eight stories from the southern region. Page 8 had television and radio schedules while Page 9 had commercial advertisements.

Page 10 was the edit page and also carried the column entitled Letters to the editor. Page 11 had 13 news stories by HS while Page 12 had five news features including *Needed: Humane options for orphaned children–an insider's view* or *Tsunami has brought about a global consciousness.* Page 13 carried 10 foreign news stories of which three were taken from AP, the Guardian and NYTNS. The rest were filed by the Hindu correspondents based in London, Dhaka, Manama, Bahrain, Colombo and Kuala Lumpur. Page 14 had six news features on the subject of Science and Technology. Page 15 had four features on agriculture including the Farmers' Notebook. Page 16 had 10 business news stories of which five were credited to PTI.

They included the following: *Mumbai: Rupee loses 31 paise on resurgent dollar overseas;* and *New Delhi: Centre to divest stakes.* Page 17 also had 10 business news stories including *New Delhi (PTI): Reliance oil and gas block in Gulf of Oman* and seven sports stories including one by Reuters from London on *Fifa to test ball device.* Page nos. 18 and 19 had 24 sports news stories of which three were credited to AP and one to PTI. They included: *London (PTI): Kallis upstage Lara; Cape Town (AP): Langerveldt ruled out of series* and *Berlin (AP): Schumacher's generous gesture.* Page 20 had two news features by HS. The issue included four pages of Metroplus. The total news stories in this edition were 139 of which 19 were credited to various news agencies including 12 taken from PTI and UNI wires.

The Hindu, Delhi, Friday, January 7, 2005: *Jakarta: Navy on alert for relief efforts, says Natwar Singh (Hindu); New Delhi (PTI): US may increase H1B visa for professionals* and *New Delhi: Awareness can prevent AIDS, says Manmohan (Hindu)* were among the 15 news stories on the front page of this edition. Of the eight news briefs here, two were credited to PTI and three to UNI. Page 2 entitled Life had the column–Talk of the town while Page 3 called City had 14 stories from in and around the capital filed by HS. Page 5 had three news stories by HS while page nos. six and seven carried 13 news stories from the south. Page 8 carried television and radio schedules while Page 9 called variety had today's engagements and sponsored commercial features.

Page 10 was the edit page. Page 11 had 10 news stories including Jakarta datelined story on *Natwar holds talks with Wen Jiabao* accompanied by a four column AP picture. Page 12 had three news stories by HS including *Somnath contributes Rs. 11 lakh for relief work.* Page 13 called News had seven news stories of which three were credited to AP, PTI and UNI respectively. The stories were: *Jirkatang (AP): We are safe, says Jarawas; New Delhi (UNI): Ambani brothers deny reports of legal split;* and *New Delhi (PTI): Nicobarese boys help rescue family.* Page 14 had 10 foreign news stories of which two each were credited to AFP, AP and Reuters while one was credited to PTI.

Another story was picked up from the Guardian. The stories included *Tokyo (PTI): Japan offers Asian nations early warning system; Washington (AP): Fresh Guantanamo probe;* and *Hong Kong (AFP): Another quake.* Page 15 had 10 business news stories including news briefs of which two were credited to PTI and one to UNI. Of the six main stories, four were taken from PTI wires and one from AP. They were: *New Delhi: Maruti rolls out Euro III versions* and *Roadmap to banking reforms soon;* and *Washington (AP): Microsoft offers free virus-removal programme.* It also had to market stories by PTI as well. Page 16 had 12 news stories including five news snippet of which one each were taken from PTI and UNI.

Page 17 to 19 had 39 sports news stories of which three were credited to PTI. Page 20 had six news stories of which two were credited to AP and one each to AFP and ANI. The rest came from HS. The issue included four pages of the

Friday Review and another four pages of the Young World, a special supplement for children. In total, the edition had 147 news stories of which 33 were taken from various news agencies including 20 taken from PTI and UNI wires.

End Notes

1. Archives, Nehru Memorial Museum and Library, Teen Murti, New Delhi.
2. Ibid.
3. Ibid.
4. Ibid.
5. The Hindu Archives, New Delhi.

8

Punjab Kesari

Punjab Kesari is a Hindi-language newspaper published from many centres in Punjab and Haryana in India. It claims itself to be the largest selling Hindi daily in India. At the time of the Punjab insurgency, its then editor Shri Jagat Narain and later his son Shri Ramesh Chandra were assassinated by militants.

The reason for selecting this sample universe is to analyze the country-wide trend in the selection and use of news agency stories by the daily newspapers. All these newspapers represent their respective regions very well. Their reach and coverage is undoubtedly the best in their respective regions.

Trends visible in these newspapers are therefore a reliable indicator of changing patterns in news selection and news coverage in leading newspapers of the country both before and after the onset of current phase of globalization and their impact on news agency functioning.

Punjab Kesari (1985)

Punjab Kesari, Delhi, Tuesday, January 1, 1985: The eight-page edition of Punjab Kesari dated 18 Paush 2041 Vikrami Samvat was priced at 60 paise only. The use of blue/indigo ink instead of black gave the newspaper a distinct appearance unlike the other newspapers considered so far. Given the fact that this daily enjoys popular mass appeal in the whole of north India, its coverage of news and views has a distinct style of its own unlike the English newspapers.

For instance, its front page has well displayed Hindi poem on '*Nav Varsha Abhinandan*' along with a feature story on the '*Bartania ke Krishna bhakta*'. It also had another story entitled '*Convent sanskriti kidhar le ja rahi hai*'. Both stories as well as the poem are in-house contributions. Page 2 had 30 news stories of which 12 were credited to Varta, the Hindi wing of UNI and 11 to Bhasha, the Hindi counterpart of PTI. Also, there was a bit of comic strip called '*Jadugar Mandrake*' along with regular features like Doordarshan schedule, daily almanac and daily forecast. Page 3 had the main news story of the day entitled '*Rajiv ke netritva mein 40-sadasyiya mantrimandal dwara shapath*'. There were total 22 news stories of which PTI had eight, UNI nine and Reuters two while there were just five stories filed by Punjab Kesari (PK) staffers.

They included two box items by PTI called '*Antarashtriya yuva varsha par Bharat ka upahaar*' and '*25 kilo ki phoolmala*'. Page 4 carried the editorial called 'Sampaadkiya' along with foreign news comprising five news stories by AP, Reuters, AFP, PL-Pool and Xinhua. Page 5 had 20 news stories of which six were by PK, five by Varta, eight by Bhasha and one by HS. They included Varta's *Gulab ka phool* and Bhasha's '*Sultanpuri ka kursi juloos*'. Page 6 had 18 news stories from the world of sports and commodities–all credited to news agencies–six to Varta, eight to Bhasha and the rest of Hindusthan Samachar. Page 7 had news stories from Phagwara and Moga–23 stories filed by PK while Page 8 had 16 news stories of which only three were credited to PK that included a Kanpur datelined story on '*Chunav charcha ka police style*'.

The remaining stories were credited to wire services–three to Hindusthan Samachar (HS), four to PTI and six to UNI. In total, the New Year edition of Punjab Kesari had 131 news stories of which 92 were credited to various news agencies that included 83 stories taken from national news agencies like PTI, UNI and Hindusthan Samachar.

Punjab Kesari, Delhi, Wednesday, January 2, 1985: The front page carried four news features on sports while Page 2 had 25 news stories from all across the country. Of these, just seven were filed by the daily and of the remaining stories five were credited to Bhasha, six to Varta and seven to HS. Page 3 carried 22 main political news stories of which just three were credited to the PK. Of the remaining, eight were filed by Bhasha, four by Varta and seven by HS. Page 4 was the editorial page and carried six news stories as well divided equally between PK and Varta. Page 5 also had 23 political news stories of which seven were filed by PK including *Akali neta desh ki akhandata mein vishwas vyakta karein.*

Of the remaining, four were credited to Bhasha, nine to Varta, three to HS. Page 6 carried 28 stories on sports and markets by the daily itself. Page 7 carried 28 news stories from Shamli, Faridabad and Chandigarh by PK. Page 8 had 30 news stories of which 12 were credited to PK, six to HS, five to Varta and seven to Bhasha. Thus, the issue had a total of 166 news stories and features of which 92 were attributed to various news agencies including 74 to national news agencies like Hindusthan Samachar–22, Varta–28 and Bhasha–24.

Punjab Kesari, Delhi, Thursday, January 3, 1985: First page of this edition was the fiction page that carried three short stories for readers' literary entertainment. Page 2 had 27 news stories of which eight were attributed to Bhasha, 10 to Varta and six to HS. Page 3 carried a medley of 23 stories from the states, foreign news, news from the business world and politics. Of these, five were credited to PK, six to Bhasha, seven to Varta and five by HS. However, New Delhi datelined story by PK correspondent G.S. Chawla entitled *Carbide company apna karkhana Indonesia lay jana chaahati thi* was the most important story. Another story was a box item-*Pranab aur Ghani Khan ka patta kyoun kata?*. Page 4 was the editorial page.

Page 5 carried 25 news stories of which five stories from Kapurthala, Lucknow and Bhopal were credited to HS. Of the remaining, another five were credited to PK, seven to Bhasha and eight to Varta. Page 6 carried 35 news stories from the world of sports and commodities. Of these, two were credited HS, six to PK and the remaining were shared between Bhasha nine and Varta eight. The HS stories included *Jammu-Tawi Express ab punah Madras tak.* Page 7 had 32 news stories of which three were credited to HS, five to Bhasha, eight to Varta and remaining to PK. Page 8 carried 27 news stories including foreign news stories. Of these, five were credited to PK, three to Bhsha, two to Varta, three to HS and one each to AP, AFP and UPI. Thus, the issue had a total of 169 news stories of which 108 were credited to various news agencies of which 105 were taken from leading domestic news agencies.

Table 8.1: Number of News Agency Stories Appearing in Punjab Kesari in the First Week of January 1985

Date	Total Number of News Stories	News Agency Stories	Stories from PTI, UNI and HS
January 1, 1985	122	90	83
January 2, 1985	166	92	92
January 3, 1985	169	108	105
January 4, 1985	150	90	59
January 5, 1985	133	91	72
January 6, 1985	130	59	52
January 7, 1985	141	80	48

Punjab Kesari, Delhi, Friday, January 4, 1985: The front page of this issue carried articles and features on miscellaneous subjects like *Chunav material supply company.* Page 2 had 31 news stories from in and around the national capital including a four-column story entitled *1999 tak Dilli vishwa ka sabse bada slum banegi* by PK. Of the remaining stories four were filed by Bhasha, six by Varta and two by HS. Page 3 had 27 news stories including PK's three column story on *Punjab samasya par teen mantriyon ki samiti gathit.* Of the remaining, five were credited Bhasha, three to Varta and four to HS.

Page 4 carried the editorial content. Page 5 had 18 news stories of which seven were credited to PK, three to Bhasha, five to Varta and three to HS. Page 6 carried 35 news stories on sports and commodities/markets by PK. Page 7 carried medley of 17 national and foreign news stories of which two each of the foreign news was credited to UPI, AP and Reuters.

Likewise, Page 8 also carried 22 news stories of which seven were credited to AP, two to AFP, five to Bhasha, six to Varta and two to HS. Bhasha's story from Kolkata–*Jab Bandar hajjam bana*–was the box item. Thus, the total news stories were 150 of which 75 were credited to various news agencies including 59 taken from national news agencies like PTI, UNI and Hindusthan Samachar.

Punjab Kesari, Delhi, Saturday, January 5, 1985: As usual, the front page of this edition carried news from the world of films and entertainment along with pictures. Page 2 had 23 news stories of which 12 were filed by city correspondents while the rest were attributed to Varta and Bhasha. Page 3 carried main political news totalling 19 stories that included a four column Varta story originating from New Delhi saying: *Pados mein hathiyaro ke jamav se asthirta paida hogi: Rajiv. Soochna tantra ka computerikaran* and *Dilli ke shahi imam ke viruddha kanooni karyavahi par vichar* were filed by PK. Bhasha's Bhopal story on *Bhopal ki vinaash lila sirf aadha kilo pani ki kartoot* was a five column banner headline on the bottom split.

Page 4 had the editorial content along with four news stories attributed one each to Bhasha and Hindusthan Samachar and two to Varta. Page 5 had 16 news stories of which four were credited to Varta, six to PTI, two to Hindusthan Samachar and one each to Bhasha and AFP. Page 6 had 16 sports stories of which three were attributed to Bhasha, four to Varta, two to HS and seven to PK. It also had eight stories about the market credited to National News Service or NNS. Page 7 had 20 news stories of which nine were credited to PTI, seven to Varta and two each to HS and Bhasha. Page 8 had 35 foreign news stories of which four were credited to Reuters and two each to Varta, UPI and AFP.

They included a two column Varta story from New Delhi saying *Rajiv ka 24 ghante chalne wali rashtriya radio seva ka sujhav*. The remaining stories were credited to PK. Thus, it had a total of 133 news stories of which 91 were credited to national and international news agencies of which 72 were credited to national news agencies.

Punjab Kesari, Delhi, Sunday, January 6, 1985: The front page of this edition carried poignant memoirs of Shri. Vijay Kumar Chopra entitled *36 varsha baad Pakistan mein.* Page 2 carried human interest features like *Krishnaavatar* and *Singapore mein paryatan suvidha.* It also carried weekly forecast and news on films. Page 3 had 24 news stories that included a four column Varta story on *Sabhi dharmo ke logo ki jaanmaal ki raksha sarvopari kartavya: Rajiv* and *Yojana Aayog mein pherbadal: Manmohan upadhyaksha niyukta* from PTI. Of these, 11 were credited to PTI, one to UNI and two to HS. Page 4 carried the editorial along with four news stories that included a box item from PTI saying *Shimla ne safed chadar odh li.*

The other stories were credited to Varta. Page 5 carried 18 commodity news stories and classified advertisements. Of the stories, 10 stories were credited to UNI and PTI. Page 6 had 30 foreign news stories of which four were credited to AP, two to Reuters and one each to PL and Tanjug. Of the remaining, four were credited to Bhasha, eight to Varta and three to HS. The rest were credited to PK. Page 7 had 29 news stories from India and abroad including tit-bits from the capital all filed by PK staffers. Page 8 had 20 sports stories and one political story on Congress's increasing vote percentage. Of these, four each were credited to Bhasha and Varta and one to HS. Page 9 and 10 carried special supplement for children. Thus, the issue had 130 news stories of which 59 were credited to various wire services including 52 to domestic news agencies.

Punjab Kesari, Delhi, Monday, January 7, 1985: The front page of this issue had a feature on *Swadhinata ki veeranganayein* while Page 2 carried classified advertisements. Page 3 had 27 news stories including eight from Bhasha and two from UNI. The stories included a Ludhiana dateline story by PTI saying *Sikh kabhi homeland ki maang nahin karenge.* Page 4 carried the editorial. Page 5 had

23 news stories of which four were credited to Bhasha, 11 to Varta, five to PTI and one to NNS and two to HS. Page 6 had 37 sports news stories of which 16 were filed by PK, four by Reuters, three each by AP and AFP, six by Bhasha, two by Varta and three by PTI. Page 7 had 18 news stories including weekly analysis of markets–all by NNS. Page 8 had 36 news stories. Of these, seven were credited to Bhasha, six to Varta, four to Reuters, two each to PTI, HS, AFP, AP, UPI and Tanjug while the remaining attributed to PK. Thus, of the total 141 news stories, 80 were credited to various wire services including 50 attributed to Indian news agencies.

Punjab Kesari (1990)

Punjab Kesari, Delhi, Monday, January 1, 1990: In its characteristic style, the front page of this edition had human interest features. Page 2 had advertisements and three news stories of which one was credited to Bhasha and two to Varta. Page 3 had 17 news stories of which 12 were credited to Bhasha, Varta and HS. They included a six column Bhasha story from Chungyang in Sikkim saying *18 hajaar foot oonchi barfani chotiyon par tainat Bhartiya jawano ke hosle Himalaya se bhi buland.* Page 4 was the editorial page while Page 5 had miscellaneous items like *Aaj ka Itihas, Akashwani, Aaj ka din, Kal kya hoga and Doordarshan* along with advertisements that covered three-fourth of the entire page. Page 6 had six news stories of which two were credited to PTI, three to UNI and the rest to PK.

Page 7 had seven news stories of which one each were credited to Bhasha and Varta while five were attributed to PK. Again, three-fourth of this page carried commercial advertisements. Page 8 had lottery results along with four sponsored features. Page 9 called Parishishta had guest articles while Page 10 had 12 news stories of which two each were credited to Bhasha, Varta, HS and AFP. The rest came from PK. Page 11 had news about bullion and commodities and three news stories credited one each to PK, NNS and Bhasha.

Page 12 had three features on the weekly market review by NNS. Thus, the issue had 51 hard news stories of which 32 were credited to various news agencies. Of these, 12 were taken from Bhasha wires, 12 from Varta and five from Hindusthan Samachar.

Punjab Kesari, Delhi, Tuesday, January 2, 1990: As usual, the front page had two features and 21 news briefs including a box item by Varta from Moscow saying *Pachas saal baad Girijaghar ka ghanta bajaa.* Bhasha's news from Guruvayur saying *Krishna to hathi bheint* was also a box item. The break-up of the news stories was as follows: seven attributed to Varta, six to Bhasha, three to Reuters and two each to AFP and AP. Page 2 had nine stories of which two were credited to Bhasha, three to Varta and one to IANS while the rest were from PK. Page 3 had 10 news items of which four were shared between Varta and Bhasha, one was credited to Varta alone and the rest were attributed to PK.

Page 4 was the editorial page while Page 5 had seven news stories of which three each were credited to Bhasha and Varta and one to HS. Page 6 carried 17 brief news stories from the world of sports and commodities including news from Delhi. Of these, four were credited to Bhasha, six to Varta, three to HS and the rest to PK. Page 7 carried sponsored features while Page 8 had 13 news stories of which six were credited to Bhasha, two to Varta and five to HS. The issue had a total of 79 news stories of which 64 were credited to various national and international news agencies that included 59 taken from Bhasha, Varta and HS wires. Of these, 23 were taken from Bhasha wires, 24 from Varta and 12 from HS.

Punjab Kesari, Delhi, Wednesday, January 3, 1990: True to its colours, this edition of Punjab Kesari had interesting articles, short stories and book review on its front page. Page 2 had 17 news stories along with cartoon strip on Mandrake. Of these, seven were credited to Bhasha, five to Varta and the rest to PK. Page 3 had 13 news stories of which two were credited to PK while the rest were taken from various news agencies such as two from Reuters, four from Bhasha, three from Varta and two from HS. Page 4 was the editorial page and had 11 news stories of which two were credited to Bhasha, three to Varta, two each to AFP and AP and one to PK.

Page 5 had news from stocks and shares as well as 11 news stories of which four were filed by PK staffers and the rest came from news agencies–three from Bhasha, two from Varta and two from HS. Page 6 had 20 news stories of which six were from PK, two from AP, six from Varta, four from Bhasha and two from HS. Page 7 gave commodity and share prices along with 13 stories of which two were credited to Bhasha, four to Varta, one each to DPA and PK and five to NNS. Page 8 had 17 news stories of which five were taken from Bhasha, seven from Varta and one each from Kyodo, Reuters, AP, AFP and IANS. This edition had a total of 102 news stories of which 77 were taken from various news agencies. Of these, six were attributed to Hindusthan Samachar, 30 to Varta and 27 to Bhasha.

Punjab Kesari, Delhi, Thursday, January 4, 1990: The front page had three human interest features along with advertisements. Page 2 carried classified ads along with five news stories attributed two each to Bhasha and Varta and one to HS. Page 3 had 14 news stories of which three were filed by PK staffers while the rest were shared between Bhasha, Varta and HS. Page 4 carried the editorial contents while Page 5 had thirteen news stories of which five were credited to Bhasha, four to Varta and two to HS. Page 6 had 23 news stories–eight.

From Bhasha, six from Varta, two from HS, one each from Reuters and AP and the rest by PK. Page 7 had stocks and shares index and commodity prices along with 14 news stories of which two were credited to Bhasha, three to Varta, one to HS and the rest to NNS. Page 8 had 21 news stories from the world sports and city news of which 10 were filed by PK while five each were credited to Bhasha and Varta and one to HS. The edition had four pages of entertainment as well. Thus, this issue had a total of 93 news stories of which 61 were taken from various news agencies. Of these, 26 were credited to Bhasha, 23 to Varta and nine to Hindusthan Samachar.

Table 8.2: Number of News Agency Stories Appearing in Punjab Kesari in the First Week of January 1990

Date	Total Number of News Stories	News Agency stories	Stories from PTI, UNI and HS
January 1, 1990	51	32	29
January 2, 1990	79	64	59
January 3, 1990	102	77	63
January 4, 1990	90	61	58
January 5, 1990	84	60	37
January 6, 1990	85	73	55
January 7, 1990	54	45	42

Punjab Kesari, Delhi, Friday, January 5, 1990: The front page had three features along with six news stories credited one each to Bhasha and PK and four to Varta. Page 2 had five news stories of which three came from Bhasha files and two from Varta. Page 3 had 20 news stories from around the world of which seven came from Bhasha, eight from Varta, three from PK and one each from AP and AFP. Page 4 carried the editorial while Page 5 had eight news stories of which one came from Bhasha and two from Varta. The rest were filed by PK from Delhi. Page 6 carried 10 sports news stories along with classified advertisements.

Of the stories, two each came from Bhasha, Varta, AP and PK. Page 7 carried 15 commodity news and share price stories of which five each were attributed to Bhasha, Varta and NNS. Page 8 had 17 news stories of which five were credited to Bhasha, six to Varta and three each to HS and PK. The issue had a total of 84 news stories of which 60 came from various news agencies. Of these, 24 were taken from Bhasha, 28 from Varta and eight from Hindusthan Samachar.

Punjab Kesari, Delhi, Saturday, January 6, 1990: The

front page of this edition had four miscellaneous articles and four news stories credited two to Bhasha and one each to Varta and AP. Page 2 carried four news stories credited to Bhasha while Page 3 had 18 news stories of which six came from Bhasha files, nine from Varta and three from HS. Page 4 carried four news stories–two from Bhasha and one each from Varta and DPA. Page 5 had eight news stories of which two each were credited to Bhasha and Varta and one each to HS, PK, NNS and AP. Page 6 had 23 sports news stories of which five came from PK and the rest from various news agencies such as Bhasha, Varta, HS, Reuters, AP, AFP and DPA. Page 7 had 11 news stories of which five were shared between Bhasha and Varta while two each came from HS, Reuters and AP. Page 8 had 12 news stories of which eight were credited to Bhasha and one each to Varta, HS, AP and DPA. Thus, the issue had a total of 85 news stories of which 73 came from various news agencies. Their break-up was as follows: 31 from Bhasha, 20 from Varta and four from Hindusthan Samachar.

Punjab Kesari, Delhi, Sunday, January 7, 1990: The front page had colourful display of entertainment features from the world of cinema and Page 2 was full of classifieds. Page 3 had 11 news stories of which three each were credited to Bhasha and PK while five were attributed to Varta. Page 4 contained editorials along with 14 news stories–five taken from Bhasha, four from Varta and one each from AP and AFP.

Page 5 had eight news items of which three came from Bhasha, two from Varta and one each from HS, PK and AP. Page 6 carried commercial advertisements. Page 7 carried news and information about commodity/market and had four specific news stories credited two to NNS and one each to Bhasha and Varta. Page 8 had 17 news stories–nine from Bhasha, three from Varta, four from HS and one from PK. The issue also had a four-page special Sunday supplement called 'Ravivaariiya'. Thus, this Sunday edition of the first week of the New Year had only 54 news stories of which 45 were taken from various news agencies. Of these, 42 were taken from leading domestic news agencies–21 from Bhasha, 15 from Varta and six from Hindusthan Samachar.

Punjab Kesari (1995)

Punjab Kesari, Delhi, Sunday, January 1, 1995: The 22-page edition of Punjab Kesari kept its readers happy by following the same old trend of providing entertainment news along with colourful pictures of Bollywood starlets in the first page itself. The first two columns carried column called *Cine Jharokha.* The hard news for which a newspaper derives its name and meaning starts from column three with main political news stories of the day. For example, *Rao ke inkaar par Tiwari in adhyaksha pad choda; Mantriparishad dwara Arjun ke aarop puri tarah khariz.*

Of these political stories, five were picked up from Bhasha and three from Varta. Page 2 carried four stories from Grozni by AP, Bhopal from Bhasha and PK stories from Delhi and Haryana. Page 3 carried the editorial page called *Sampadkiiya.* Page 4 had seven stories–three each from Bhasha and Varta and one from PK staffers along with three pictures by PK. Page 5 again had eight stories of which two each were carried from Bhasha and Varta and the rest by PK. Page 6 carried uncredited business and commodity news while Page 7 had nine news stories of which two were credited to Bhasha, one to Varta and six to National News Service. Page 8 carried commercial advertisements. Page 9 carried 17 news stories from mainly around Delhi like Modi Nagar, Gurgaon, Ghaziabad.

Of these, only three were credited to Bhasha and one to AFP from Islamabad. Page nos. 10 and 11 carried advertisements while Page 12 had 18 news stories credited three each to Bhasha, HS, Reuters, AFP and six to Varta. Page 13 had three stories taken each from AP, Varta and PK and rest of the page carried advertisements. Page 14 had 12 news stories of which one was credited to AFP, two each to Reuters and AP, three to Bhasha and five to Varta. The edition also had an eight page supplement of which two pages were devoted to entertainment news on the occasion of New Year and the last page was meant for children. The remaining pages were sponsored and carried advertisements.

Punjab Kesari, Delhi, Monday, January 2, 1995: The 12-page edition priced at ₹ 2 could be called the advertisement special as its every page carried the major share of advertisements and advertisements alone with bits of news stories here and there. In all the, issue carried 26 news stories of which five were taken from Bhasha, four from Varta, three from HS, three each from AP and Reuters and the rest from PK. The main headlines included: *Uttar Bharat mein karake ki thand; Bihar chunav sthagit ho sakte hain: Chunav Aayog; ISRO jasoosi kaand: Sandigdha vyaktiyon ke khilaf koi surag nahin mila;* and *Rao ke khilaf muhim tej.*

Punjab Kesari, Delhi, Tuesday, January 3, 1995: The edition also had 12 pages of which the first page was devoted to human interest features and Bollywood news. Page 2 carried five main political news stories of which two were credited to Bhasha and three to Varta. Page 3 carried the editorial page while Page 4 had nine stories–two each from Bhasha and Varta, one each from HS and AP and the rest by PK. Page 5 and six carried advertisements as did Page nos. 9 and 10. Page 7 had business and commodity news while page carried medley of news from around the world credited three each to Reuters and AP, two to AFP and UPI and one each to Bhasha, Varta and HS. Page 11 had 12 stories from in and around Delhi by PK staffers while page 12 again carried human interest features.

Punjab Kesari, Delhi, Wednesday, January 4, 1995: As usual, the front page carried human interest features while Page 2 had 17 news stories of which six were taken from Bhasha and four from Varta and the rest by PK. The stories originated from as far as Ahmedabad and Dhaka and Mewalamaharajpur in Faridabad. Page 3 had 21 stories of which 8 each were taken from Bhasha and Varta, 4 from HS and the rest were filed by PK. Page 4 carried the editorial page while Page 5 had 17 news stories of which one each were credited to Bhasha, Varta and HS while the rest were credited to PK. Page nos. six and seven were devoted to business and finance and 18 stories in total.

Table 8.3 Number of News Agency Stories Appearing in Punjab Kesari in the First Week of January 1995

Date	Total Number of News Stories	News agency Stories	Stories from PTI, UNI and HS
January 1, 1995	102	57	43
January 2, 1995	56	28	22
January 3, 1995	77	24	13
January 4, 1995	143	82	62
January 5, 1995	96	30	23
January 6, 1995	84	24	16
January 7, 1995	103	69	58

Page 8 had 13 stories of which four were taken from Bhasha and two from Varta while the rest came from PK. Page 9 had 18 stories of six were credited to Bhasha, five to Varta, two each to AP and AFP and three to Reuters. Page 10 had 14 news stories of which four were taken from Bhasha and one from Varta while the rest came from PK. Page 11 had 16 sports news stories of which two were taken from Bhasha and Reuters, four each from Varta, AP and AFP. Page 12 had nine stories taken one each from Bhasha, Varta, AFP and Reuters and the rest from PK. It also carried standard features like Doordarshan Schedule, Today's events and Astro column.

Punjab Kesari, Delhi, Thursday, January 5, 1995: The front page, as usual carried human interest features on subjects like religion and spirituality with coloured pictures of various deities and saints. Page 2 had a sprinkling of soft and hard news such as *Aarthik sudhar nahin rukenge: Rao; England ke videsh manti Bharat daure par* and *Bihar chunav sthagit* along with advertisements. Page 3 carried the editorial column along with guest article. Page 5 again had a medley of news stories numbering 15 of which five were credited to Bhasha and two each to Varta and HS.

The rest were filed by PK staffers from in and around Delhi. Page nos. six and seven carried business and corporate news along with commodity prices. Page 8 had foreign news from around the world of which 3 were filed by Bhasha, 4 by Varta, 2 each by AP, Reuters and AFP. Page 9 had 11 sports stories mainly filed by PK staffers and two by AFP. It also carried an AP picture.

Punjab Kesari, Delhi, Friday, January 6, 1995: *Jitendra Prasad UPCC ke naye adhyaksha bane; Rai Arjun ke paksha mein bole* and *Bhartiya bazaar nivesh ke liye upayukt* - were some of the main political headlines of this issue. Page 2 had eight stories of which three were credited to Bhasha, one each to Varta and HS and the rest to PK. Page 3 carried the editorial content while Page 4 had a medley of news stories by PK staffers from in and around Delhi. Page 5 had again had 11 stories from across the nation of which four were credited to Bhasha, three to Varta and four to HS.

Page 6 and seven carried business and financial news as well as commodity prices. Page 8 and nine carried advertisements while page 10 and 11 had sports news stories numbering 18 of which four were taken from Reuters, three each from AP and AFP while the rest were PK in-house contribution. Page 12 again had a sprinkling of advertisements, human interest features and astro column.

Punjab Kesari, Delhi, Saturday, January 7, 1995: The Saturday edition had 14 pages and a four page sponsored supplement. The front page was, as usual colourful, with interesting serialized stories and articles on Hindi films. Page 2 had 17 news stories of these, 7 were credited to Bhasha, 5 to Varta and the rest to PK. Page 3 was the editorial page while Page 4 had 13 news stories of which two were credited to PK while the rest were taken from various news agencies such as two from Reuters, four from Bhasha, three from Varta and two from HS.

The main headlines included *Britani Videsh mantri Bharat yatra par; Japan dwara ek billion dollar ki madad;* and *Ayodhya case mein sarkar ki naa.* Page 5 had 11 news stories of which five were credited to Varta, two each to AFP and AP and one to PK. Page 6 and seven news from stocks and shares as well as 11 business news stories of which four were filed by PK staffers and the rest came from news agencies–3 from Bhasha, 2 from Varta and 2 from HS. Page 8 and 9 had 20 news stories of which 6 were from PK, 2 from AP, 6 from Varta, 4 from Bhasha and 2 from HS. Page 10 and 11 carried advertisements while page 12 carried seven news stories of which two were credited to Bhasha, four to Varta, one to DPA. Page 13 and 14 had 17 news stories of which five were taken from Bhasha, seven from Varta and one each from Kyodo, Reuters, AP, AFP and IANS. The issue had a four page special supplement containing commercial advertisements.

Punjab Kesari (2000)

Punjab Kesari, Delhi, Saturday, January 1, 2000: The hostage crisis of Y2K compelled the newspaper management of Punjab Kesari to use the front page for presenting main news of the day as is done all over the world. For a change, it carried an eight column banner headline: *Teen durdaant aatankvaadiyon ke badle 154 bandhak yatri mukt*–jointly credited to Varta, Bhasha, Reuter and PK correspondent.

It also had a box item entitled: *Sabse achha sauda* credited to Bhasha. In all, it had 10 stories credited one to DPA, two to Reuters, three to Bhasha and four to Varta. Page 2 was the editorial page while Page 3 had 10 news stories of which four were credited to Bhasha and two each to Varta, Reuters and PK. Page 4 had 14 stories from in and around Delhi of which two each were credited to PTI and UNI. The rest were filed by PK staffers. Page 5 also carried seven news stories from Delhi of which one was credited to Bhasha.

Page 6 carried five business and commodity news of which two each were credited to Bhasha and NNS while one to

Varta. Page 7 had three news stories of which two were credited to Varta and one to PK. The rest of the page carried classified advertisements. Page 8 had six stories from the share market while Page 9 was sponsored. Page 10 carried five PK stories from neighbouring states of Delhi along with day's events, Doordarshan schedule and Astro column. Page 12 called Parishishta had four foreign stories filed by Reuters, AP, IANS and Bhasha.

Page 13 carried six sports news of which three were filed by Bhasha and Varta while one came from AP. Page 14 had 10 news stories including Bhasha's Beijing story on *Unsuljhe seema vivaad ke bawjood Cheen Bharat ke saath behtar sambandhon ka icchuk.* Page 15 and 16 carried sponsored features while Page 17 carried five PK stories from Haryana. Page 19 carried advertisements while page 20 had eight news stories including two credited to Bhasha and one to IANS. The rest were filed by PK.

Punjab Kesari, Delhi, Sunday, January 2, 2000: Of the 17 stories in the front page, the main carried a four column headline saying *Nai Dilli: Vimaan kand ke liye Pakistan jimmevar; Bharat uske khilaf 'uchit samay par uchit kadam uthayega': Jaswant Singh.* The credit for this story was shared by Bhasha and Varta. Another box item entitled: *Humne jindgi ka sabse bada jokhim uthaya*–was exclusively credited to Bhasha. Another prominent story was *Apharta teen aatankvadiyon ke saath Pakistan pahunche.* This was a two column story shared by various news agencies like PTI, UNI and Reuters.

The break-up of stories was as follows: seven credited to Bhasha, six to Varta and one each to Reuters, DPA, AP and PK. Page 2 was the editorial page while Page 3 carried 16 news stories of which seven were taken from Bhasha and nine from Varta. Page 4 had 20 news stories from in and around Delhi of which one was credited to Bhasha and two to Varta. The rest were filed by PK staffers. Page 5 also had 22 news stories from in and around Delhi of which two each were credited to Bhasha and Varta while one was taken from IANS.

They included a two column Bhasha story saying: *Apharan kaand mein ek ke baad ek galati se koi vikalpa nahin bacha tha.* Page 6 had 15 business news stories along with commodity prices of which two were credited to Bhasha, six to Varta and five to NNS. Page 7 had 24 news stories of which just two were taken from Bhasha and five from Varta. The rest were filed by the growing network of PK staff correspondents from various states. Page 8 carried classified advertisements while Page 9 had 12 news stories of which three came from Bhasha, two from Varta, one each from Reuters, AP and DPA and the remaining from PK. Page 10 had 19 news stories of which two were credited to Bhasha, four to Varta and one to Reuters. Page 11 had 17 sports news stories of which three were taken from Varta, two each from Bhasha, AFP and Reuters and the rest from PK.

Table 8.4: Number of News Agency Stories Appearing in Punjab Kesari in the First Week of January 2000

Date	Total Number of News Stories	News Agency Stories	Stories from PTI, UNI and HS
January 1, 2000	101	43	38
January 2, 2000	93	54	36
January 3, 2000	110	63	44
January 4, 2000	104	40	32
January 5, 2000	106	34	20
January 6, 2000	103	28	17
January 7, 2000	94	36	20

Punjab Kesari, Delhi, Monday, January 3, 2000: The front page carried the weekly column *Parishishta* with human interest features and news about film industry. Page 2 had nine stories including a four column IANS story from New Delhi saying: *Vimaan apharkartaon ke khilaf kanooni karyavahi ki sambhavana nahin ke barabar.* Other stories included Washington datelined story on Clinton visit and a story from Lahore saying *Sarkar aur Sharief ke beech koi samjhota nahin.*

The credit break-up for these nine stories is as such–four by Bhasha, three by Varta and two by IANS. Page 3 had 17 news stories of which three were credited to Bhasha, six to Varta, one each to AP and IANS and six to PK.

They included an eight column Bhasha story from Islamabad saying *Pakistan ke liye mushkil ho raha hai munh chhipana.* Varta also had a New Delhi datelined box item entitled: *Bagal mein chhuri, munh mein Ram Ram.* Page 4 was the editorial page called *Sampaadkiya.* Page 5 had nine stories from in and around Delhi by PK while Page 6 had 10 business news stories credited two to Bhasha and HS and three each to Varta and IANS. Page 7 had 16 corporate news stories of which 10 were credited to PK, one to Bhasha, two to Varta and three to NNS.

It also had three foreign news stories credited two to Reuters and one to DPA. Page 8 had 12 stories from Delhi of which one each was taken from Bhasha and Varta, the rest came from PK. Page 9 had 10 news stories including a four column feature by Varta saying: *Khush hoon kyunki jinda hoon, jyada khushi hoti yadi apharta bhi pakde jate.* Of these, four each were credited to Bhasha and Varta and one each to PK and HS. Page 10 had 13 sports stories of which one was taken from AFP and four each from Reuters, Bhasha and Varta. Page 11 had 11 news stories of which five were credited to Bhasha, three to Varta and one to AFP while two came from PK. Page 12 carried pictures of starlets, human interest features, schedules of events etc.

Punjab Kesari, Delhi, Tuesday, January 4, 2000: *Pakistan ki parmanu bam dagne ki dhamki*–this five column headline of an IANS story from Islamabad was prominently displayed on the front page. This was among the five stories published on this page. The other stories came two each from Bhasha and Varta. Page 2 had 15 news stories of which four each were credited to Bhasha and Varta while the rest came from PK. Page 3 had 14 news stories including a four column IANS story from Washington saying: *Pakistan ke aatankvadi* *hone ke saboot nahin: America.*

The other stories included four each from Bhasha and Varta and three from HS and two from PK. Page 4 was the editorial page while Page 5 carried nine stories from various states by PK. Page 6 and seven carried 17 business news items and commodity prices by PK. Page 8 had 19 stories from in and around Delhi by PK. Page 9 carried advertisements while Page 10 had 11 news stories including a human interest story from Baitul saying *Jamunabai ne teesri shatabdi mein kadam rakha.* Page 11 had 14 news stories of which four came from Reuters, three from AFP and two each from Bhasha and Varta. The stories included a Reuters story from Sydney saying–*Bharat teeno test hara.* Page 12 called Manoranjan had human interest features.

Punjab Kesari, Delhi, Wednesday, January 5, 2000: *Apharta Pak mein hi, Bharat la kar mukaddama chalayenge: Vajpayee (Varta/Bhasha)); Apharit vimaan ko Amritsar se jane dena sabse badi chook: Jethmalani (Varta)* and *Nepal ne jali mudra ke dhandhe mein lipt Pak rajnayik ko nikala (Bhasha)*–these were among the seven main news stories on the front page of this edition. The rest came from PK. Page 2 had eight news stories of which two each were credited to Varta, Bhasha, Reuters and AFP. Page 3 had 12 stories from in and around Delhi by PK while Page 4 carried the editorial contents.

Page 5 had 13 stories from various states of which two came from Bhasha and one each from Varta and HS. The rest were filed by PK. Page 6 and seven carried 17 business and commodity news stories of which four came from Bhasha and two each from Varta and HS and nine from NNS. Page 8 carried advertisements while Page 9 and 10 had 21 sports stories credited five each to Reuters and AFP, one to AP and Bhasha and three to IANS. The rest were uncredited. Page 11 had a medley of 12 news stories by PK while page 12 had religious and other human interest features and columns.

Punjab Kesari, Delhi, Thursday, January 6, 2000: The

front page had news stories including Varta's New Delhi datelined story saying *Fernandis Pakistan prayojit aatankvad ki undekhi ke liye America par barse; Kashmir hathiyane ke liye parmanu yudh ki dhamki de raha hai Pak: George (Varta)* and *Akela Saboor nahin, poora Pak dootavas jaali noto ke dhandhe mein.* Page 2 carried nine stories of which two were credited to Bhasha and one each to AFP and Reuters. The rest came from PK. Page 3 had 14 news stories from in and around by PK; Page 4 carried the editorial content and five had 11 stories from in and around Delhi filed by PK.

Page 6 and seven carried 21 news stories from the world of business and finance including commodity prices and stock index. Page 8 carried advertisements. Page 9 and ten carried 16 sports news stories credited two each to Bhasha and Varta, five to AP and three to Reuters. Page 11 had a medley of nine foreign and domestic news stories of which four were credited to Bhasha, two each to Varta and HS and one to Reuters. Page 12, as usual, contained human interest news and features along with colourful pictures of Bollywood starlets, the Hindi version of Page 3.

Punjab Kesari, Delhi, Friday, January 7, 2000: The main headlines of the front page included *Vimaan apharan ki saajish mein shamil char ISI agent giraftar* and *Desh seemit yudh ke liye tayyar rahe: Gen Malik.* The page also carried a picture of Masood Azhar in Karachi. Page 2 had five news stories related to the Kandhar hijacking plus regular features. Page 3 carried 15 news stories from Delhi and its neighbourhood. Page 4 was the editorial page while Page 5 carried eight news stories from various states credited two each to Bhasha and Varta and the rest to PK.

Page 6 and seven carried business and corporate news including commodity price index and share prices of which five were filed by NNS, two each by Bhasha and Varta and one by Reuters. The rest came from PK staffers. Page 8 carried advertisements while Pages 9 and 10 had 23 sports news stories credited five to Reuters, two each to AP and AFP and one to DPA. The rest came from PK. Page 11 again had a medley of foreign and domestic news of which two came from Bhasha, one from Varta, HS, Reuters, AP, AFP and DPA. The rest came from PK. Page 12 had human interest news and features.

Punjab Kesari (2005)

Punjab Kesari, Delhi, Saturday, January 1, 2005: Post tsunami, all Indian newspapers were full of related news stories. Punjab Kesari was no exception. Its front page had five tsunami related news stories including a five column news jointly credited to Bhasha and Varta saying *Ab jwalamukhi phatne ki ashanka; Kachh for toofan ki chetavani;* and *Andhra ko sau karore ki sahayata, Andaman ke liye rahat dal* both by Varta. For a change, it also carried an editorial column saying: *Alvida 2004, Swagat 2005.* Page 2 called Vividha had a medley of entertainment features along with classified advertisements. Page 3, also entitled Vividha, had seven news stories of which five were taken from Bhasha wires, two from Varta and one from IANS.

Page 4, as usual, was the editorial page and had five stories –two each from Bhasha and PK and one from IANS– alongside the lead articles. Page give called Pradeshik, Aas Paas evam anya gatividhiyan five news stories of which three were credited to Bhasha and two to Varta. Page 5 entitled Sthaniya Mahanagar Kone Kone se had eight stories from in and around Delhi filed by PK staffers. Page 7 carried advertisements while Page 8 called Artha Jagat had news from the world of business and finance including share index and commodity prices. Page 9 called Mahanagar, had 12 news stories from Delhi along with advertisements. Page nos. nine and 10 carried 31 sports news of which 11 were credited to Bhasha, four to Varta, three to AFP, two to Reuters and the rest to PK. Page 12 called Vishwa Darshan had six foreign news stories credited two each to AFP, Bhasha and Reuters.

Punjab Kesari, Delhi, Sunday, January 2, 2005:

Tsunami continued to dominate the news headlines including *Nagapattanam ke rahat shiviro mein afratafri* among the six main news stories on the front page of the issue. Of these, two were credited to Bhasha, one to Varta and the rest to PK. Page 2 had eight news stories of which Bhasha had two, Varta three and PK three stories to their credit. Page 3 called Desh had 15 news stories from all over the country of which seven were credited to Varta, six to Bhasha and two to PK. Page 4 carried the editorial content along with two PK stories while Page 5 called Mahanagar had 20 storied by PK staffers from in and around Delhi.

Likewise, Page nos. 6 and 7 also had 24 more stories from the capital and the surrounding areas. Page 8 called Artha Jagat had 18 news stories from the world of business and finance credited two to AFP, four to IANS, five to Bhasha and six to Varta. Page 9 also called Mahanagar, had 10 news stories emanating from the national capital including one filed by Bhasha. Page nos. 10 and 11 had 32 sports news stories of which four were credited to Reuters, 13 to Bhasha, 10 to Varta, three to AFP and the rest came from PK. Page 12 had nine foreign news stories of which one was credited to AP, two to AFP and three each to Bhasha and Reuters. The stories included an AFP story from Banda Aceh saying *Bhookamp ke jhatko se kaamp raha hai Banda.* The issue also had four pages of classifieds and another four pages of Sunday supplement.

Punjab Kesari, Delhi, Monday, January 3, 2005: *Sena jindagi ko patari par lane mein juti* were among the 11 news headlines and a special editorial on the front page called 'Vishesh Sampadkiya' that began thus:

Tu na ainth madmaati Dilli
Mat phir youn itraati Dilli
Avidit nahi hame teri
Kitni kathor hai chhati Dilli

Of these, three were credited to Bhasha, two to Varta, one each to Reuters and AFP and the remaining to PK. The following Page 2 had five stories–two each picked up from

Bhasha and Varta files and one from PK. Page 3 had 15 news stories under the title Desh-Videsh. Of these, seven were credited to Varta, three to Bhasha, two to AFP and three to PK. Page 4 was the editorial page while Page 5 seven news stories of which two were credited to Bhasha and one each to Varta, AFP, Reuters, IANS and PK.

Page nos. 6 and 7 called 'Sthaniya' had 31 news stories by PK while Page 9 also carried 17 local news stories filed by PK. Page 8 carried 15 stories from the world of business and finance of which eight were taken from IANS wires and two from Varta while the rest were filed by PK staffers.

Page 10 had seven sports news stories of which two were credited to Bhasha and one each to Varta, Reuters, AP, AFP and Tanjug. Page 11 called Atirikta had 27 news stories four were credited to Bhasha, five to Varta, three each to AFP and AP and the rest were filed by PK. Page 12 carried 15 foreign news stories from various parts of the world. They were credited thus: four each to AP and AFP, three to Reuters and two each to Bhasha and Varta. The issue also had four page of 'Som Varta'–a special supplement devoted to Dharma and Adhyatma.

Punjab Kesari, Delhi, Tuesday, January 4, 2005: *Global Trust bank mein bhari golmaal, case darja; CBI ne jaanch shuru ki* was the main headline of the front page of this issue that otherwise carried a total of eight news stories credited equally to Bhasha and Varta.

Page 2 also had eight news stories of which four were credited to Bhasha, three to Varta and one to PK along with classified advertisements. Page 3 called Desh had just one story by PK while the rest of the page only carried revenue generating commercial advertisements that included the bottom split advertisement of Abu Dhabi's Ettihad Airways. Page 4 carried the editorial page and Page 5 also called Desh had 10 news stories including a six column shared story by Bhasha and Varta on tsunami from Chennai, Port Blair and New Delhi.

Table 8.5 Number of News Agency Stories Appearing in Punjab Kesari in the First Week of January 2005

Date	Total Number of News Stories	News Agency Stories	Stories from PTI, UNI and HS
January 1, 2005	97	44	33
January 2, 2005	108	42	31
January 3, 2005	150	70	41
January 4, 2005	121	38	26
January 5, 2005	116	55	41
January 6, 2005	131	60	52
January 7, 2005	144	52	39

Page 6 carried 22 sthaniya or local stories by PK. Likewise, Page 7 had 19 such stories of which only one was credited to Varta. Page 8 carried 11 business and financial news stories along with share index and commodity prices. Of these, two were taken from Bhasha, eight from Varta and one from AP. Page 9 again had 19 stories from Delhi and its neighbourhood under the title Sthaniya. Page nos. 10 and 11 23 sports stories of which six were credited to Bhasha, five to Varta, three to AP, two to Reuters and one to AFP. The rest were credited to PK. Page 12 only carried advertisements. The issue also had four pages of Mangal Varta, a special supplement on Dharma and Adhyatma.

Punjab Kesari, Delhi, Wednesday, January 5, 2005: Bhasha's story from Port Blair on *Car Nicobar mein dobara vayu sena adda nahin* was the five column main headline of the front page that otherwise carried nine news stories of which five were attributed to Bhasha, one each to Varta and HS and two to PK. Likewise, Page 2 had seven news stories of which four were credited to Bhasha, two to Varta and one to HS. Page 3 had a medley of 12 news stories under the title Desh Videsh of which four each came from Bhasha and Varta, two from IANS and one from PK. Page 4 carried four news stories from AP, AFP, IANS and Reuters along with the editorial space.

Page nos. 6, 7 and 9 entitled Sthaniya carried 34 stories

from in and around Delhi while Page 8 carried 16 stories from the world of business and finance of which only one each was credited to Bhasha and Varta. The rest were credited to PK. Page nos. 10 and 11 carried 25 sports stories 11 were credited to Bhasha, three to AP, five to Varta and three to Reuters. The rest came from PK. Among the stories were five column headline saying *Ponting ke dohre shatak se Australia ka vishal score.* The edition also had a four page supplement called Budh Varta that carried three guest articles and Society Jharokha, a human interest feature.

Punjab Kesari, Delhi, Thursday, January 6, 2005: *Bihar mein farar apradhiyon ki suchi Patna High Court talab* from Patna by Bhasha was among nine main news stories on the front page of this issue. Of the remaining stories, three were also credited to Bhasha, two to Varta and one to PK. Page 2 had five PK stories and classified advertisements. Page 3 had seven stories from Desh Videsh of which three were credited to Bhasha and two each to Varta and Reuters.

Page 4 carried the editorial contents along with six news stories credited three to Bhasha, one each to Varta, HS and PK. Page nos. five, six and seven carried 46 local news under the title Sthaniya while Page 8 had 16 business news stories of which five were credited to Bhasha, six to Varta, one each to IANS and Reuters and three to NNS. Page 9 also had 14 stories from in and around Delhi of which three were credited to Bhasha, one to Varta and the rest to PK. Page 10 and 11 had 20 sports news stories of which five were credited to Bhasha, nine to Varta, two each to AFP, Reuters and PK. Page 11 also had a KBK graphic on *Bharat mein tsunami ka prabhav.* Page 12 called Videsh had eight foreign news stories of which four were credited to Bhasha and two each to Varta and Reuters. The edition also had a four page supplement called Manoranjan.

Punjab Kesari, Delhi, Friday, January 7, 2005: Bhasha's *Supreme Court ne hatya mein Shankaracharya ki sanliptata ke thos saboot mange* was among the nine news stories on this page of which four were credited to Bhasha, two to Varta and three to PK. Page 2 called Vividha had six stories by PK while Page 3 had 12 news stories–seven by Bhasha, two by Varta and one each by HS, IANS and PK. Page 4 was the editorial page and also carried to Bhasha stories including one five column news from Islamabad on Indo-Iranian pipeline.

Page nos. five, six, seven and nine carried 52 stories from in and around Delhi by PK while Page 8 had eight business news stories of which one each was credited to Bhasha and Varta while the rest came from PK. Page nos. 10 and 11 had 42 sports stories of which seven came from Bhasha, eight from Varta, three each from AP, AFP and Reuters and the rest from PK. Page 12 carried 12 foreign news stories of which one was credited to Bhasha, four to PTI, three to AP, two to AFP and one each to IANS and Reuters. The edition also had a four page supplement of which two pages were called Shukra Varta and the other two Nayee Rahein and focused on new products and window to the industry.

9

Data Analysis and Interpretation

This chapter analyses various trends visible over a period of 20 years from 1985 to 2005 to test the validity of the hypothesis, i.e. the globalisation has given way to a new trend in Indian news media where the once leading news agencies are steadily losing their traditional hold on daily newspapers and slowly getting marginalised in the process. The news agencies considered for this study are the Press Trust of India, the United News of India and the Hindusthan Samachar and the newspapers are the Times of India, the Tribune, the Statesman, the Hindu and Punjab Kesari.

The Times of India:

Analysis and interpretation of the Times of India from 1985 to 2005.

The Times of India, Bombay (1985): A close examination through content analysis of the newspaper for the week starting from January 1, 1985 to January 7, 1985 has revealed that in the issue of January 1, 1985, the number of stories published stood at 103 of which news agency stories culled from various domestic and foreign news agencies were 39 of which 32 were taken from PTI and UNI wires.

Of these, 24 were PTI stories while 8 came from UNI. Thus the agency stories were just 19.12 percent of the total news stories of which the percentage of PTI and UNI stories were 20.76. Likewise, the January 2, 1985 edition had 149 news stories of which 67 were total news agency stories including 50 from PTI and UNI combine. Of these, 27 were PTI stories while 23 were taken from UNI. In terms of percentage, this stands at 57.7 percent for the total news agency stories and 33.45 percent for PTI and UNI stories. The next day edition of January 3, 1985 had 160 news stories of which 81 were taken from various news agencies including 58 from PTI and UNI. Of these, 27 were attributed to PTI and 31 to UNI. In terms of percentage, it stood at 50.6 percent and 36.25 respectively.

The January 4 edition had 129 news stories of which 50 were attributed to various news agencies (39 percent) including 33 (25.56 percent) from PTI and UNI. Of these, 15 were taken from PTI and 18 from UNI. The January 5 issue had 133 news stories of which 49 (36.85 percent) were taken from various news agencies while 38 (28.57 percent) were attributed to PTI and UNI. Of these, 21 were credited to PTI while 17 to UNI. The January 6 edition had a total of 135 news stories of which 43 (31.85 percent) were taken from various news agencies including 27 (17.77 percent) from PTI and UNI.

Of these, 19 were credited to PTI while 8 to UNI. Likewise, the January 7 issue had a total of 147 news stories of which 51 (34.69 percent) were credited to various news agencies while 35 (23.81 percent) were credited to PTI and UNI. Of these, 17 were attributed to PTI and 18 to UNI. Thus, the average percentage of news agency stories for the aforementioned week was 45.51 percent while that of PTI and UNI stories stood at 33.28 percent.

The main headlines in all the seven issues of 1985 examined were contributed by newspaper's staff correspondents. For instance, the January 1, 1985 edition had an eight-column banner headline saying 'Rajiv and 39 ministers sworn-in'. However, the next important headline was a PTI story saying '8th Lok Sabha formed' along with another significant story about the 'List of Portfolios'. Likewise, a UNI story from Kohima on 'Nagaland seat goes to Congress' along with '20 killed as quake hits Assam' from Guwahati was also well-displayed. Thus, one could see that priority was given to in-house stories as compared to wire stories. However, the wire stories were picked up on the basis of merit and were given due weightage as per their content.

The same trend was visible in other issues as well. For instance, in the January 3 issue, the main headines were contributed by the staffers on stories like Delhi wants Hegde to continue or Government seized of services' woes or MGR will write to governor from Madras. While stories like PTI's Dhawan quits or Apang sworn in as Arunachal CM or Rajya Sabha to meet on January 17 were mainly taken for their sheer news value and were given as little space as possible.

An important point noticed was the kind of treatment given to news features in terms of space and display. As we know, news features are essentially soft news stories that go beyond mere accounts of events and happenings. Unlike the hard news stories that are primarily 'event cantered' and aim at providing the basic information, the soft news stories go beyond the 5 Ws and one H. While the hard news is the mainstay of all three modes of daily journalism–newspapers, radio and television, the importance of features as the essential and often the main ingredient of colourful and picturesque weekend pull-outs, backgrounders and supplements in a daily newspaper is no less significant. Features are often interpretative, give background or play-up human interest and convey the colour of an event.

For example, a PTI feature from Beijing on 'Icons of Shiva, Vishnu found in Chinese town' of Quanzhou in Fujian province of south-east China was better displayed than most other hard news stories from the news agency. This story was not featured alone on along with an AP/PTI picture on the world page. The same trend was visible all through.

The same trend continued in 1990 as well. The agency stories were given due weightage in their selection and display. For instance, in January 1st issue of 1990, out of total 124 news stories, 69 (55.64 percent) were from news agencies and of these, 44 (35.48 percent) were from PTI and UNI. Likewise, the next issue of January 2 had 115 total news stories of which 47 (41 percent) were taken from various wires of which 33 (28.69 percent) were from PTI and UNI. The January 3rd issue had 93 news stories of which 39 (41.93 percent) were taken from various news agencies while 30 (32.25 percent) were credited to PTI and UNI. The January 4 issue had 110 total news stories of which 63 (57.27 percent) were taken from various national and international news agencies while 35 (31.18 percent) were credited to PTI and UNI.

The next issue had 131 total stories of which 38 (29 percent) were from various wire services while 32 (24.42 percent) were taken from PTI and UNI. Likewise, January 6th issue had a total number of 103 news stories of which 40 (38.83 percent) were taken from various news agencies while 30 (29.12 percent) were taken from PTI and UNI. The January 7th issue had a total number of 153 news stories of which 38 (24.83 percent) were taken from various news agencies while 33 (21.56 percent) were taken from PTI and UNI. Thus, the average percentage of news agency stories for the aforementioned week stood at 41.21 while that of PTI and UNI stood at 28.95.

The importance given to news agency stories was most evident from the January 1st issue of 1990. Its front page had 10 news stories and a signed featured. Of these, the main headline 'Document soon on Agriculture policy' and four other stories were credited to PTI while two were taken from DPA and one from AFP. Likewise, the January 6th issue's front page had 10 news stories of which two were credited to PTI and five to UNI and all were well displayed. The page also carried a news analysis on Indian Airlines hits rock bottom by the newspaper staffer.

Thus, the important point to note was that agency stories continued to occupy a place of pride in the news selection and display of daily newspapers notwithstanding its commercial success.

However, from 1990 to 1995, many changes took place that had an important bearing on the news coverage worldwide. The most important change was the creation of worldwide web in 1991 that enabled instant communication around the world. Another important development was the coming into being of World Trade Organisation or WTO, a new multilateral trade body replacing the General Agreement on Tariffs and Trade (GATT) in order to better enforce a global free trade regime.

The WTO brought into being the multilateral trading system along with commercial activities such as trade in services as well as the exchange of ideas in the context of intellectual property protection and investment. The resultant liberlisation, privatization and globalization of world economy in general and Indian economy in particular had a significant impact on the news coverage of newspapers. The extent of this impact can be measured in the overall selection and presentation of news stories, both hard and soft, in daily news papers as they now had many new avenues of news gathering, thanks to the instant connectivity to the worldwide web and the avalanche of information available therein.

All this had a definite bearing on news agency stories in daily news papers. For instance, the 36-page issue of January 1st of 1995 of TOI had a total 35 news stories of which just one (2.85 percent) was taken from PTI in the name of news agencies. The reason for such a small number of news stories was the excessive presence of advertisements and sponsored pages numbering 17 including Sunday review. The next day edition had a total of 114 news stories of which 41 (35.96 percent) were taken from various news agencies while 27 (23.68 percent) were credited to PTI and UNI. January 3rd issue had a total of 117 news stories of which 51 (43.8 percent) were from news agencies and 36 (30.76 percent) from PTI and UNI.

In January 4th issue, there were a total of 82 news stories of which 24 (29.26 percent) were from various news agencies while 21 (25.60 percent) were credited to PTI and UNI. In January 5th issue, the total number of stories was 93 while those taken from news agencies was 21 (22.58 percent) and those from PTI and UNI 10 (10.75 percent). The January 6th edition had a total of 65 news stories of which 21 (32.30 percent) was taken from various news agencies while 16 (24.61 percent) were taken from PTI and UNI. Likewise, the January 7th issue had 120 news stories of which 30 (25 percent) were taken from various national and international news agencies while 16 (13.33 percent) were taken from PTI and UNI. Thus, the average percentage of news agency stories for the aforementioned week stood at 26.98 while that of PTI and UNI was at 18.79.

Likewise, analyses of The Times of India during the first week of 2000 from January 1st to January 7th showed a marked upswing in the stories credited to their own staffers as compared to news agencies whether national or international.

For instance, the January 1st issue had a total of 102 news stories out of which 36 (32.29 percent) were from various news agencies while just 17 (16.66 percent) were from PTI and UNI. Likewise, the next issue had out of 114 news stories, only 41 (35.96 percent) stories credited to news agencies of which 27 (23.68 percent). The January 3rd issue had a total of 102 news stories of which 36 (35.29 percent) were culled from news agencies and 20 (23.68 percent) from PTI and UNI wires.

Similarly, the next day's edition had a total of 120 news stories of which 52 (43.33 percent) were from various news agencies and 21 (17.5 percent) from PTI and UNI. January 5 edition had a total of 92 news stories of which 34 (36.95 percent) were credited to various news agencies while 14 (15.21 percent) were attributed to PTI and UNI. January 6th edition had a total of 99 news stories of which 31 (31.31 percent) were attributed to various news agencies while 13 (13.13 percent) were taken from PTI and UNI. Likewise, January 7th edition had a total of 89 news stories of which 22 (24.71 percent) were credited to various news agencies while 14 (15.73) were attributed to PTI and UNI.

The same trend was visible in the 2005 issue where the percentage of news agencies stories showed a marked decline as also the stories attributed to PTI and UNI. Take a look. Of the total 81 news stories in the January 1st, 2005 edition of

Times of India, Mumbai, just 24 (29.62 percent) were from various news agencies while only 7 (8.64 percent) were from PTI and UNI. The next day edition had a total of 80 news stories of which 11 (13.75 percent) were from various news agencies while just 6 (7.5 percent) were from PTI and UNI.

Likewise, the January 3rd edition had a total of 75 news stories of which 22 (29.33 percent) were from various news agencies and 7 (9.33 percent) were from PTI and UNI. The January 4th edition had a total of 67 news stories of which just 17 (25.37 percent) were from various news agencies while 7 (10.44 percent) were from PTI and UNI. January 5th edition had a total of 69 news stories of which 15 (21.73 percent) were from news agencies while 13 (18.84 percent) were from PTI and UNI. Likewise, the January 6th edition had a total of 67 news stories of which 14 (20.89 percent) were from news agencies while 9 (13.43 percent) were from PTI and UNI. The January 7th edition had a total of 60 news stories of which just 11 (18.33 percent) were from various news agencies while 5 (8.33 percent) were from PTI and UNI.

Thus, the percentage-wise analysis of news agency stories appearing in the Times of India showed a steady downtrend in their number in the time span of 20 years. This trend was visible both in the number of news agency stories in general and stories credited to PTI and UNI, the two national news agencies of India, in particular. This downward trend, as can be seen from the graph, takes a nosedive in the five year period from 1990 to 1995. This was the period when the process of globalization was set into motion around 1991 and together with the effect of worldwide web in instant communication, its impact could be easily felt. For instance, the decline was the lowest at 1995 and from thereon took an upward leap around 2000. This was the time when the Times of India came up with many new editions.

Today it enjoys the largest circulation of 3,433,000 copies daily among all English-language newspapers in the world, across all formats–broadsheet, tabloid, compact, Berliner and

Online. With daily editions coming out from all over India namely Ahmedabad, Bangalore, Bhopal, Bhubaneshwar, Chandigarh, Chennai, Coimbatore, Delhi, Goa, Hubli, Hyderabad, Indore, Jaipur, Kanpur, Kolkata, Lucknow, Mumbai, Mysore, Nagpur, Patna and Pune, The Times of India continues to give an extensive local flavour to its news reporting in its own inimical style.

The Tribune

The trends visible in the west of India in the 20 year time period from 1895 to 2005 were more or less also evident in the north via the leading daily newspaper The Tribune published in English, Hindi and Punjabi. First launched on February 16, 1881 in Lahore a by noted philanthropist Sardar Dyal Singh Majithia, The Tribune is the oldest daily to cover the regions of Punjab, Haryana, Himachal Pradesh and Jammu & Kashmir. Today, it has six editions coming out from Chandigarh, New Delhi, Bhatinda, Jammu, Jalandhar and Dehradun besides two editions namely the Dainik Tribune in Hindi and Punjabi Tribune in Punjab.

The Tribune has been in the forefront of news dissemination since its inception in the pre-independence era. Since then, it has played a major role in complementing the role and function of various foreign and national news agencies particularly the PTI and UNI. This was evident from a close study of its various editions from 1985 to 2005. It showed the mutually beneficial symbiotic relationship between daily newspapers and the news agencies.

For instance, in the 1985 editions examined for content analysis, the percentage of news agency stories stood at 48.21 percent of the total news stories. This was the time when winds of liberalization and accompanying privatization had not touched the Indian media scene. This was the time when print media depended heavily on news agency inputs for its news coverage. This was clearly visible from the fact that the 51.58 percent of news agency stories in the 1990 editions of January

1st to 7th were taken from various news agencies and the number of PTI and UNI news stories grew from 36.64 percent in 1985 to 39.55 percent in 1990.

For example, in the January 2 issue of 1990, of the 10 stories on the front page, four were credited to PTI, one was shared between PTI and UNI while one was attributed to UNI. This was a standard pattern in almost all issues of the daily considered for content analysis thus far. More so, this pattern was not confined to the front page alone. For instance, page 16 had a total of five news stories of which two were credited to PTI and one to DPA while the remaining two were in-house contribution.

However, the decline in news agency stories was evident in the 1995 edition which revealed a downward trend in the percentage of total number of news agency stories in the daily editions of The Tribune. For instance, the average percentage of total number of news agency stories stood at 45.80 as against 51.58 in 1990. Likewise, the average percentage of total number of stories taken from PTI and UNI wires stood at 33.78 which was nearly two percent down from 39.55 percent in 1990.

This trend was further visible in the year 2000 editions where the percentage of total news agency stories plummeted to 32.96 from 45.80 in 1995. Likewise, the number of PTI and UNI stories too dropped to 20.09 percent from 33.78 in 1995. In 2005, further sharp decline was evident when the total number of news agency stories stood at dismal 18.19 percent while the number of PTI and UNI stories went down to 12.90 percent.

This percentage-wise trend is a reflection of the number of news agency stories appearing on the pages of The Tribune from time to time in the aforementioned time period. For instance, the issue of January 1, 1985 carried a total number of 103 stories of which the number of news agency stories, both domestic and international, stood at 48. Of these, 25 came from PTI and UNI. Likewise, the January 2, 1985 edition of

The Tribune had a total of 118 news stories of which 63 were news agency stories of which the number of PTI and UNI stories was 53. In the January 3, 1985 issue, the total number of news stories was 137 of which the news agency stories were 63 while the PTI and UNI stories were 49.

The next day edition of January 4, 1985 had 123 news stories of which 53 were taken from various news agencies including 38 from PTI and UNI. The January 5, 1985 issue had 87 news stories of which 57 came from various news agencies including 52 from PTI and UNI. The following day's issue of January 6, 1985 had a total of 95 news agency stories of which 46 were from various news agencies including 30 from PTI and UNI. The January 7, 1985 issue had a total of 116 news stories of which 40 were taken from news agencies including 34 from PTI and UNI. Thus, the average percentage of total number of news agency stories that appeared in the 1985 edition of The Tribune stood at 48.21 while the percentage of PTI and UNI stories at 36.64 percent.

Despite such high percentage of news agency stories, the front page headlines in The Tribune were found to be a mixed baggage. Unlike Times of India where all major headlines were in-house contribution, the Tribune would give credit to a news agency only when it did not have the same story in its kitty. For instance, the story on the list of ministers in the Rajiv Gandhi cabinet issued by UNI was duly acknowledged while the swearing-in of Rajiv Gandhi that also appeared on the front page of the Chandigarh edition of January 1, 1985, carried a by-line of the daily's special correspondent although both PTI and UNI did a fine job on it. Likewise, a story on speaker entitled 'B.R. Bhagat may be Speaker' appearing in the issue of January 5, 1985, was credited to the special correspondent of The Tribune while 'Sympathy wave' led to debacle: BJP was duly credited to PTI.

Foreign news briefs appearing on the front page remained the hot property of foreign news agency with domestic wire services chipping in here and there. The regional flavour, found in abundance, remained within the ambit of newspaper's reach and access. For example, stories from Patiala, Ludhiana, Jalandhar and other places in the states of Punjab and Haryana were widely covered by the daily itself.

However, this did not in any way affect the daily's dependence on news agency stories. This could be seen from the fact that of the nine stories appearing on the page two of the aforementioned issue, only one story was credited to the daily as its dateline was Jalandhar and it talked about some NIMPA office bearer.

The same trend was visible in the issues of 1990 as well. The news agency stories were give due weightage in their selection and display but not at the cost of their own stories. For instance, the issue of January 1, 1990, had a mixed baggage of major headlines with five of the nine stories being credited to news agencies while the rest coming from their own correspondents. Thus, of the total 82 news stories, 38 were credited to news agencies including 32 from PTI and UNI. In the following day's issue of January 2, of the 97 news stories, 45 were taken from various news agencies including 36 from PTI and UNI.

As regards the headlines, six of the 10 news stories on the front page were credited either to PTI or UNI. The major headlines included Punjab bandh near total, Farm pricing method to change, Bomb blast in the valley and Wijeratne coming on Thursday. The January 3rd issue had a total of 105 news stories of which 48 came from news agencies including 29 from PTI and UNI. The January 4 issue also had 105 news stories of which 62 were credited to various news agencies including 7 from PTI and UNI. The following day's edition had a total of 106 news stories of which 58 were credited to news agencies including 49 from PTI and UNI. The January 6, 1990 issue had a total of 101 news stories of which 57 were credited to news agencies including 42 from PTI and UNI. Interestingly, the January 7 issue also had the same number of 101 news stories of which 53 were credited to various news agencies including 41 from PTI and UNI.

In the meantime, the globalization and its impact on the Indian media scene could be felt in the interregnum of 1990 to 1995. As soon as the realization dawned that the entire global news was available on one platform with the touch of a button thanks to satellite news channels, the traditional rivalry between print and the electronic media too took a new turn. This was the time for the print media to pause and ponder. It was a struggle for survival and only the fittest could win the race. The clock was ticking away.

The Indian print media carried out a random analysis of its strengths, weaknesses, opportunity and threats and hammered out a solution to get out of this morass. Having identified its lacunae and recognized the inherent threat perception that had begun to make its very existence meaningless, it went on to focus on its strengths and opportunities in terms of readership and its reach and access. The resultant emphasis on local news coverage as an answer to growing ambit of globalization of news is often dubbed as Glocalisation which is a hybrid of Glocal+Local.

According to media professionals and experts, glocalisation was the new found solution that rescued the print media particularly the daily newspapers from the imminent onslaught of breaking news phenomenon of the electronic media that had virtually rendered the existence of daily morningers almost pointless. [1]

Aided by growing spread of literacy in the country, the newspapers resorted to diversification through intense local coverage unavailable on the so called 24-hour satellite news channels. The Tribune too joined the bandwagon and started giving more emphasis to regional news in its pages to meet the challenge of globalization. [2] The 1995 editions of The Tribune amply bore this fact out.

For instance, the January 1, 1995 issue of the Chandigarh edition of The Tribune had a new page called 'Chandigarh and Around' that had a barrage of stories from in and around the state capital. Also, it had added another page called the 'Business Tribune' focusing on the country's burgeoning corporate sector under the new trade regime. These changes, did not, in any way, affected the routine flow of news agency stories into the newspaper columns. For instance, the percentage of news agency stories appearing in the pages of The Tribune in 1995 remained more or less same at 54.65 as compared to 54.33 in 1990. However, the percentage of PTI and UNI stories dipped to 39.20 percent as compared to 43.47 percent in 1990. This was primarily due to growing local coverage by the daily of the areas in and around Chandigarh where the PTI or UNI network was either weak or unavailable.

The additional six-page supplement of the Chandigarh Tribune in the Chandigarh edition of the Tribune in January 2000 opened a new window on Chandigarh and its surrounding areas in Haryana and Himachal Pradesh. It now covered areas like SAS Nagar, Panchkula, Patiala, Ambala, Rajpura, Kalka, Dera Bassi, Kurali, Parwanoo, Kharan, Zirakpur, Baddi, Barotiwala and Lalru. This almost added 50 to 60 news stories to its pages and lured equal if not more number of advertisers to help consolidate the newspaper's financial position.

This was in addition to already existing three pages on Punjab, Haryana and Himachal besides two pages on the rest of the region that included the District Diary. These pages were solely dedicated to big political news and relates issues while the Chandigarh Tribune focused on the nitty gritty of local coverage.

This trend further affected the number of news agency stories in general and PTI and UNI stories in particular in the 2000k issues of The Tribune. For example, the January 1, 2000 issue had a total of 163 news stories of which only 44 were credited to news agencies including 34 to PTI and UNI at 20.85 percent. Likewise, of the total 169 stories in the next day's issue, only 63 were credited news agencies including 44 to PTI and UNI at 25.88 percent.

The January 3rd issue had a total of 204 news stories of which only 68 were taken from various news agencies including 56 from PTI and UNI at 27.45 percent. The following issue had a total of 191 news stories including 74 from news agencies of which 53 (27.74 percent) were credited to PTI and UNI. The January 5th issue had a total of 175 news stories including 50 from news agencies of which 32 were taken from PTI and UNI at 18.28 percent of the total. The January 6th issue had a total of 177 news stories of which 51 were credited to various news agencies including 43 from PTI and UNI at 24.29 percent while the January 7th issue had a total of 180 news stories of which 67 were taken from various news agencies including 43 from PTI and UNI at 23.89 percent. This brings the average percentage of news agencies stories in general to 32.96 percent and the PTI and UNI stories together to 20.59 percent of the total.

This sharp downturn did not stop here. The number of news agency stories in the 2005 issues of The Tribune showed further decline as the local news coverage system of the daily got further strengthened. For instance, the January 1st issue had a total of 176 news stories of which 42 (23.86 percent) came from news agencies including 25 from PTI and UNI at 14.20 percent. The January 2nd issue had a total of 184 news stories of which 30 (16.30 percent) were taken from news agencies including 22 (11.96 percent) from PTI and UNI. Likewise, the January 3rd issue had a total of 191 news stories of which 48 (25.13 percent) were taken from news agencies including 32 (12.32 percent) from PTI and UNI.

The following day's issue had three more stories making the total number of news stories 194 including 34 (17.52 percent) from news agencies with 32 (16.49 percent) taken from PTI and UNI. The January 5th issue had a total of 181 news stories including 23 (12.71 percent) from news agencies of which 16 (8.84 percent) were credited to PTI and UNI. January 6th issue had a total of 176 news stories of which 28 (15.91 percent) were taken from news agencies of which 17

(9.66 percent) were taken from PTI and UNI. The January 7th issue had a total of 177 news stories of which 38 (21.47 percent) were credited to various news agencies including 22 (12.43 percent) from PTI and UNI. Thus, a constant decline in news agency stories over the years was noticed in The Tribune as well.

The Statesman

Very much like The Times of India and The Tribune which showed a steady downtrend with regard to news agency stories, the research findings of The Statesman, one of the oldest English dailies in the country known for its anti-establishment stance, showed a similar pattern. Despite its heavy dependence on the news agency news stories for its daily reporting of national and international affairs, The Statesman could not remain untouched by the winds of change sweeping the Indian media scene.

This was clear from the percentage-wise data generated through content analysis of its various issues from 1985 to 2005. For instance, in 1985, the percentage of total number of news agency stories used by it stood at 56.39 percent while in 1990 it stood at 54.33 percent. In 1995, this figure stood more or less same at 54.65 percent while in the year 2000, it went down to 44.27 percent. In 2005, it hovered around 43.81 percent. The percentage of total number of PTI and UNI stories reported in this period plummeted from 42.26 percent in 1985 to 22.99 percent in 2005. In between it hovered at 39.20 percent in 1995 to come down at 30.37 percent in 2000.

A detailed analysis of this data further clarifies the point. For instance, of the 78 news stories published in the January 1st issue of 1985, 37 were credited to news agencies of which 27 were taken from PTI and UNI. Percentage-wise this works out to be 47.43 percent for the news agency stories and 34.61 percent for the combined total of PTI and UNI stories. The January 2nd issue in which 32 of the 83 stories were taken from news agencies including 14 from PTI and UNI, the percentage of news agency stories stood at 38.55 percent while that of PTI and UNI stories at 16.86.

Likewise, the next day's issue had a total of 98 news stories of which 54 (55.10 percent) were credited to various news agencies while just 14 i.e. 16.86 percent was taken from PTI and UNI. In January 4th issue this percentage stood at 53.84 and 40.38 respectively. The following day's issue had a total number of 104 news stories of which 56 or 53.84 percent stories were credited to various news agencies including 47 i.e. 47.96 percent to PTI and UNI. The January 5th issue had a total number of 103 news stories of which 70 or 67.96 percent were credited to various news agencies including 56 i.e. 54.37 percent to PTI and UNI. In January 6th issue, the total number of stories were 108 of which 82 came from various news agencies including 60 from PTI and UNI. Percentage-wise this figure stood at 75.93 percent and 55.56 percent respectively. The January 7th issue had a total number of 102 news stories of which 57 i.e. 55.88 percent were credited to various news agencies including 47 i.e. 46.07 percent from UNI and PTI.

However, true to its character, almost all the main news stories that required astute political analysis in all the seven issue of 1985 examined for the study were in-house contribution. For instance, the January 1, 1985 edition of The Statesman had an eight-column banner headline in bold letters saying 'New union ministry sworn in'. The story had two more headlines of decreasing boldnewss saying Pranab, Ghani Khan and Kaushal dropped/Bansi Lal, Arun Nehru, Pant and Scindia in. The other such stories included ADMK is seeking Delhi's advice and Janata chief to retain post.

However, due care was taken in the selection and presentation of news agency stories which were essentially picked up on the basis of their merit and given necessary treatment. For instance, the UNI story from Shillong saying Earthquake kills 16 in Assam was given a two-column display on the right upper corner of the front page. [3] Likewise, the front page of the January 7, 1985 edition had a two-column stepped headline of a story from Washington saying 'Geneva talks to seek a starting point.

This story filed by special correspondent Warren Unna discussed the resumption of talks between the USA and Soviet Union on nuclear disarmament. Thus, despite its financial constraints, The Statesman managed to provide an inside view of all the major national and international issues, events and affairs for the benefit of its discerning readers that included policy and opinion makers as well as keen observers of Indian polity and current affairs. So far, its objective and no holds bar reporting has gone down very well with critics and analysts alike. For instance, the January 1, 1990 issue had a special box item by M.L. Kotru urging 'Drastic action needed in J&K'. The importance given to this kind of incisive news reporting remains the unique selling proposition of The Statesman.

At the same time, The Statesman has also displayed a marked propensity towards news featurization which, according to Keith Flory [4], was a direct result of intense localization of news. While dailies like The Tribune could very well afford to experiment and add supplements like the Chandigarh Tribune to enhance their regional coverage to tackle the impact of globalization on news media, newspapers like The Statesman could ill-afford to do so. Hence, to retain their readers' interest, the only option left with them was to give news features more and more space to build up their daily stock of soft news as against hard news and more particularly spot news which had become the monopoly of cable and satellite news channels.

Thus, going by these statistics, one can easily surmise that the spirited newspapers like The Statesman are the real users or beneficiaries of national news agency stories primarily because they don't have the financial muscle to support a wide network of staffers and correspondents both within and outside the country to fulfil their obligation towards their readers. Therefore, there mainstay continues to be the agency stories as proven by the research findings.

The Hindu

Content analysis of The Hindu, one of the oldest newspapers of India, over a period of 20 years from 1985 to 2005 revealed how it has managed to remain the leading English daily of the country by virtue of its distinctive style of news presentation and analysis. Unlike many other dailies that have resorted to page three phenomenon to bolster their sagging readership and resorted to 'advertorials' to gain attention and revenue, The Hindu has been steadfast in its puritanic approach towards presentation of news and views. Its strict adherence to a self-imposed code of conduct vis-à-vis news selection and presentation has won it an ever-widening base of loyal readership and the maximum number of advertisers at any given point in time in the entire newspaper industry of the country.

Notwithstanding its pro-left, pro-China and anti-America stance, its gross income touched US$ 40 million in 2010 with an impressive readership of 21.59 lakh [5] next only to the Times of India and Hindustan Times. [6] Currently, it is being published from 14 centres and locations within India. They are: Bangaluru, Chennai, Coimbatore, Delhi, Hubli, Hyderabad, Kochi, Kolkata, Madurai, Mangalore, Thiruvananthapuram, Tiruchirapalli, Vijayawada and Vishakhapatnam.

The Hindu's financial strength and stylistic boldness (it does not, till now, believes in resorting to Page 3 allurements to woo readers) over other newspapers was amply borne out by a close examination of its contents for the week starting from January 1 to 7, 1985. For instance, the 32-page issue of January 1, 1985 priced at less than a rupee at 90 paise only had 12 pages full of advertisements and the remaining 20 pages had a total number of 80 news stories of which 22 or 27.5 percent were taken from various news agencies while 14 were credited to PTI and UNI at 17.5 percent.

Likewise, the 28 page January 2nd issue had again 10 pages devoted to advertisements and the remaining 18 pages had 116 news stories of which 38 or 32.75 percent were credited to news agencies while just 28 or 24.13 percent were credited to PTI and UNI. The January 3rd issue had 95 news stories of which 26 or 27.36 percent were credited to news agencies while 17.89 or 17 were taken from PTI and UNI. The January 4th issue had a total of 109 news stories of which 23 were taken from various news agencies at 21.10 percent and 13 or 11.92 were credited to PTI and UNI. Likewise, the next day's issue had a total of 96 news stories including 17 taken from various news agencies at 17.70 percent while just 10 at 10.41 percent from PTI and UNI.

The January 6th issue had a total number of 85 news stories of which just five or 5.88 percent of the total news content were taken from various news agencies of which just three or 3.53 percent were credited to PTI and UNI. The January 7 issue had total of 77 news stories of which 20 or 25.97 percent were credited to various news agencies including 12 or 15.58 percent taken from PTI and UNI. So, the average percentage of total news agency stories was at 22.60 percent including 14.42 percent.

This low percentage of news agency stories particularly from PTI and UNI in the pages of 1985 issues of The Hindu not only proved its financial supremacy over other newspapers but also the fact that it was just not dependent upon wire services for its news reporting. It had a wide network of reporters and correspondents to cover the entire spectrum of national and international news reporting. Unlike other newspapers, big or small, that were directly downloading news stories from news agency wires, The Hindu was way ahead in its style of news selection and presentation.

This trend could be seen in the subsequent issues of January 1990 as well. The news agency stories were no doubt given due weightage in their selection and display but not at the cost of its own news stories. For instance, the January 1st issue of 1990 had a total of 77 news stories of which 28 (36.36 percent) were taken from news agencies including 17 (22.07

percent) from PTI and UNI. Likewise, the January 2nd issue had a total of 96 news stories including 23 or 22.77 percent of the total from various news agencies including 11 or 10.89 percent from PTI and UNI.

The next day's issue had a total of 117 news stories including 30 or 25.64 percent from news agencies that included 21 or 17.94 percent credited to PTI and UNI. The January 4th issue had a total of 101 news stories that included 28 or 28.28 percent taken from various news agencies including 16.16 percent taken from PTI and UNI while the following day's issue had a total of 137 news stories of which mere 23 or 22.11 percent were taken from news agencies including 16 or 15.38 percent from PTI and UNI. The January 6th issue had a total of 97 news stories including 27 or 27.83 percent from news agencies of which 20 or 20.61 percent were taken from PTI and UNI.

The January 7th issue had a total of 90 news stories of which 12 or 13.33 percent were credited to news agencies including 8 or 8.89 percent taken from PTI and UNI. Thus, the average percentage of news agency stories stood at 25.19 while that of PTI and UNI at 15.99. Interestingly, little difference could be seen in the percentage of news agency stories for the year 1985 and 1990.

In 1995, The Hindu became the first Indian newspaper to offer an online edition. It was a major break-through. Its online edition proved to be a trendsetter and greatly helped the Indian newspaper industry to directly confront the challenge posed by electronic media with its non-stop 24-hour news channels. Thus, with ever-widening reach of computer literacy in urban India, this was a welcome move that enormously helped the print media to compete with its arch-rival–the all pervasive electronic media. It was no mean achievement.

However, this had a telling effect on the selection and presentation of news stories in general and news agency stories in its daily morning edition. Since, the online edition required continuous updating of spot news as well as developing news stories, the daily newspaper became all the more finicky about selecting news agency stories. For instance, for the week starting from January 1st to 7th, 1995, the average percentage of the total news agency stories went down to 19.59 percent while that of PTI and UNI dipped to 14.02 percent from the previous percentage points of 25.19 and 15.99 respectively in 1990. The reason was simple. It had begun to rely all the more on soft news stories and news features as against hard news stories or spot news dished out by news agency wires.

The soft news stories were preferred as they dissected, analysed and interpreted the previous day's news stories, events and issues to provide a new perspective or throw more light on them for the benefit of newspaper readers who expected something new and unusual than what the 24-hour news channels had been continuously dinning in their ears. No wonder, it was a hard task that required more than a straight jacket approach of the type usually seen in reporting a fire accident or writing a crime story. "It needed more meat, more masala and therefore more intellectual labour". [7]. It also required, tie-ups with global news and features syndicates to get news features and articles to provide an exclusive peek into matters of national and international importance.

The seven-column front page story on 'Hostages swapped for three militants' by Harish Khare in the January 1st, 2000, edition of The Hindu proved the point. It was indeed a hard story written as an interpretative narrative to convey the mixed feelings of relief for the freed hostages and distress at surrendering to terrorist demands. This was the general pattern followed through out. Consequently, the news agency stories continued to figure poorly in the issues from January 1 to 7, 2000. The number of news agency stories dipped further to 18.29 percent while that of PTI and UNI stood at 13.24 percent.

Five years down the line, the January 2005 issues of The Hindu diligently followed the same pattern of sparingly using news agency stories. For instance, of the 134 total news stories appearing in the issue of January 1st, 2005, only 23 stories were taken from news agency wires that included 17 from PTI and UNI at a dismal 12.69 percent of the whole. The next day's edition had a total of 109 stories of which 30 including 14 from PTI and UNI were taken from news agencies. In January 3rd issue, there were just 10 stories from UNI and PTI out of 120 total news stories at 8.33 percent.

The January 4th issue had a total of 129 news stories of which 29 at 18.60 percent were credited to various news agencies including 10 or 12.40 percent to PTI and UNI. Likewise, the January 5th issue had a total of 134 news stories of which just 31 or 23.13 percent were credited to various news agencies of which 15 or 11.19 percent were taken from PTI and UNI. The January 6th issue had only 8.63 percent of news stories credited to PTI and UNI out of the total of 139 news stories of which 19 were taken from various wire services. The January 7th issue had out of 147 news stories only 20 credited to PTI and UNI at 13.60 percent. Thus, the average percentage of news agency stories dipped to 12.95 percent while that of PTI and UNI stood at 10.38.

Punjab Kesari

One of the oldest Hindi dailies of India, Punjab Kesari has made a niche for itself in states like Punjab, Haryana, Himachal Pradesh and Jammu-Kashmir. It is still in a process to establish a complete hold over Delhi, Rajasthan, Uttar Pradesh, Uttarakhand, Madhya Pradesh, Bihar, Jharkhand and Chattisgarh. At present it is published simultaneously from Delhi, Jalandhar, Ambala and Jaipur. It comes out in 10 regional editions along with a mushroom growth of various sub-editions. All these editions and sub-editions are meant to provide intensive local coverage from various nodal points in the state/s as part of Hind Samachar Group's wider strategy to establish its sway over the entire Hindi belt of north India by meeting the challenge of globalization head-on.

All through, Punjab Kesari's approach to news selection

and presentation has been a little different from other newspapers. This included its bizarre use of blue-black ink instead of black and an off-beat approach towards the front page. Instead of publishing major news stories of the day, its front page would invariably publish titillating pictures of Bollywood and Hollywood starlets. No wonder, it is so very popular among the not so literate section of society like the neighbourhood chaiwalla and his horde of customers mainly the daily wage earners, car mechanics, vendors, rickshaw pullers or scooter-rickshaw wallahs and their ilk.

At the same time, Punjab Kesari has somehow managed to enjoy considerable goodwill among the educated mainly due to its incisive editorials and pithy comments on the political situation of the day. It could feel the pulse of the nation and connect with the nationalist citizens of the country who had not forgotten the trauma of motherland's tragic vivisection on the eve of independence from the British Raj. The credit for this goes entirely to its patriotic editors two of whom lost their lives during the reign of terror in Punjab.

However, in its approach to news coverage, Punjab Kesari is the proverbial story-teller. Like a compulsive narrator, it has to tell and tell all. Unmindful of the source, its approach to news dissemination has remained the same–share everything you know with your readers no matter from where the story comes. This has been a defining feature of its relationship with various news agencies particularly PTI-Bhasha, UNI-Varta and Hindusthan Samachar or HS. The 20-year period from 1985 to 2005 bears it out.

In the week considered for analysis in 1985, one could see at least 50 percent of the total news stories or at times, one-third of them, taken straight from news agencies. For instance, in the January 1, 1985 issue, 90 of the total 122 news stories credited to various news agencies making it 73.77 percent. In the same proportion, the stories taken from Indian news agencies namely PTI-Bhasha, UNI-Varta and HS stood at 68 percent of the total news stories published in that issue. The

January 2nd issue had 96 of the total 169 news stories credited to news agencies including 92 credited to Indian news wires. Likewise, the January 3rd issue had a total of 169 news stories of which 105 were credited to Indian news agencies.

The January 4th had out 150 news items published 90 were credited to various national and international news agencies including 59 credited to the Indian wire services. The following day's issue had a total of 133 news stories of which 71 were credited to PTI-Bhasha, UNI-Varta and Hindusthan Samachar. Likewise, the January 6th issue had a total of 130 news stories of which 69 including 52 were credited to news agencies. The January 7th issue had 141 news stories of which 48 of the 80 news agency stories were credited to Indian news agencies. Thus, the average percentage of news agency stories for the week considered for 1985 stood at 52.75 percent while that for stories taken from Indian news agencies stood at 50.61 percent.

The same pattern continued in 1990 as well where the average percentage of news agency stories used stood at a whopping 75.38 percent while that of Indian news wires at 63.46 percent of the total news content. For instance, the January 1st issue had a total of 57 news stories of which 32 were credited to various national and international news agencies of which 29 were credited to Indian news agencies. Similarly, the January 2nd issue had a total of 79 news stories of which 59 were credited to PTI, UNI and HS. The January 3rd issue had a total of 102 news stories of which 77 i.e. 75.49 percent were taken from various news agencies.

This included 63 news stories from the Indian news agencies. Likewise, the January 4th issue out of 90 news stories 61 credited to various news agencies that included 58 taken from Indian wires. The January 5th issue had a total of 84 news stories including 60 from various news agencies of which 37 came from Indian ones. Likewise, the January 6th issue had a total of 85 news stories including 73 taken from news agencies i.e. a whopping 85.88 percent of the total news input. Of these, 55 were credited to the Indian news agencies. The January 7th issue of Punjab Kesari had a total of 54 news stories of which 45 i.e. 83.33 percent of the news stories published were credited to various news agencies including 42 or 77.77 percent taken from Indian news agencies.

End Notes

1. H.K. Dua, Editor-in-Chief, The Tribune.
2. Ibid.
3. Xerox Picture.
4. Special Correspondent, The Statesman, Delhi.
5. Indian Readership Survey
6. http://en.wikipedia.org/wiki/The-Hindu.
7. Ms. Kalyani Shankar, Sr. Journalist and Columnist.

10

Conclusions

Globalisation, as a process, dates back to antiquity. The economic, political and cultural processes of globalisation have roots in early history. However, as a widely used critical term, its genesis can be traced to back to mid-1980s when economic reforms began to shape the world economy. India, in its keenness to participate in the globalisation wave, readily went through several structural and policy changes in early 1990s, although the awareness for the need for opening up to world economy had dawned in late 1980s.

Although the on-going process of globalisation has left an indelible mark on every aspect of human life, its most profound impact was felt on the media. Media systems along with their production and dissemination of news and information networks the world over came under its sway. Globalisation of media has resulted in concentration of media ownership through a series of mega mergers into a handful of transnational media corporations (TNMCs) like Time Warner, Sony, Viacom, AT&T/Liberty Media, Disney and Seagram etc. [1] This concentration of media ownership has centralised power amongst media organisations into the hands of a small minority both within states and globally.

Thus, globalisation has redistributed resources within nations to the domestic elite and internationally to the TNMCs. [2] Hence, together with the policies of liberalisation and privatisation, globalisation has created 'a second tier' of corporations with 'national and regional strongholds' or 'to specialise in global niche markets'. [3]

The impact of globalization on Indian media was felt in the interregnum of 1990 to 1995 when a spate of economic reforms opened up the Indian economy to foreign investment and by 2003, media was identified as one of the top five priority sectors for investment. The five-year period from 2000-2005 recorded a dramatic growth of electronic media in the country with over 200 television channels available to subscribers as against just 10 channels a decade or so back. Of these, 25 were dedicated 24-hour news channels. The presence of these news channels was enough to upset the equation between print and electronic media in the country where the mainstay of television news happened to be the daily eight p.m. and nine p.m. news telecast by national television called Doordarshan.

This had a far reaching effect. As soon as the realization dawned that the entire global news was available on one platform with the touch of a button thanks to dedicated news channels, the traditional rivalry between print and the electronic media took a new turn. This was the time for the print media to pause and ponder. It was a struggle for survival and only the fittest could win the race. The clock was ticking away. It was time for the Indian print media to carry out random analysis of its strengths, weaknesses, opportunity and threats and hammer out a solution to get out of this morass.

Having identified its drawbacks, the Indian newspaper industry went on to focus on its strengths and opportunities in terms of readership and its reach and access. The resultant emphasis on local news coverage as against a blizzard of global news was the answer. Thus, combination of global with local or glocalisation was the new found solution that rescued the print media particularly the daily newspapers from the imminent onslaught of breaking news phenomenon of the electronic media that had virtually rendered the existence of daily morningers almost meaningless.

Aided by growing spread of literacy in the country, the newspapers resorted to rapid diversification through intense local coverage unavailable on the so called 24-hour satellite news channels. While dailies like the Times of India and the Hindu were already at it, newspapers like The Tribune too joined the bandwagon and started giving more emphasis to regional news in its pages to meet the challenge of globalization.

The 1995 editions of The Tribune amply bore this fact out. For instance, the January 1, 1995 issue of the Chandigarh edition of The Tribune had a new page called 'Chandigarh and Around' that had a barrage of stories from in and around the state capital. Also, it had added another page called the 'Business Tribune' focusing on the country's burgeoning corporate sector under the new trade regime. These changes, did not, in any way, affect the routine flow of news agency stories into the newspaper columns.

For instance, the percentage of news agency stories appearing in the pages of The Tribune in 1995 remained more or less same at 54.65 as compared to 54.33 in 1990. However, the percentage of PTI and UNI stories dipped to 39.20 percent as compared to 43.47 percent in 1990. This was primarily due to growing local coverage by the daily of the areas in and around Chandigarh where the PTI or UNI network was either weak or unavailable.

This trend was further visible in the year 2000 editions when the percentage of total news agency stories plummeted to 32.96 to 45.80 in 1995. Likewise, the number of PTI and UNI stories too tripped to 20.09 percent from 33.78 in 1995. In 2005, further sharp decline was evident when the total number of news agency stories stood at a dismal 18.19 percent while the number of PTI and UNI stories went down to 12.90 percent.

Not to be left behind, even modest and conservatives newspapers like The Statesman were forced to change their strategy. Given their inability to widen their reporting network or bring out as many more editions as they wanted, it resorted to providing more detailed inside view of all the major national and international issues, events and affairs for the benefit of its discerning readers that included policy and opinion makers. Thus it displayed a marked propensity towards news featurization as direct outcome of intense localisation of news. This was a welcome change.

With an eye on circulation figures and advertisement revenue to widen their readership base, dailies like The Tribune could manage to bring out additional zonal supplements like the Chandigarh Tribune. This was not the case with newspapers like The Statesman that could ill-afford to do so in view of their limited finances. Hence, the only option left before them to retain their readership base was to give more space to soft news in terms of news features and analysis as distinct from spot news which had become the mainstay of cable and satellite news channels.

Since news agency stories are often considered 'bland' and 'straight jacket' due to highly constrained and homogenous nature of their news content, they could find little or no room in this market driven or market-oriented news industry where circulation figures and advertising revenue were taking precedence over the editorial policies and practices. As a result, the conventional pyramid of news journalism with editorial department at the top and commercial interests at the bottom was turned upside down. No wonder then if one finds commercial advertisings and advertorials appearing right in the middle of the editorial space. As a result, the news agency stories known for their agenda setting influence on other media started faring badly in newspaper columns.

This was clearly evident from the analysis of the data painstakingly generated from five newspapers over a 20-year time-frame. The inference drawn indicated a distinct down turn in the usage of news agency stories, particularly the national news agencies like the PTI, UNI and Hindusthan Samachar by Indian newspapers. This decline is clearly visible across the wide spectrum of newspapers picked up on the basis of their representative nature for a pan-Indian perspective. The dailies considered for a simple, descriptive and analytical content analysis through quantitative estimates of their entire news contents before and after the onset of globalization from

1985 to 2005 on a quinquennial basis were–Times of India (Mumbai), The Hindu (Chennai/Delhi), The Tribune (Chandigarh), The Statesman (Kolkata/Delhi)–along with Punjab Kesari, a leading Hindi daily from the north. This decline validates the research hypothesis that globalization has given way to a new trend in Indian news media where the once leading news agencies may lose their hold on daily newspapers in terms of news coverage.

This process of marginalisation of news agency stories from the pages of newspapers coincided with the paradigm shift taken by the Indian print media to meet the challenges of globalisation. This included strategic adaptation to the demands of the liberalised, privatised and globalized media scenario ushered in by economic reforms during 1991-96 and thereafter. Consequently, no effort was spared to consolidate print media's hold on the growing market share. The Indian newspaper industry undertook wide ranging structural changes and technological modifications in the production processes.

Once undertaken, it was now possible to reformat the newspapers by improving their page design, page make-up including coloured mastheads and pages, increased number of pages, appearance of special news and feature supplements each day under different categories. All this was done to widen the readership base and cater to the advertising needs of the large and small business establishments including domestic and foreign enterprises, banks and other financial sector institutions among others.

'All this has resulted in an unprecedented competition among national and regional newspapers to attract the readers both by way of slashing the prices (Samir Jain's–The Times of India formula of fixing price for each day's paper differently) and increasing the number of pages in the form of special daily supplements'. [4] Consequently, the print media took giant strides towards strengthening itself and emerged a winner in the process.

The decline in the news agency stories from the newspaper

columns was aided and abetted by another development. This was the emergence of web journalism in the form of on-line editions of important newspapers. The lead in the cyberspace was taken by none other than the Hindu.

In 1995, The Hindu became the first Indian newspaper to offer an online edition. It was a major break-through. Its online edition proved to be a trendsetter and greatly helped the Indian newspaper industry to directly confront the challenge posed by electronic media with its non-stop 24-hour news channels. Thus, with ever-widening reach of computer literacy in urban India, this was a welcome move that enormously helped the print media to compete with its arch-rival–the all pervasive electronic media. It was a no mean achievement.

However, this had a telling effect on the selection and presentation of news stories in general and news agency stories in particular. Since, the online edition required continuous updating of spot news as also developing stories, the Hindu preferred news stories filed by its own wide network of correspondents over those put out by national wire services. Its gate-keepers showed marked preference for international stories filed by global news agencies like the BBC, AP, AFP and Reuters over those filed by PTI or UNI.

This was clear from a look at the mean percentage of news agency stories in its columns. For instance, for the week starting from January 1st to 7th, 1995, the average percentage of the total news agency stories went down to 19.59 percent while that of PTI and UNI dipped to 14.02 percent from the previous percentage points of 25.19 and 15.99 respectively in 1990. The reason was simple. It had begun to rely all the more on soft news stories and news features as against hard news stories or spot news dished out by news agency wires.

The soft news stories were preferred as they dissected, analysed and interpreted the previous day's news stories, events and issues to provide a new perspective or throw more light on them for the benefit of newspaper readers who expected something new and unusual than what the 24-hour news channels had been continuously dinning in their ears. No wonder, it was a hard task that required more than a straight jacket approach of the type usually seen in reporting a fire accident or writing a crime story. In the words of a well-known columnist, Ms. Kalyani Shankar, it needed more meat, more masala and therefore more intellectual labour.

This also explains why newspapers were tying up with global news and features syndicates like the New York Times Service to get news features and articles to provide an exclusive peek into matters of national and international importance. [5] This further explained as to why news agencies stories, often written on predictable lines, were either rejected or thrown into the bin. And, if at all they were considered, they were used only as backgrounders or for padding up stories filed by their own correspondents.

However, the final blow to news agency stories came in the form of mushroom growth of various zonal editions in the regional editions of dailies like the Punjab Kesari in the Hindi heart land and going on-line with them. Once solely dependent on news agency stories for its news coverage in 1985, Punjab Kesari in 2005 had very little space for them in its growing number of pages, editions and sub-editions. It was speeding away on its own.

This is evident from the declining percentage of news agency stories from 1985 to 2005. For instance, in 1985, the average percentage of news agency stories in general stood at 52.75 while that of PTI, UNI and Hindusthan Samachar or HS stood at 50.61. This figure moved up to 75.38 percent and 63.46 percent in 1990. But plummeted to 38.75 and 34.44 percent respectively in 1995 when the impact of global media began to be felt on the Indian media. In 2000, the mean percentage of news agency stories went up to 41.99 but that of domestic news agency stories tripped to 30.46. This is because by now the local news coverage had begun with full vigour and only international news from foreign wire services were used for publishing. This pattern was maintained in 2005 also when the mean of total news agency stories stood at 41.66 percent while that of national news agency stay put at 30.52 percent.

Thus, Punjab Kesari with all its on-line editions or e-papers, had managed to transcend the barrier of time, space and speed to reach its readers worldwide. All this was part of the original paradigm shift in news coverage to meet the challenge of globalization head-on. So far, this strategy had paid rich dividends. The platform provided by these regional editions for advertisers had proved a very lucrative bargain for the newspaper. It resulted in an ever-widening readership base for the daily. Some therefore argue that readership base has encouraged advertisers and not vice versa. Somehow, notwithstanding this egg and hen debate as to what came first, the fact of the matter is that today Punjab Kesari is reaping rich harvest from its new strategy of intensive local news coverage.

For instance, the 12-page Punjab edition of Punjab Kesari published from Jalandhar for the last 41 years today has 11 sub-editions being published from various towns and cities of the state. They include the Amritsar and Ludhiana editions comprising additional eight pages each entitled Amritsar Kesari and Ludhiana Kesari respectively along with four page editions being published from Kapurthala, Ropar, Hoshiarpur, Gurdaspur, Moga, Firozpur, Sangroor, Bhatinda and Patiala in Punjab. They are entitled: Kapurthala Kesari, Ropar Kesari, Hoshiarpur Kesari, Gurdaspur Kesari, Firozpur Kesari, Sangroor Kesari, Bhatinda Kesari and Patiala Kesari. These pages provide intensive local news to the readers at no extra cost and are delivered along with the main Punjab edition. Alongside news, these pages provide excellent opportunity to advertisers and are a good source of revenue for the newspaper as well.

Similarly, the 12-page Himachal Pradesh edition has eight zonal being published simultaneously from Bilaspur, Shimla, Hamirpur, Mandi, Chamba, Kangra, Una and Sirmaur. These regional centres bring out four pages each to be tagged along the main edition. Similarly, the 12-page Haryana edition being published from Ambala has 15 zonal editions getting published from Bhiwani, Jind, Kaithal, Kurukshetra, Panipat, Rohtak, Sirsa, Yamunanagar, Fatehabad, Gurgaon, Hissar, Karnal, Sonipat and Faridabad. All these editions cover the Haryana state in minute detail. For instance, the physical distance between Sonipat and Panipat is hardly 50 kms.

However, both these towns have separate editions called the Sonipat Kesari and Panipat Kesari respectively. While Sonepat is located just on the outskirts of Delhi, Panipat is famous for not just for its historic battles, but also for being a leading textile hub of the country. Their separate editions thus provide intense local coverage of these townships to make the readers abreast of their neighbourhood along with national and international news from the world of politics, sports, science, entertainment and society in general.

The 12-page Jammu-Kashmir edition also has two separate four page zonal editions called the Jammu Kesari and Kashmir Kesari. Interestingly, both of them are published in Jammu but are distributed as per there requirement along with the main edition to the readers in Jammu and Kashmir regions of the state daily. Likewise, the 10-page main edition of Uttrakhand Punjab Kesari has six zonal editions covering areas like Dehradun, Mussorie, Haridwar and Rishikesh; Roorkie, Rudra Prayag and Shri Nagar; Joshi Math, Kotdwar, Pauri Garhwal; Nainital, Haldwani, Almora and Rani Khet; and Ram Nagar, Udham Singh Nagar, Kharima and Champawat.

Its UP edition called the Uttar Pradesh Punjab Kesari covers various towns and cities like Lucknow, Banaras, Moradabad, Rampur, Bareilly, Badayun, Bijnaur, Agra, Kanshiramnagar, Ghazipur, Khurja, Dehradoon, Saharanpur, Aligarh, Hathras, Bulandshahar, Firozabad, Muzaffarnagar, Hapur and Meerut. It also has a separate Noida edition to cover adjoining areas like Meerut, Modinagar, Greater Noida and Noida.

However, this phenomenon is not confined to Hindi

heartland alone. Big newspapers like the Times of India, Hindustan Times and the Hindu are setting new record both in terms of circulation figures and gross revenue generated through advertisements. The Times of India which enjoys a circulation of over 2.14 million and is read by over 7.4 million peoples is published from eight centres across the country. Its electronic edition is one of the most popular on-line editions in the world accessed by millions everyday. It is published by India's largest media group, Benett, Coleman & Co. Ltd. This company along with its other group companies is more popularly known as The Times Group that also publishes The Economic Times, the Navbharat Times and the Maharashtra Times. It has also forayed into electronic media and runs a leading news channel, Times Now.

Likewise, The Hindu, with a circulation of 1.45 million, is the third largest circulated English daily in India after The Times of India and The Hindustan Times. Headquartered in Chennai, it's the largest newspaper in south India and is published from 13 locations. It is known to be the best pay master in the print media so far. Other smaller newspapers too are expanding including the Tribune which is now being published from six centres and also has an on-line edition.

Their success proves the point that globalisation has indeed created a second tier of corporations with national and regional strongholds. This concentration of media ownership into the hands of a small minority of domestic elites within states in response to the threat posed by concentration of international media conglomerates globally is a major development with far reaching consequences for journalism and mass communications in the days to come.

Thus, our research work has shown a shrinking presence of once leading news agencies like the PTI and UNI in newspapers despite their growing number of pages and editions. This inverse proportion of news agency stories with newspaper expansion is indicative of rapid commercialisation and commodifaction of news in what some communication scholars like Leslie Sklair called the culture-ideology of consumerism.

The natural response of news agencies to these developments has been one of caution. Afraid of losing revenue as a result of their shrinking subscriber base, the news agencies particularly the affluent ones like the PTI took some drastic measures to off-set the negative impact of growing consumerism in newspaper industry. Since news agencies are only bulk suppliers of news and do not publish any newspaper, they had to tread cautiously to retain their market share. And if need be, step into new frontiers like advertising on its web site to earn additional revenue.

According to PTI sources, PTI could manage to steer clear of this crisis on account of its shrewd business strategy as it had already foreseen the fall out of media globalisation in the days to come. The strategy took into account factors like content creation and content delivery on the one had and revised subscription rates as well as advertisement tariff on the other.

By going on internet in March 1999 on the occasion of its Golden Jubilee, PTI had bravely stemmed the onslaught of 24-news channels controlled by global media conglomerates by providing all its major services like PTI-Mag, PTI-Graphics, PTI-Science Service on the net. By September 2003, when the winds of globalisation were blowing hot and cold, it had launched its internet delivery of news and photo services to make up for the losses incurred on the newspaper front.

Since news agencies are the original and therefore more reliable producers of news, PTI like Reuters, AP, AFP and BBC can now easily by-pass the intermediary processors of news or so called 'news aggregators' like Yahoo and Google News in cyberspace to reach mass news audience directly. [6] Since online news needs to be continuously updated, the other news portals floated by almost major newspapers like the www.hindustantimes.com or www.IBNlive.com are more than willing to subscribe to its online service as it saves them labour and revenue. They can thus get quality service at a reasonable cost. Thus PTI and Bhasha's loss in the newspaper columns is more than made up by its online service.

Also, the detour made by PTI in terms of carrying advertisements and providing entertainment news with an eye on Page 3 phenomenon in newspapers is also paying rich dividends with its annual turnover touching somewhere between ₹ 2.5 and ₹ 5 crore. Today, any one can access PTI online by becoming a subscriber–be it an individual or a news aggregator or an advertiser.

Thus, PTI could manage to steer clear of this challenge and come out a winner in this race. But how about smaller and not so fortunate news agencies like the UNI or Hindustan Samachar. As against PTI's privileged position in terms of monetary resources and bigger network of journalists and correspondents within India, these less privileged agencies could not rise to the occasion to meet the challenge head on.

The failure is particularly glaring in case of UNI. Launched in March 1961 with an objective of providing healthy competition to PTI and sponsored by 40 leading newspapers of India including the Statesman, the Times of India and the Hindu, UNI could have done well in the present scenario had it concentrated on its broader objectives with which it was established and not remained mired in endless infighting. Even efforts by private players like Zee to take it over and corporatise it have failed. Today, it continues to play a marginal role in its limited sphere of influence.

The case of Hindusthan Samachar is even more pathetic. Despite noble intentions of its founder and missionary zeal of its workers, lack of financial resources and state patronage has resulted in its present plight. A venture started in December 1948 by a great patriot late Shivram Shankar Apte, Hindusthan Samachar, the only multi-lingual news agency in the country, could have had a better future if only the political masters of the day been more sympathetic to its onerous task of nation building.

The sad plight of news agencies like UNI and Hinduthan Samachar and the government apathy towards them is a fit example that vindicates the assessment of the current phase of globalisation by scholars like Amartya Sen. According to him, globalisation has turned the McLuhanesque global village into 'a global landscape of gross inequalities.' "The central issue of contention is not globalisation itself, nor is it the use of the market as an institution, but the inequality in the overall balance of institutional arrangements–which produces very unequal sharing of the benefits of globalisation. The question is not just whether the poor, too, gain something from globalisation, but whether they get a fair share and fair opportunity". [7]

Seen in the context of national news agencies, only the financially stronger and 'politically correct' players are getting favours from the ruling elite while the less privileged ones like UNI and Hindusthan Samachar are victims of government bias and apathy. This is despite the fact that everything is not hunky dory within these few privileged organisations. At least, this is the impression one gets by the growing unionisation of these organisations and the public utterances of their disgruntled employees in accounts like PTI-Diary.

While PTI's commands 90 percent of the news agency market in India, thanks to its clever marketing tactics, small players like UNI and Hindusthan Samachar are on the verge of extinction. The gross inequality that exists between them is also reflected in the imbalance in the overall news flow both within and outside India.

Within India, both newspapers and news agencies have failed to cover the imbalances and inequalities existing since long. Despite rapid horizontal expansion witnessed in the newspaper world and section of the news agencies, the share of rural coverage as part of developmental reporting continues to lurk around two to five percent of the total news coverage. It seems like Indian media is totally unaware of concepts like diffusion of innovation and their role in developmental process. Hopefully, the elevation of Shri Jairam Ramesh as the Union Cabinet Minister for Rural Development may bring some change as he himself has been a writer and journalist of note on business and economic affairs.

Since global and regional news agencies are important for their agenda-setting influence on other media through their international stories that other media choose to carry for distribution to their clients, their role in conflict zones and developing regions of the world for breaking news stories which the other major media miss is bound to increase in the days to come. Since India is one of the major developing economies of the world and shares geographical proximity with conflict zone in the Af-Pak region and is a consistent victim of terrorism exported from Pakistan that happens to be the epicentre of global terrorism, the role of Indian news media especially national agencies in providing Indian perspective on important issues and developments in the region and shaping world opinion in its favour increases manifold. Even the Prime Minister, Dr. Manmohan Singh, has voiced a similar concern at a recent meeting with senior editors of the print media saying "we need our own CNNs and BBCs–a global Indian channel with global perspective and reaching out to global audience" to stress the point further.

This concern has been raised earlier as well. A study made by the Indian Institute of Mass Communication in 2009 clearly points to the fact that domestic news agencies, particularly the dominant ones, have failed to provide a strong Indian perspective to the outside world. The dominant global multi-media information conglomerates like AP and Reuters still rule the roost and players like PTI which have all the financial resources and government patronage at their beck and call, have not been able to play the desired role expected of them.

If India is keen on having a strong news agency like the BBC then it must seek true objectivity from news agencies. For instance, UNI could face stiff competition from PTI in its initial years primarily on the basis of its objective news coverage outside the pale of government influence. It made a good impact as an agenda setter within India by covering and providing all shades of views and opinions ranging from anti-establishment to ultra nationalist to its clients. Today, the same grit and courage is required of those who truly and genuinely aspire to be India's global news agency.

End Notes

1. McChesney, R. (1999), The New Global Media, The Nation, USA, November 29, 1999, pp. 265-266.
2. Artz, L. and Kamalipur, K. 2003 (ed.), The Globalisation of Corporate Media Hegemony, State University of New York Press, New York, p. 86.
3. McChesney, R. (1997), The Global Media Giants, *Extra*, USA, November 1997, p. 2.
4. Sonwalkar P (2002), "Murdochization" of the Indian Press: From By-line to Bottom line, Media, Culture and Society, 24 (6), pp. 821-834.
5. Ms. Kalyani Shankar, Sr. Journalist and Columnist.
6. McNair, B. (2003), From Control to Chaos: Towards a New Sociology of Journalism, Media, Culture and Society, 25, pp. 547-555.
7. Sen, Amartya (2002), How to Judge Globalism?, The American Prospect, 13, January 1-14.

Bibliography

Bibliography

A. Primary Sources

List of Newspaper Microfilms

1. The Times of India:
- 1985 – Roll no: 6,713
- 1990 – Roll no: 7,032
- 1995 – Roll no: 7,525
- 2000 – Roll no: 10,070
- 2005 – Roll no: 12,072

2. The Tribune:
- 1985 – Roll no: 8,234
- 1990 – Roll no: 8,110
- 1995 – Roll no: 7,525
- 2000 – Roll no: 11,481
- 2005 – Archives, The Tribune, Chandigarh.

3. The Statesman:
- 1985- Roll no: 6,937
- 1990 – Roll no: 6,979
- 1995 – Roll no: 9,077
- 2000 – Roll no: 11,506
- 2005 – Archives, The Statesman, New Delhi.

4. The Hindu:
- 1985 – Roll no: 8,559
- 1990 – Roll no: 7,511
- 1995 – Roll no: 7,875
- 2000 – Roll no: 11,942
- 2005 – Archives, The Hindu, New Delhi.

5. Punjab Kesari:
- Archives, The Punjab Kesari, New Delhi.

Reports, Documents and Articles

A Manual of News Agency Journalism (1980), Indian Institute of Mass Communication, New Delhi.

ASSOCHAM-ICRIER Joint Conference on Globalisation (2006), Report and Recommendations.

Fegusson, M. (2007), The Mythology About Globalisation,

European Journal of Communication, 7, 1, 69-93.

Galtung, J. and Ruge, M.H. (1965), The Structure of Foreign News, *Journal of Peace Research*, Vol. 2, pp. 64-91.

Gauhar, A. (1981), Third World: An Alternate Press, *Journal of International Affairs*, 35, pp. 165-177.

Many Voices, One World: The McBride Commission Report on International Communication Problems (1982), Paris: UNESCO.

Mohammadi, A. and Sreberny (1995), International Newsflows in the Post-Cold War World, *Electronic Journal of Communication*, 5, pp. 7-17.

Murdock, G. and Golding, P. (1989), Information Poverty and Political Inequality: Citizenship in the Age of Privatised Communications, *Journal of Communication*, Vol. 39, pp. 180-195.

Nye, J. and Owens, W. (1996), America's Information Edge, *Foreign Affairs*, March/April, pp. 20-36.

Paterson, C. (2006), Papers in International and Global Communication, Centre for International Communication Research, No. 01/06.

Peterson, S. (1980), A Case Study of Third World News Coverage by the Western News Agencies and The Times, London, *Studies in Comparative International Development (CSID),* New York: Springer, pp. 62-98.

Rao, B and Vasanti, P. N. (2005) Media Scene as India Globalises. Centre for Media Studies, India, New Delhi.

Ray, Alok (1993), External Sector Liberalisation in India, Economic and Political Weekly, October 2, p. 2161.

Robertson, R. (1994), Globalization and Glocalization, *The Journal of International Communication,* 1, pp. 33-52.

Rothkopf, D. (1997), In Praise of Cultural Imperialism, *Foreign Policy*, Summer, pp. 38-53.

Sen, Amartya (2002), How to Judge Globalism?, *The American Prospect*, 13, 1, January 1-14.

Sonwalkar, P. (2002), "Murdochization" of the Indian Press: From By-line to Bottomline, *Media, Culture and Society,* 24(6), pp. 821-834.

Tomlinson, J. (1994), Mass Communication and the Idea of a Global Public Sphere, *The Journal of International Communication*, 1, pp. 57-70.

UN, Our Global Neighbourhood, The Report of the Commission on

Global Governance, (1995), Oxford: Oxford University Press.

UNESCO (1997), World Communication Report: The media and the challenges of the new technologies, Paris.

Waters, R. (2000), A New Media World, *Financial Times*, 11 January, p. 22.

Weaver, D., Wilhoit, G., Stevenson, R., Shaw, D. and Cole, R. (1980), The News of the World in Four Major Wire Services, Paris: International Association for Mass Communication Research, UNESCO.

White, D.M. (1950), The Gatekeeper: A Case Study in the Selection of News, *Journalism Quarterly*, 27, pp. 383-390.

B. Secondary Sources

Allan, S. and Zelizer, B. (2002), Journalism after September 11, London: Routledge.

Appadurai, A. (1996), Modernity at Large: Cultural Dimensions of Globalization, Minneapolis: University of Minnesota Press.

Archibugi, D. and Held, D. (eds.) (1995), Cosmopolitan Democracy, Cambridge: Polity Press.

Bagchi, A.K.; Sinha, D.; Bagchi, B. (eds.) (2005), Webs of History, Information, Communication and Technology from Early to Post-Colonial India, Indian History Congress in association with Institute of Development Studies Kolkata, New Delhi: Manohar Publishers.

Barber, B. (1996), Jihad vs. McWorld, New York: Ballantine Books.

Beck, U. (2000) What is Globalisation?, Oxford: Polity Press.

Bhattacharya, A. (1972), The Indian Press: Profession to Industry. New Delhi, India: Vikas.

Bloom, W. (1990), Personal Identity, National Identity, and International Relations, Cambridge: Cambridge University Press.

Boyd-Barrett, O. and Rantanen, T. (eds.) (1998), The Globalization of News, London: Sage.

Boyd-Barrett, O. and Thussu, D.K. (1992), Contra-flow in Global News, London: John Libbey/UNESCO.

Boyd-Barrett, O. (1979), The World-wide News Agencies: Development, Organization, Competition, Markets and Product, Open University, Milton, Keynes, U.K.

Boyd-Barrett, O. (1980), The International News Agencies, London: Constable.

Carey, J.W. (1989), Communication as Culture: Essays on Media and Society, Boston: Unwin Hyman.

Castells, M. (1996), The Information Age: Economy, Society and Culture, Oxford: Blackwell.

Chalapathi Rau, M. (1974), The Press: National Book Trust, India, New Delhi.

Cheah, P. and Robbins, B. (eds.) (1998), Cosmopolitics: Thinking and Feeling beyond the Nation, Minneapolis: University of Minnesota Press.

Clarke, I. (1997), Globalisation and Fragmentation: International Relations in the 20th century, Oxford: Oxford University Press.

Crawley, David and Heyer, Paul (1995), Communication in History –Technology, Culture, Society, New York: Longman Publishers.

Desai, A.R. (1976), Social Background of Indian Nationalism, Bombay: Popular Press.

Desmond, R. (1978), The Information Process: World News Reporting in the Twentieth Century, Iowa City: University of Iowa Press.

Drucker, P. (1993), Post-Capitalist Society, New York, NY: HarperCollins.

Eagleton T. (1990), Nationalism, Colonialism, and Literature, Minneapolis, MN: University of Minnesota Press.

Gerbner, G. and Marvanyi, G. (1981), The Many Worlds of the World's Press, in J. Richstad and M. Anderson (eds.), Reading the News, pp. 109-15, New York: Pantheon Books.

Giddens, A. (1990), The Consequence of Modernity, Cambridge: Polity Press.

Golding, P. and Murdoch, G. (eds.) (1997), The Political Economy of the Media, Cheltenham: Edward Elgar.

Grossberg, L. et al. (eds.) (2006), Media Making, Mass Media in a Popular Culture, New Delhi: Sage.

Hale, J. (1975), Radio Power: Propaganda and International Broadcasting. London: Paul Elek.

Harasim, L. (ed.) (1994), Global Networks: Computers and International Communication, Cambridge, MA: MIT Press.

Harris, C. (1997), International Communication: Global Market and Morality, in A. Mohammadi (ed.) International Communication and Globalization, pp. 92-118, London: Sage.

Harvey, D. (1989), The Condition of Post-modernity: An Enquiry into the Origins of Cultural Change, Oxford: Blackwell.

Headrick, D. (1981), The Tools of Empire: Technology of European Imperialism in the Nineteenth Century, New York: Oxford University Press.

Herman, E.S. and Chomsky, N. (1988), Manufacturing Consent: The Political Economy of the Mass Media, New York: Pantheon Books.

Hester, A. (1978), International Information Flow, in H. Fischer and J.C. Merrill (eds.), International and Intercultural Communication, pp. 242-250, New York: Hastings House.

Hirst, P. and Thompson, G. (1996), Globalisation in Question: The International Economy and the Possibilities of Governance, Cambridge: Polity Press.

Hjarvard, S. (ed.) (2001). News in a Globalised Society, Goteberg: NORDICOM.

Kavoori, P. (1999), The Global Dynamics of News: Studies in International News Coverage and News Agendas, Stanford: Ablex Publishing Corporation.

Kerlinger, F. N. (1986), Foundations of Behavioural Research, New York: Holt, Rinehart & Winston.

Kleinwachter, W. (1993), Three Waves of the Debate in Global Media Debate: Its Rise, Fall and Renewal (eds.) Gerbner, G.; Mowlana, H. and Nordenstreng, K., Norwood, NJ: Ablex Publishing Corporation.

Kofman, E. and Youngs, G. (eds.) (1996). Globalization: Theory and Practice, London: Pinter.

Lasswell, H. (1927), Propaganda Techniques in the World War, New York: Alfred Knopf.

Lerner, D. (1958), The Passing of Traditional Society, New York: Free Press.

Lerner, W. and Walters, W. (eds.) (2004), Global Governmentality, London: Routledge.

Lull, J. (1995), Media Communication and Culture: A Global Approach, Cambridge, England: Polity Press.

Malik, R. (1992), The Global News Agenda. *Intermedia*, 20, pp.12-29.

Mankekar, D.R. (1981), Whose Freedom? Whose Order? New Delhi: Clarion Books.

Mansell, R. and When, U. (eds.) (1998), Knowledge Societies: Information Technology for Sustainable Development, Report of the UN Commission on Science and Technology for

Development), Oxford: Oxford University Press.

McLuhan, M. (1964), Understanding Media, London: Methuen.

McLuhan, M. (1960), Explorations in Communication.

McQuail, D. (1994), Mass Communication Theory: An Introduction, London: Sage.

Melkote, S. and Steeves, H.L. (2001), Communication for Development in the Third World, London: Sage.

Mevlyn, D. and van Leeuwen (eds.) (2002), Global Media Discourse: A Critical Introduction, New York: Routledge.

Mohammadi, A. (ed.) (1997), International Communication and Globalization, London: Sage.

Mooney, A., and Evans, B. (eds.) (2007), Globalisation: The Key Concepts, New York: Routledge.

Mosco, V. (1996), The Political Economy of Communications, London: Sage.

Mowlana, H. (1996), Global Communication in Transition, London: Sage.

Murthy, Nadig Krishna (1966), Indian Journalism, University of Mysore Press, Mysore, pp. 66-67.

Musa, M. (1997), From Optimism to Reality: An Overview of Third World News Agencies, in P. Golding and P. Harris (eds.), Beyond Cultural Imperialism, pp.117-146, London: Sage.

Nayyar, D. (1988), "Globalisation: What Does it Mean for Development?" in Bibek Debroy (ed.), Challenges of Globalisation, New Delhi, p. 15.

Newbold, C.; Boyd-Barrett, O.; Belck, Hilde van Den (eds.) (2002), The Media Book, Oxford University Press: London.

Nordenstreng, K. and Schiller, H. (eds.) (1993), Beyond National Sovereignty: International Communications in the 1990s, Norwood, NJ: Ablex Publishing.

Pisarek, W. (1983), "Reality" East and West, in H. Davis and P. Walton (eds.), Language, Image, Media, pp. 156-164, Oxford, England: Blackwell.

Pye, L. (1963), Communications and Political Development, Princeton, NJ: Princeton University Press.

Read, D. (1992), The Power of News: The History of Reuters, 1849-1989, Oxford: Oxford University Press.

Robertson, R. (1978), Meaning and Change: Explorations in the Cultural Sociology of Modern Societies, Oxford: Basil Blackwell.

Robertson, R. (1992), Globalisation: Social Theory and Global Culture, London: Sage.

Robertson, R. (1995), 'Glocalisation: Time, Space and Homogeniety-heterogeniety' in M. Featherstone, S. Lash and R. Robertson (eds.) Global Modernities, London: Sage.

Rogers, Everett M. (1962), Diffusion of Innovations, New York: Free Press.

Rosenblum, M. (1993), Who Stole the News? New York: John Wiley.

Schiller, H. (1971), Mass Communication and American Empire, Boston, Beacon Press.

Schiller, H. (1989), Culture Inc.? New York: Oxford University Press.

Schiller, H. (1996), Information Inequality, New York: Routledge.

Schramm, W. (1964), Mass Media and National Development: The Role of Information in the Developing Countries, Stanford, CA: Stanford University Press.

Schramm, W. (1964), Mass Media and National Development: The Role of Information in the Developing Countries, Stanford, CA: Stanford University Press.

Schramm, W. and Atwood, E. (1981), Circulation of the News in the Third World, Hong Kong: The Chinese University Press.

Schudson, M. (1995), The Power of News, Cambridge, MA: Harvard University Press.

Servaes, J. (1996), Media and Development: Alternate Perspectives, Leicester, UK: Centre for Mass Communication Research, University of Leicester.

Siebert, F.S., Peterson, T. and Schramm, W. (1963), Four Theories of the Press, Urbana, IL: University of Illinois Press.

Simons, T, W., Jr. (1993), Eastern Europe in the Post-War World, New York: St. Martin's Press.

Singer, P. (1993), One World: The Ethics of Globalisation, New Haven, CT: Yale University Press.

Smith, A. (1973), The Politics of Information, London: Macmillan.

Somavia, J. (1976), The Transnational Power Structure and International Information, Development Dialogue, 2, pp. 15-28.

Soros, G. (2000), Open Society: The Crisis of Global Capitalism Reconsidered. London: Little, Brown.

Sreberny-Mohammadi, A. (1992), The Global and the Local in International Communication, in J. Curran and M. Gurevitch

(eds.), Mass Media and Society, London: Edward Arnold.
Stehr, N. (1994), Knowledge Societies, London: Sage.
Stevenson, R. and Cole, R. (1980), "Foreign News and the New World Information Order" debate, Part 2: Foreign News in Selected Countries, Washington, DC: Office of Research, International Communication Agency.
Swamy, Dalip S. (1994), The Political Economy of Industrialisation, New Delhi: Manohar Publishers.
Thompson, J. (1993), The Theory of the Public Sphere, Theory, Culture and Society: 10, pp. 173-189.
Thussu, D. (ed.) (1998a), Electronic Empires: Global Media and Local Resistance, London: Arnold.
Thussu, D.K. (1998), Electronic Empires: Global Media and Local Resistance. London: Arnold.
Toffler, A. (1980), The Third Wave, London: Collins.
Tomlinson, J. (1991), Cultural Imperialism: A Critical Introduction, London: Pinter.
Tuchman, G. (1980), Making News, New York: The Free Press.
Waters, M. (1995), Globalisation, London: Routledge.
Waters, M. (1995), Globalisation, London: Routledge.
Weaver, D., Wilhoit, G., Stevenson, R., Shaw, D. and Cole, R. (1980), The News of the World in Four Major Wire Services, Paris: International Association for Mass Communication Research, UNESCO.
Winseck, D. (1997), The Shifting Contexts-International Communication: Possibilities for a New World Information and Communication Order, in Bailie, M. and Winseck, D. (eds.), Democratizing Communication? Cresskill, NJ: Hampton Press.
Youngs, G. (1999), International Relations in a Global Age: A Conceptual Challenge. Cambridge: Polity Press.

Index

Index

A
Aden, 16
Agence France Presse (AFP), 17
All India Radio, 31
Amartya Sen, 2
Annie Besant, 30
Aparna Caur, 182
Asian News Network, 145
Associated Press (AP), 17
Associated Press of India (API), 28, 32

B
Bay of Bengal, 138
Benett Coleman & Co. Ltd., 249
Bernard Wolff, 18
Bombay; 16
British Empire, 11

C
Cairo, 16
Cape Town, 16
Ceylon, 16
Charles Wheatstone, 11
Cold War, 1, 19
Contingency Compensatory Financing Facility (CCFF), 35
Crimean War, 11

D
D.R. Mankekar, 44
Dainik Tribune, 83
Daniel Lerner, 42
Director General of Posts and Telegraphs, 28
Douglas Hurd, 100
Dow Jones, 17
Durban, 16

E
Economic Times, 48
Edward Hulton, 31

F
First World War, 9, 12, 16
Foreign Exchange Regulation Act, 34
Free Press Journal, 30
Free Press of India News Agency, 29

G
G.D. Birla, 30
George Soros, 2
Gherardo of Cremona, 8
Globe News Agency, 31
Goran Verzic, 45

H
H.K. Dua, 239
Hindu Magazine, 181
Hitler's Propaganda

Ministry, 13
Hong Kong, 16

I
I.K. Gujral, 94
Indian Daily News, 28
Indian Institute of Mass Communication, 46
Indian News Bureau, 29
Indian Ocean, 12
Industrial Revolution, 10
International Media and Globalization, 5
International Monetary Fund (IMF), 34
International News Service (INS), 18
International Radio Telegraph Union, 12

J
Jagat Narain, 188
Jairam Ramesh, 253
Johann Gutenberg, 10, 11
Josef Goebbels, 13

K
K.C. Roy, 28, 29
Kalyani Shankar, 239
Keith Flory, 231
Korean Herald, 149

L
League of Allied Agencies, 15
Leslie Sklair, 250
London, 16
Ludhiana Tribune, 109

M
M.L. Kotru, 231
M. Chalapathi Rau, 29
M.R. Jayakar, 30
MacBride Commission, 21, 44
Maharashtra Times, 48
Manchurian Crisis of 1931, 13
Manmohan Singh, 253
Mauritius, 16
Mediterranean, 16
Ministry of Information and Broadcasting, 132
Mombasa, 16

N
Naomi Ackerman, 182
Navbharat Times, 48
New York Times News Service (NYTNS), 183
News Agency of Thailand, 25
Novosti Press Agency (APN), 19

O
Orient Press of India, 31
Oxford Dictionary of New Words, 3

P
Paul Julius Reuter, 16

Persian Gulf, 12
Peter Singer, 2
Phiroze Sethna, 30
Port Blair, 212
Praful R. Desai, 103
Press Trust of India, 25
Publishers' Press Association, 18
Punjabi Tribune, 83
Purushottamdans Thakurdas, 30
Puspa Girimaji, 103

R

R. N. Lakhotia, 103
Radio Free Europe, 13
Radio Liberty, 13
Radio Moscow, 13
Rajinder Puri, 129
Ramesh Chandra, 188
Rashtriya Samachar Seva, 25
Rupert Murdoch, 39
Russian Telegraph Agency (ROSTA), 19

S

S.S. Apte, 33
Samuel Morse, 11
Sardar Dyal Singh Majithia, 83
Second World War, 13
Seychelles, 16
Singapore, 16
Sophia Peterson, 45
Soviet Union, 1
St. Petersburg Telegraph Agency (SPTA), 19
Strait Times, 149
Sunil Kumar Mukhopadhyaya, 46
Swaraj Paul, 182
Syed Mohammad, 31

T

Telegrafnoi Agentsvo Sovetskavo Soyusa (TASS), 19

U

UNESCO's World Communication Report, 1
Union of Soviet Journalists, 19
Union of Soviet Writers, 19
United Nations Educational, Scientific and Cultural Organisation (UNESCO), 24
United Press International 18
United Press of India (UPI), 30
Usha Nath Sen, 28

V

Voice of America (VOA), 13

W

Walchand Hirachand, 30
West Virginia University, 45
Wilbur Schramm, 42
World Bank, 34
World League of Press Associations, 15
World Trade Organization (WTO), 37

Z

Zanzibar, 16